The Political Identities of
EZRA POUND & T. S. ELIOT

Has Eliot or have I wasted the greater number of hours,
he by attending to fools and/or humouring them, and I
by alienating imbeciles suddenly?

Ezra Pound, 1938

WILLIAM M. CHACE

The Political Identities of
EZRA POUND & T. S. ELIOT

Stanford University Press
STANFORD, CALIFORNIA
1973

Stanford University Press
Stanford, California
© 1973 by the Board of Trustees of the
Leland Stanford Junior University
Printed in the United States of America
ISBN 0-8047-0843-6
LC 73-80620

To the Memory of My Brother
David Christopher Chace
1952-1969

Acknowledgments

I thank Guy Davenport, who first taught me to see the poetry of Ezra Pound and T. S. Eliot. In addition, I owe many thanks for advice and encouragement to two Berkeley friends, Thomas B. Flanagan and Alex Zwerdling, under whose guidance this book began as a doctoral dissertation. My colleagues at Stanford, particularly Yosal Rogat, George Dekker, Donald Davie, Wilfred H. Stone, and Albert J. Gelpi, have been enormously helpful in showing me what good prose and good sense might be like. David Levin, once of Stanford and now of the University of Virginia, has schooled me in patience and integrity. Νῦν δ'αἶνον ἀνδράσιν ἐρέω φρονέουσι καὶ αὐτοῖς.

For the meticulous, even-tempered, and consistently good judgments of my editor at the Stanford University Press, Autumn J. Stanley, I am deeply appreciative. No author could ask for more expert help.

My parents should not be forgotten here. They have supplied me with, among other things, valuable research information from the Library of Congress and the National Archives.

I would also like to thank Robert von Hallberg and Michael D. Channing for their care in searching out errors, large and small, in the manuscript. For the errors that may remain, none of those named above can be blamed.

Albert H. Hastorf, Annamaria Napolitano, Ronald Mellor, Gary Ward, and William P. Allan have each contributed something helpful to the making of this book.

James Siena, Iris Brest, and Daryl Dawson deserve my gratitude, and that of other scholars, for helping to resolve some of the practical matters attendant upon publication of the book.

My wife JoAn and our children Billy and Kate have known for some time that it is the life that is so long to learn. I am grateful to them for allowing me so much time with the craft.

I am grateful to the publishers of Eliot's and Pound's works, in England and in the United States, for permitting me to quote from the poetry in their volumes. The passages from T. S. Eliot's poems are taken from *Collected Poems 1909-1962* by T. S. Eliot (London: Faber & Faber Ltd., 1963) and *The Complete Poems and Plays 1909-1950* by T. S. Eliot (New York: Harcourt Brace Jovanovich, Inc., 1963). The excerpts from the Ezra Pound poems are reprinted from *Personæ: Collected Shorter Poems of Ezra Pound* by Ezra Pound (London: Faber & Faber Ltd., 1952), from *The Cantos of Ezra Pound* by Ezra Pound (London: Faber & Faber Ltd., 1954), from *Personæ: The Collected Poems of Ezra Pound* by Ezra Pound (New York: New Directions Publishing Corporation, 1926), and from *The Cantos* by Ezra Pound (New York: New Directions Publishing Corporation, 1948). The Pound material appearing in Appendix B is reprinted by permission of the Estate of Ezra Pound, copyright owner.

W.M.C.

Contents

Abbreviations

WORKS BY POUND

ABC   *ABC of Economics*. Tunbridge Wells, England: Peter Russell, 1953; first published in London: Faber and Faber, 1933.

GK   *Guide to Kulchur*. Norfolk, Conn.: New Directions, n.d. (1952).

J/M   *Jefferson and / or Mussolini: L'Idea Statale: Fascism As I Have Seen It*. London: Stanley Nott, 1935.

LE   *Literary Essays of Ezra Pound*. Norfolk, Conn.: New Directions, 1954.

PM   "Patria Mia," *New Age*, 11 (Sept. 5-Oct. 10, 1912); in six parts.

PM   *Patria Mia* and *The Treatise on Harmony*. London: Peter Owen, n.d. (1962).

SA   "The Serious Artist," in LE.

SC   *Social Credit: An Impact*. London: Peter Russell, 1951; originally published in London: Stanley Nott, 1935.

WORKS BY ELIOT

ASG   *After Strange Gods, A Primer of Modern Heresy*. New York: Harcourt, Brace, 1934.

ICS   *The Idea of a Christian Society*, in *Christianity and Culture: The Idea of a Christian Society* and *Notes towards the Definition of Culture*. New York: Harcourt, Brace, n.d.

NTDC   *Notes towards the Definition of Culture*, in *Christianity and Culture: The Idea of a Christian Society* and *Notes towards the Definition of Culture*. New York: Harcourt, Brace, n.d.

Introduction

This study of Ezra Pound and T. S. Eliot confronts the fact that two of the most artistically influential writers of our time were reactionaries. At crucial moments in his career, Eliot was an advocate of regressive social planning and a snob who saw Jews as an unwholesome and alien presence. Pound, always more flamboyant than Eliot, climaxed his public career by broadcasting on wartime radio his support of Benito Mussolini and Italian fascism. Years before, he had given himself over to simplistic economic thinking and become snarled in his own perfervid forms of anti-Semitism.[1]

All this is well known. Many studies have dealt with the anti-liberalism of these two men, albeit more often using the rhetoric of outrage than the tools of inquiry.[2] What is not often confronted

[1] Late in his long life, Pound saw error and failure everywhere in his career. "Io tutto quello che tocco, guasto. Io ho sbagliato sempre...." (Everything I touch, I destroy. I have always blundered) were his words to the Italian journalist Grazia Livi ("Vi Parla Ezra Pound," *Epoca*, March 24, 1963). To Allen Ginsberg in 1967 Pound said, "Any good I've done has been spoiled by bad intentions—the preoccupation with stupid and irrelevant things.... But the worst mistake I made was that stupid, suburban prejudice of anti-Semitism" (Michael Reck, "A Conversation Between Ezra Pound and Allen Ginsberg," *Evergreen Review*, June 1968). Pound as an old man would have forsaken all his work, and the anti-Semitism along with it. His writing, however, is now a part of history and will always carry with it the sentiments out of which it was, in part, formed. Also a part of history are his apologies. Welcome as they are, they cancel nothing; the poetry and the prejudice are forever united.

[2] John R. Harrison, for instance, who has written a book about the general problem of reaction and modern writers, has asked, "Why is it that great creative artists can totally reject a liberal, democratic, humanitarian society, and prefer a cruel, authoritarian, bellicose society?" He has but limited success

is the fact that Pound and Eliot were also radicals. They both believed that something was deeply wrong with the world around
them and that most of the solutions offered by the liberal political
leaders of their day were hopelessly shallow. Their own solutions
would have meant fundamental changes in the structure of society,
and both men were probably aware of this, although Pound sometimes denied it and Eliot usually ignored it. Offended by the crassness of their native land and by the puerile idealism of those who
sought to make it genteel, they became expatriates. Yet as radicals
they were only sporadically satisfied by the success of reactionary
politics in the lands to which they had traveled. They did not fit,
and yet they sought to fit. Eliot, in England, at last ascended to a
political station above England and its mundane problems; he had
become "plus anglais que les anglais." Pound, in Italy, at last entered a world of delusions and poetic beauties that, at war's end,
became darkly colored by his despair at the collapse of fascism.

Nor were they alone among great modern artists in their anti-
liberalism. The fiction that they were alone has its origin in the
assumption that writers should be liberal, one of several virtually
unquestioned assumptions that have impeded a rational assess-
ment of Pound's and Eliot's politics in the past. Lionel Trilling is
one of the few to question it:

> If we name those writers who, by the general consent of the most serious
> criticism, by consent too of the very class of educated people ... are
> thought of as the monumental figures of our time, we see that to these
> writers the liberal ideology has been at best a matter of indifference.
> Proust, Lawrence, Joyce, Yeats, Mann (as novelist), Kafka, Rilke, Gide
> (also as novelist)—all of them have their own love of justice and the
> good life, but in not one of them does it take the form of a love of the
> ideas and emotions which liberal democracy, as known by our educated
> class, has declared respectable.[3]

Trilling's observation can serve, in the very names adduced, not
only to refute the assumption that Pound and Eliot were uniquely

in answering his own question. See *The Reactionaries* (London: Gollancz,
1966), p. 15.

   [3] Lionel Trilling, *Beyond Culture: Essays on Literature and Learning* (New
York: Viking, 1965), pp. 166-67.

illiberal, but to introduce two other unquestioned assumptions about the two poets that will concern me here: that they were uniquely political, and that they were uniquely unwise in their views.

James Joyce, whom Trilling mentions, is now and again cited as an enviable model of political disengagement. Joyce reached out to no ideology and sought nothing save his art. Irish politics had shown him that politics is a nightmare. Whether Joyce is to be seen as a wise man who stepped around the snare of politics or as a very selfish man who husbanded all his energy for his art may be debatable; but his apolitical stance was certainly exceptional. If, as William Carlos Williams once said, "poetry is a rival government always in opposition to its cruder replicas," we find many poets, and indeed many novelists, preoccupied with the cruder replicas. Moreover, we find them preoccupied from different vantage points at different times in their lives.

There is André Malraux, for example, attacking liberalism from the left at one stage of his life and from the right at another stage. There is D. H. Lawrence, in his novel *Kangaroo*, attacking virtually simultaneously from both right and left and at last developing a wrathful repugnance toward all politics. And there is Yeats, descending from the tower of his imagination to write marching songs for General Eoin O'Duffy and his Blueshirts. They, strong individualists, would lead Ireland violently toward the future of legendary strength. "A Fascist opposition is forming behind the scenes to be ready should some tragic situation develop," Yeats wrote in 1933; "I find myself urging the despotic rule of the educated class."[4] Just as quickly as Yeats offered this encouragement, however, he took it away, saying in his poem "Church and State," "That were a cowardly song, / Wander in dreams no more."[5] Malraux's spectacular alternations, Lawrence's restless fluctua-

---

[4] Allan Wade, ed., *The Letters of W. B. Yeats* (London: Rupert Hart-Davis, 1954), pp. 811-12.

[5] See Conor Cruise O'Brien, "Passion and Cunning: The Politics of W. B. Yeats," in A. N. Jeffares, ed., *In Excited Reverie* (London: Macmillan, 1965) for the most significant discussion of Yeats and politics. O'Brien sees Yeats's profascism and his phases of detachment as equally real and powerful.

tions, Yeats's contradictions—and Thomas Mann's movement from the conservative feelings he expressed during World War I to the clearly antifascistic attitudes of his later life[6]—are all more indicative of how artists of this frenzied century have responded to pressures from within and without than Joyce's steadfast refusal to enter the arena at all.

Several further examples, both of engagement in politics and of political unwisdom if judged by hindsight, can be furnished from among Pound's and Eliot's contemporaries in the United States. More than fifty of the most highly esteemed American writers of the time went on record in support of the Communist Party's candidates for President and Vice-President in 1932. Edmund Wilson, Sherwood Anderson, Lincoln Steffens, Langston Hughes, John Dos Passos, and Malcolm Cowley were among them.[7] But one by one, largely in reaction to the Moscow Trials of 1936-38 and to the signing of the Nazi-Soviet nonaggression pact of 1939, these men withdrew their support of communist aims. The peculiar combination of doctrinaire zeal and naive moral idealism that had characterized American partisanship with the left lay dormant by the end of the decade. Fluctuations began again, and those who did not fit sought again to fit. Dos Passos, once a spokesman against the crudities of America, now praised its Jeffersonian past and shut his eyes to its exploitative lusts.

These many examples should remind us that it is foolish to look to most of the writers of our time for political wisdom. It should also show us that Pound and Eliot were not really unique. (Liberals would of course be pleased if they were: if writers in general were, to use Trilling's word, at ease with liberals' own "respectable" ideas and emotions. But they are not. And their not being so has hampered liberals in their defense of literature as a valuable

---

[6] See Mann's *Betrachtungen eines Unpolitischen* (1918) for his feelings during the war. His feelings against the right (as expressed in, for instance, *Mario and the Magician*, 1930) were given strong impetus by the murder of Walther Rathenau, Germany's foreign minister, in 1922 by anti-Semitic nationalistic terrorists.

[7] See *Culture and Crisis* (New York: Workers Library Publishers, 1932), p. 32.

medium of human expression. This fact tells us much about the powerful spectre that Pound and Eliot continue to raise; it also gives us some insight into the malaise and disarray of conventional liberal thought.)

Having made the point that Pound and Eliot were not unique, I must go beyond it to say that they can be seen as special cases in the general context. They were more than interested in politics; they were entangled in, even obsessed by, politics. Much of their time was devoted to creating political responses, arguments, and visions. Their "pure" literary pursuits were apparently often dislodged by other pursuits. And these other pursuits, over the years, reveal the two poets as cognate expressions of an extreme revulsion against liberal democracy and an elitism paralleled in few other writers of the century.

Whether Pound and Eliot will in the end be found more like or more unlike their contemporaries awaits a more careful examination of their politics than has yet been attempted. The difficulties in such an examination, which will be attempted here, are considerable. Pound's political identity is hard to evaluate because evaluation slips so easily into confusions about his controversial "case" and his worthiness as a recipient of literary prizes. Eliot's political identity is elusive because his politics shades so easily into his religion, and his religion is so transcendent that it leaves no shade at all.

Not only their politics, of course, but the intellectual context in which they operated must be more thoroughly understood. Nineteenth-century England had a strong tradition of partisanship among its greatest writers: Dickens, William Morris, Ruskin, Charles Kingsley, and Carlyle all entertained firm and explicit political opinions. The English Romantics may have changed from young revolutionaries to old conservatives, but they were political always. Coleridge sided early with the French Revolution and later with the Established Church of England, but he remained the political animal described by Aristotle. In the United States during the same period, writers such as James Fenimore Cooper, Mark Twain, Emerson, Thoreau, Whitman, and Henry Adams held political sentiments, some well formed and some not, all crucial to their careers. But there could be no smooth transition between such men and Pound and Eliot because the Symbolist and Aesthetic movements—of which the two poets themselves were once a part—intervened with the dictum that the poet must shut his door to the world of streets and speeches. Thus in rejecting this dictum, as both poets did, Pound and Eliot were attempting to revive a tradition of partisanship about which they knew little.

If we see Pound's and Eliot's partisan activities in part as an awkward emergence from the Symbolist quarantine, we may gain more understanding of their predicament. And if we see in their preoccupations an implicit challenge to another kind of "dissociation of sensibility," we may also understand not only these preoccupations but why a dispassionate look at them is not an unlikely departure for a literary critic. As Pound and Eliot united things, so may we.

PART ONE

EZRA POUND

If I am introducing anybody to Kulchur, let 'em take the two phases, the nineteen teens, Gaudier, Wyndham L. and I as we were in *Blast*, and the next phase, the 1920's.

The sorting out, the *rappel à l'ordre*, and thirdly the new synthesis, the totalitarian.

—*Guide to Kulchur*, 1938

CHAPTER ONE

The Early Writings: The Sorting Out

The critical treatment of Ezra Pound and his highly unorthodox political and social concerns is beset by great difficulty, controversy, and, in some quarters, ill feeling of the bitterest kind. Pound has the questionable distinction of having carried political theory and belief more directly into action than any other major poet of his time. Since some of his actions were criminally liable, many of his most passionately held ideas have for some years remained beyond the purview of critical respectability. Pound's public career, climaxed by his attachment to Mussolini and his twelve-year term in a federal mental institution, reminds us of two melancholy facts. The first is that artists make mistakes and that great artists may make great mistakes. The second and more pertinent here is that social stigma can inhibit the study of ideas that by virtue of their idiosyncrasy alone, to say nothing of the fame of their spokesmen, would otherwise irresistibly intrigue us.

By becoming an idiosyncratic supporter of fascism, and a most unusual kind of anti-Semite, Pound exiled himself from the bounds of balanced, dispassionate discussion to a country of extremes. The most helpful of the early investigations of his poetry, that by Hugh Kenner,[1] completely ignores the political and economic ideas of that poetry, particularly the *Cantos*. It takes, in fact, no interest in any of the poem's ideas as ideas. Content is thus reduced to the level of an arbitrarily chosen raw material on which the poet, for unspecified reasons, chose to exercise his con-

---

[1] *The Poetry of Ezra Pound* (London: Faber and Faber, 1951).

summate constructive skills. Kenner's recent book,[2] by turns brilliant and crotchety and therefore somehow an appropriate monument to Pound, also gives short shrift to politics. Its quasi-scientific approach, stressing pattern and design, would purify a body of work whose very impurity, its mixture of unresolved fragments, is its essence.

At the other extreme, George P. Elliott focuses on the Pisan cantos and angrily reminds us that when they were written, "the Auschwitz ovens were scarcely cool."[3] For Elliott, the true test of Ezra Pound is the way in which ideas that he espoused have issued in violent action and underlain a sordid chapter in history. With Auschwitz in our memories, the poet and all he has made must be condemned. And so he has been, by those who stood so solidly against him when he received the Bollingen Prize for Poetry from the United States Library of Congress in 1949[4] and, lately, by those who denied him the 1972 Emerson-Thoreau Medal of the American Academy of Arts and Sciences on the ground that he did not deserve a humanistic award.[5]

Until recently, then, critics have for the most part preferred either to analyze Pound's work without reference to his ideas or to analyze his ideas without reference to his work, producing in the first instance largely formalistic analyses and in the second, scathing attacks.[6] The studies done in the 1960's by George Dek-

---

[2] *The Pound Era* (Berkeley: University of California Press, 1971).

[3] George P. Elliott, "Poet of Many Voices," in Walter Sutton, ed., *Ezra Pound, A Collection of Critical Essays* (Englewood Cliffs, N.J.: Prentice-Hall, 1963), p. 153.

[4] Beverly J. G. Loftus provides a detailed survey of how American periodicals stood on the questions of Pound himself, the award, and government sponsorship of the award. See "Ezra Pound and the Bollingen Prize: The Controversy in Periodicals," *Journalism Quarterly*, 39 (Summer 1962): 347-54, 394.

[5] See *New York Times*, May 25 and July 9, 1972.

[6] There is a third camp. Ironically enough, it does Pound the greatest disservice of all. That is, it simply agrees with him—about banks, China, Italy, the Jews, the United States, Provence, or whatever. Clarence Eustace Mullins, *This Difficult Individual, Ezra Pound* (New York: Fleet, 1961) is the most extreme example, but the books by Harry M. Meacham (*The Caged Panther* [New York: Twayne, 1967]) and Michael Reck (*Ezra Pound: A Close-Up* [New York: McGraw-Hill, 1967]) reveal the same sycophancy.

ker, Donald Davie, Daniel Pearlman, and Herbert Schneidau,[7] however, suggest that one may discuss, with understanding and good grace, and within the usual sort of literary analysis, the ideas underlying Pound's *Cantos* and the vast majority of his prose writings.

Formalistic criticism, although extremely helpful in a work as intricately structured as the *Cantos*, is incapable of confronting the poem's will to action, Pound's desire to bring political awareness to the minds of its readers. "For forty years I have schooled myself," he wrote in 1944, "not to write the Economic History of the U.S. or any other country, but to write an epic poem which begins 'In the Dark Forest,' crosses the Purgatory of human error, and ends in the light, 'fra i maestri di color che sanno.' For this reason I have to understand the NATURE of error."[8] And the nature of error, which is what his epic poem and many of his other writings study so obsessively, is, he believes, rooted in specific historical, political, and economic events. The full comprehension of these events cannot but transform our understanding of the world. Whether it be the perfidy of privately owned banks, the collapse of the American political ideal, or the defeat of Napoleon, Pound demands that we found our sense of human nature upon specific events. "Nothing," he has said, "is without efficient cause." The error is there, it can be located. Only when it is located will the world change, or, more precisely, can one know enough of the world to work changes upon it. A poetry, or a poet, attempting anything less than this entire process, from accurate perception to consummated action, fails the art.

With these sorts of distinctions in mind, it seems to me that the

[7] George Dekker, *Sailing After Knowledge, The Cantos of Ezra Pound* (London: Routledge, 1963); Donald Davie, *Ezra Pound: Poet as Sculptor* (New York: Oxford University Press, 1964); Daniel Pearlman, *The Barb of Time: On the Unity of Pound's* Cantos (New York: Oxford University Press, 1969); Herbert Schneidau, *Ezra Pound, The Image and the Real* (Baton Rouge: Louisiana State University Press, 1969).

[8] *An Introduction to the Economic Nature of the United States,* trans. from Italian by Carmine Amore (London: Peter Russell, n.d. [1950]), p. 5; reprinted, with some changes, in Noel Stock, ed., *Impact: Essays on Ignorance and the Decline of American Civilization by Ezra Pound* (Chicago: Regnery, 1960).

best way to understand Pound is to try to answer the questions
he posed in 1933 in an essay discussing the failure of certain nations to support their artists:

What drives, or what can drive a man interested almost exclusively in
the arts, into social theory or into a study of the "gross material aspects"
videlicet economic aspects of the present? What causes the ferocity and
bad manners of revolutionaries?

Why should a peace-loving writer of Quaker descent be quite ready
to shoot certain persons whom he never laid eyes on?[9]

These questions—which can be seen as parts of a single question
—are the ones I pose here. In search of answers, I examine Pound's
political writings, including a number of the cantos, and try to
understand the pressures that shaped his political vision. I also
ask about the consistency of that vision over the years. Kenner
speculated more than twenty years ago about a future study that
would be "a separate anthology of passages throwing light on the
contents of the epic."[10] This study is not such an anthology, but
it does gather passages and examine them in the hope that light
will be thrown on the *Cantos* and on Pound. The "sextant" of
this investigation will be Pound's own writings, but I will also step
outside them to talk about certain political and historical situations that left their mark on the poet.

We can begin with "Patria Mia." Pound's long career amid
ideas and visions of politics, economics, and society began pub-
licly with the appearance of this work, a discussion of the future
possibilities of the United States, in particular the possibility of a
Risorgimento. Writing in late 1912, Pound described his visit to
the United States in 1910-11 and his mixed hopes for "the most
ruthless and the most energetic people" (PM/I 445) in the world.
The chances for an American Renaissance, although theoretically
good because of "the size and vigor of 'this new strange people,'"
were, he told his English readers, threatened by the insidious
growth of a mercantile ideal that defined success in terms of the

---

[9] "Murder by Capital," *Criterion*, 12 (July 1933): 586-87.
[10] Kenner, *Poetry*, p. 334.

"nickel-plated cash register" (*PM* 21). The early pioneer, a bold and adventurous Anglo-Saxon, was being overwhelmed by other races and was gradually losing his identity in a welter of alien forces. One of these "forces" was the Jew. Discussing the strong effect of climate upon "mongrel" peoples such as those who had come to America, Pound states that "the Jew alone can retain his detestable qualities, despite climatic conditions" (PM/II 466).[11] Anti-Semitism came early to Pound—perhaps as a direct legacy of his family background and social class, Protestant professional and upper-middle class—and stayed late.

The tension created between two radically different kinds of settlers on American soil has been, he says, a decisively unhealthy one. He suggests, moreover, that without a strong central authority, and hampered by a social system demanding the agreement of a multitude of people before it can act, the United States can only remain deep within the Dark Ages he sees as its present condition. But the matter does not rest there. Although not certain that promise could outweigh despair in the face of the destructive tides of democratization and mongrelization, Pound predicts that if art be salvaged, the nation will regain its health. Since, as he announces, "letters are a nation's foreign office," it follows that "by the arts, and by them almost alone do nations gain for each other any understanding and intimate respect" (*PM* 23). The only problem was that America, according to Pound, had no interesting art. One is reminded of Henry James's devastating remarks on Hawthorne's America, or of his comments about "the extent of the Hebrew conquest of New York."

The explanations Pound gives for America's cultural bleakness

[11] There are a number of interesting differences between "Patria Mia" as originally published in A. R. Orage's *New Age* and as republished, after long and mysterious delay, by Ralph Fletcher Seymour (Chicago, 1950) and Peter Owen (London, 1962). Donald Gallup, in *A Bibliography of Ezra Pound* (London: Rupert Hart-Davis, 1963), p. 108, says that the manuscript was revised before it was sent to Seymour in 1913. In any case, the book version omits this reference to the Jews, as well as certain topical allusions. I will distinguish between references to the original and to the book by italicizing the abbreviation of the latter in in-text citations.

are characteristic of his thinking throughout his life. "Pseudo-artists" and "a system of publishing control" (*PM* 24) are to blame. A powerful conspiracy, involving venal publishing houses and empty literary traditions ("Messrs Harper and Co" and the style of 1870 are the particular culprits), creates bad or mediocre art. The publishing monopoly releases this inferior art on a duped public in such a flood that good art and sensitivity to good art are lost. The characteristic turn of argument is to refuse to blame a general weakness for the deplorable condition he witnesses, and to focus upon a particular instrument: in this case, publishing. Along with this affinity for the specific goes an unwillingness to recognize complexities—here, the historical forces at work. He exonerates ignorance and indifference—as many other critics would not have done—yet he does so in a work describing a national culture marked by both.

Pound is as eager to recommend a specific remedy as he is to find a specific cause. If America is to overcome her cultural deficit, she must begin a determined struggle to synthesize her resources. Once the true resources, particularly the artistic ones, are put to work, she will become a center of artistic activity. But this can only happen, Pound says, if she learns the one lesson the Ptolemies have to teach: "Art was lifted into Alexandria by subsidy, and by no other means will it be established in the United States" (*PM* 52-53).

Before concluding his argument, however, he hints at a remedy that was ultimately to become more important to him than notions of patronage could ever be—a veritable panacea. This was an end to all forms of unearned increment. After dismissing state socialism as impracticable and syndicalism and the workings of the I.W.W. as unknowns (PM/VI 564), he says that true justice among men can come only with recognition of the essential difference between two sorts of property: "property passive, which is, in a sense, consumed or used by its owners, and which they must labour to keep in condition," and "property active, the value of which depends almost entirely upon the labour of others" (PM/VI 564). The latter, he says, should be taxed and the taxes used to support the state whereas the former must be exempt from all taxes. This distinction between two sorts of property is rich with ethical implications. Pound seeks to penalize those "who make a profit on the labour of other men" and he views with reverence "the land which *gives,* and which *should* be cheap."[12]

Here, at age twenty-seven, Pound has already formed the basis upon which the rest of his economics will, like a ziggurat, be constructed. What is added hereafter will always reflect the differences he sees between the untaxable generosities of nature and the taxable, criminally suspect activities of men using, or exploiting, other men. The theories of Major C. H. Douglas, which Pound began to praise some eight years later, in 1920, are not far to seek.

"Patria Mia" makes a good introduction to Pound's thinking. Its callow effusiveness—sometimes reminiscent of Whitman—is not repeated in Pound's work, but certain political and cultural assumptions central to this early work recur again and again:

(1) democracy weakens that synthesis of human resources out of which alone true culture can come;

(2) alien forces, represented by crude mercantilism, enfeeble a nation;

(3) nature gives forth bounty;

(4) cultural maladies have simple, specific, and tangible solutions rather than complex, abstract ones;

(5) the arts make a nation strong, and are the best index of the nation's strength.

Later works retain these assumptions even while they reveal changes in Pound's mind about the true origin of the alien forces or the nature of the specific solution.

One year after "Patria Mia," Pound published "The Serious Artist," an essay important to us because of the light it throws on his subsequent attitudes toward the political and social significance of poetry. He was concerned at the very outset of his career, as this essay shows, about the role of poetry and the other arts in a good society. Asking himself what should be the relation of the arts to economics, and what position the arts should hold in

[12] "Through Alien Eyes I," *New Age,* 12 (Jan. 16, 1913): 252.

the ideal republic, he assumes, as Sir Philip Sidney assumed in the sixteenth century, the superiority of poetry to all other things. But whereas Sidney says that "the Poet he nothing affirms, and therefore never lyeth," Pound contends that the primary responsibility of the poet is to affirm. There is a truth to be told, and the poet must tell it; to do anything else is to engage in irrelevancies. And if he lies, he commits an act as serious as that of the physician who falsifies a clinical report or refuses to excise a malignancy: "his offence is of the same nature as the physician's and according to his position and the nature of his lie he is responsible for future oppressions and for future misconceptions." Hence he should be "punished or despised in proportion to the seriousness of his offence" (LE 44). Poetry, as Pound argues here and in his later writings, rests at the very center of a nation's well-being. Going beyond Sidney's contention about the poet's status, he espoused Shelley's more ambitious and just as dubious claim that poets are the "unacknowledged legislators of the world." By so doing, he was led inevitably to believe that his function in a sick world was to bring healing through poetry.

The seriousness of this belief tells us much about the extraordinary ambition of the *Cantos*: to trace the ways in which financial inequity has been a cancer in the body of civilization and at the root of all human decay. This ambition is at times subverted, one may feel, by Pound's prose writings, but it is an ambition seldom surpassed by any poetry in the language.[13] The *Cantos* cannot properly be evaluated without understanding how serious Pound felt the serious artist must be, and how far his aspirations should reach: "It is true that the great artist has in the end, always, his audience, for the Lord of the universe sends into this world in each generation a few intelligent spirits, and these ultimately manage

---

[13] Indeed, Pound (like Eliot) waged a strenuous campaign against John Milton and *Paradise Lost* for several years. In Pound's case it was apparently not only because of the syntactical irregularities he saw in Milton's poem, but also because Milton's aims rival his own in grandeur. For a particularly uncompromising assertion of Pound's view, see Hugh Kenner, "New Subtlety of Eyes," in Peter Russell, ed., *An Examination of Ezra Pound* (Norfolk, Conn.: New Directions, 1950), pp. 84-99.

the rest."[14] Clearly, these aspirations should draw the poet deeply into social and political concerns.

Among the first social concerns to absorb Pound, at once serious and portentous in his declarations, was the aimlessness of the public: "But this rest—this rabble, this multitude—does *not* create the great artist. They are aimless and drifting without him. They dare not inspect their own souls."[15] One of the first campaigns he therefore embarked upon, with his newly acknowledged comrade Percy Wyndham Lewis, was to provide direction for this drifting public. The campaign was launched under the banner of Vorticism. Announced in April 1914 as the "End of the Christian Era,"[16] Vorticism set out its program for change in the pages of *Blast*, first published as "A Review of the Great English Vortex" on June 20, 1914. Self-dramatized and self-conscious, ringing with denunciations, leavened by praise of a few worthies, the magazine ran, as we know, for only two issues. Herbert Schneidau has quite correctly pointed out that *Blast*'s manic hostilities—its cover was a paintpot hurled in the face of the public—can even now obscure from us the fact that neither the magazine nor the movement it spoke for was actually revolutionary. They were both, on the contrary, essentially conservative.[17] Whereas their foreign rivals the Futurists wanted to dump the entire past into the nearest ashcan, the Vorticists wanted to uphold the "real" traditions, the traditions amid which great artists and true innovators "always" work. Their savage rage was reserved exclusively for the men in the street, the mob, and the meretricious artists serving them.

The campaign of the Vorticists, begun only weeks before the

---

[14] *Poetry*, 5 (Oct. 1914): 29-30. Pound's exultations at this time were so much a product of youthful afflatus, so clearly the sign of the poet not yet thirty, that his pronouncements on his direction, or on the direction of poetry in general, have a suspiciously oracular ring. (In Eliot's opinion, and to his dismay, they would continue to sound that way for the rest of Pound's life.)

[15] *Ibid.*

[16] See Noel Stock, *The Life of Ezra Pound* (New York: Pantheon Books, 1970), p. 159.

[17] *Image and Real*, pp. 149-50.

outbreak of the First World War, was, as Schneidau has observed, strongly flavored by belligerent diction. Among other things it was a fight against "unsatisfactory democracy." Lewis thought of himself, along with Pound, Eliot, and Joyce, as "the men of 1914." Pound drew his readers' attention to the fact that Lewis was a "man at war," and the war he fought, that between the artist and the public, was one without truce. The magazine portrayed ideas as intrinsically violent, the collection of such ideas at the point of their maximum energy as the "vortex," and the force guiding them to the vortex as what Pound called "RACE, RACE-MEMORY, instinct."[18] The group's great concern with race can be seen in its manifesto in the first number of *Blast*, declaring that "the art for these climates, then, must be a northern flower," and, moreover, that "the Modern World is due almost entirely to Anglo-Saxon genius,—its appearance and its spirit."[19]

The artist was seen as antagonistic to the material with which he worked—the material was crude and chaotic, and the artist was obliged to use force as well as genius and artistic energy to wring beauty from it. As long as Pound saw himself as a "creator agonistes," as long as he perceived himself at odds with an inchoate universe that had to be brought to heel by the artist's superior, and violent, intelligence, he would be receptive to a politics that embraced some of the same heady notions; and Schneidau's contention that fascism was already, in 1914, in the air[20] seems reasonable.

Pound's poem "Salutation the Third," originally published in *Blast*, is suggestive here. It embodies all of the themes of *Blast*—*épater le bourgeois*, death, and race—and typifies the magazine's belligerence and violent diction.

> Let us deride the smugness of "The Times":
> GUFFAW!
>   So much the gagged reviewers,
> It will pay them when the worms are wriggling in their vitals;
> These were they who objected to newness,

[18] *Blast*, 1 (June 20, 1914): 153.
[19] *Ibid.*, 36, 39.
[20] *Image and Real*, p. 157.

HERE are their TOMB-STONES.
   They supported the gag and the ring:
A little black BOX contains them.
   SO shall you be also,
You slut-bellied obstructionist,
   You sworn foe to free speech and good letters,
You fungus, you continuous gangrene.
Come, let us on with the new deal,
   Let us be done with Jews and Jobbery,
Let us SPIT upon those who fawn on the JEWS for their money,
Let us out to the pastures.
PERHAPS I will die at thirty,
Perhaps you will have the pleasure of defiling my pauper's grave,
I wish you JOY, I proffer you ALL my assistance.
It has been your HABIT for long to do away with true poets,
You either drive them mad, or else you blink at their suicides,
Or else you condone their drugs, and talk of insanity and genius,
BUT I will not go mad to please you.
   I will not FLATTER you with an early death.
OH, NO! I will stick it out,
   I will feel your hates wriggling about my feet,
And I will laugh at you and mock you,
And I will offer you consolations in irony,
   O fools, detesters of Beauty.
I have seen many who go about with supplications,
   Afraid to say how they hate you.
HERE is the taste of my BOOT,
   CARESS it, lick off the BLACKING.[21]

When, in 1918, Pound turned to Henry James and began his long memorial essay on the novelist, he found himself once again considering how a serious artist should conduct himself. The connection between artistic activity and politics is again explored. Responding to that approach to James which concentrates excessively upon his stylistic delicacies, Pound writes (LE 296):

I am tired of hearing pettiness talked about Henry James's style. The subject has been discussed enough in all conscience, along with the minor James. Yet I have heard no word of the major James, of the hater

---

[21] *Blast*, 1 (June 20, 1914): 45. Later republished in *Personæ* (New York: New Directions, 1926), pp. 145-46, with the more offensive language expunged and other revisions made.

of tyranny; book after early book against oppression . . . the domination of modern life. . . . The outbursts in *The Tragic Muse*, the whole of
The Turn of the Screw, human liberty, personal liberty, the rights of the
individual against all sorts of intangible bondage.

He goes on to say that he has no wish to "drag in political con-
notations, from which H. J. was, we believe, wholly exempt," but
he does suggest that James was so finely attuned to cultural and
political reality that he was able to do no less than prophesy the
"Armageddon" of World War I. Concerning the sense of prophecy
that possesses artists, Pound then quotes Flaubert on the War of
1870: "If they had read my *Education Sentimentale*, this sort of
thing wouldn't have happened" (LE 297). As Pound says, "artists
are the antennae of the race, but the bullet-headed many will
never learn to trust their great artists."[22] If only they would trust
them, and respect their efforts to carry on communication between
peoples, peace would come.

The people who prevent communication are the same people
who remain oblivious to a prophetic spirit like James. Even when
James chose to become an expatriate, and to adopt British citizenship, American readers did not "know what they lost. They have
not stopped for eight minutes to consider the meaning of his last
public act" (LE 295). This biting censure shows that Pound in
1918 is not the man he was in 1912. "Patria Mia" had revealed
him as a descendant of Walt Whitman eagerly awaiting a Risorgimento of letters in America. Six years later he castigates America
for its slothful refusal to appreciate the loss of one of its great
novelists. In addition, then, to a commentary on James, Pound
provides in this essay some understanding of his own expatria-
tion.[23] It was a political act, an act, like that of James himself or

[22] This belief in artists as prophets persisted throughout Pound's life. In
the *Paris Review*, no. 28 (Summer-Fall 1962), p. 40, he is quoted: "The great
war came as a surprise, and certainly to see the English—these people who
had never done anything—get hold of themselves, fight it, was immensely im-
pressive. But as soon as it was over they went dead, and then one spent the
next twenty years trying to prevent the second war."

[23] Pound never officially lost his American citizenship. The proceedings
against him in 1945 make that clear. He was nevertheless an expatriate in all
but this technical sense.

of the painter Whistler, reflecting deep disappointment in a national atmosphere of mass insensitivity. The values of the nickel-plated cash register must have been, in his view of things, in the ascendant.

As we can see in these early works, Pound was being drawn in a direction similar to that taken by another young expatriate, T. S. Eliot. Both men felt vulgar forces pressing upon their better instincts. Both sought an authority that could define and control aesthetic responses. And in late 1919, Pound announced that he was taking the path of elitism: "The function of an 'aristocracy' is largely to criticise, select, castigate luxury, to reduce the baroque to an elegance. For this there is need of only a limited number of functionaries."[24]

Thus it is not surprising that Pound developed, as years went on, a political position responsive to the attractions of totalitarian control. Pound's affinity for theories of elite governance was not to be based wholly upon a disenchantment with the masses,[25] but also on an initial assumption, never made by Eliot, that the arts "carry" society and that the best artists must ultimately be recognized as the most important social pioneers. When Pound later urged artists to "make it new," therefore, his campaign was to embody an important implication for those who are not artists, for those who are to be pulled along by the avant-garde. He explains that the masses must often wait some time before benefiting from the achievements of that avant-garde: "The arts, explorative, 'creative,' the 'real arts,' literature, are always too far ahead of any general consciousness to be of the slightest contemporary use. A coal strike, with 2,000,000 orderly strikers happens . . . half

[24] "Pastiche. The Regional. XV," *New Age*, 25 (Oct. 30, 1919): 448.

[25] In 1922, he wrote to William Carlos Williams: "Aristocracy is gone, its function was to select. Only those of us who know what civilization is, only those of us who want better literature, not more literature, better art, not more art, can be expected to pay for it. No use waiting for masses to develop a finer taste, they aren't moving that way." Quoted in D. D. Paige, ed., *The Letters of Ezra Pound* (New York: Harcourt, Brace, 1950), p. 172. In 1928, he wrote to James Vogel: "It takes about 600 people to make a civilization." *Letters*, p. 221.

a century after the 'creator's,' or discoverer's concept of labour in orderly organisation."[26]

But even with his dedication to the avant-garde, he was not prepared to endorse the idea that a cultural elite should be given political power. His indecisive and self-contradictory nature can be seen very clearly on this issue. Pound is, in fact, so uneasy about the coercions involved in political life that it is difficult to see how his political alliances could ever be strong or permanent ones. Emphasizing repeatedly the importance of those philosophies permitting the ultimate degree of personal freedom within the social order, he envisioned a cultural elite that would manage to lead and influence, but would not be subject to any of the deleterious consequences of political power.

His aversion to any kind of coercion can be seen in the distinction he drew in 1917 between the kinds of social order inspired by Confucius and by Christ. Confucius had recognized "the value of personality, . . . man's right to preserve the outlines of his personality," and man's "duty not to interfere with the personalities of others," but Christianity "has become the slogan of every oppression, of every iniquity. From saving your own soul, you progress to thinking it your duty or right to save other people's souls, and to burn them if they object to your method of doing it."[27] Confucian order, we know from Canto 13, means freedom ("They have all answered correctly, / That is to say, each in his nature"); Christianity means meddling. The ideal government must allow for that great latitude of human freedom in which the arts most happily flourish.

But the achievement of this ideal is a problem. As we can see from these early exploratory essays, Pound had dealt with the question of how much freedom for whom: the elite would function with perfect liberty, and the masses would function with a liberty consonant with Confucian social ideals, but the one would not mix with the other. Pound seems almost to anticipate our retrospective judgment of such a scheme as born of vague and un-

[26] "Provincialism. The Enemy. II," *New Age*, 21 (July 19, 1917): 268.
[27] *Ibid.*

resolved musings, for he says somewhat defensively of it that "it is a long way ahead of any working economic system that any of our contemporaries will be able to devise or to operate."[28] He was sure of the artist's ability to lead the way for everyone else, and he was also sure that the artist, just like everyone else, should leave others alone and should himself be left alone. But how were the masses to be led and yet left alone? Was the artist a free man, or was he responsible to society, obligated to lead? Pound was not ready, in these early years, to set forth his answer to such thorny questions, but it is interesting that he then looked forward to a "working economic system" as the most likely solution. Such a system seemed to be provided in the teachings of Major Douglas and Social Credit, to which he was so soon to turn.

[28] *Ibid.*

CHAPTER TWO

C. H. Douglas: The Rappel à l'Ordre

It would be well to pause after our initial exposure to Pound's early political prose and consider the extent to which the man's politics grew naturally out of his life, his American birth and heritage, his early life in the United States, and his long years as an expatriate in Europe. This issue has been raised most directly by those who see a connection between the poet's attitudes and the American environment in which he was reared.[1]

Pound's family had settled early on American soil. His mother was related indirectly to Longfellow; his paternal grandfather, Thaddeus Coleman Pound, was an ambitious frontiersman and lumber merchant who sat in Congress and at times during his quite successful life advocated the cause of "money reform." Pound lived in Philadelphia for almost the first twenty years of his life.[2] His father was a civil servant in the United States Mint. Although the general tone of the Pounds' life was upper-middle class, there was, as his biographer points out, "no money to spare and Ezra was sometimes conscious of the fact that some of his friends and acquaintances were better off than he was."[3] Indeed, with such occasional anxieties, a mother who has been described

---

[1] Victor Ferkiss, "Ezra Pound and American Fascism," *Journal of Politics*, 17 (May 1955): 173-97; John R. Harrison, *The Reactionaries* (London: Victor Gollancz, 1966), p. 121.

[2] He was born in Hailey, Idaho, in 1885, but left there in 1887 at eighteen months of age. He was never a Midwesterner, although it has pleased many commentators to imagine him as one.

[3] Noel Stock, *The Life of Ezra Pound* (New York: Pantheon Books, 1970), p. 6.

as "uppish" or remarkably "formal," and a father whose claim upon the world could in no way match that of his own father, Ezra Pound's family could be described as nouveau-poor: refined, with pretensions to gentility, with a memory of rather better times, with little room for social mobility. Such families contrasted sharply with those alien or immigrant families who were arriving by the thousands on America's Eastern shores during Pound's formative years and were rapidly transfiguring American life. It was this process, of course, that so repelled Pound when he came home to the United States in 1910. The process was to become more intense as the "strangers" achieved greater vertical mobility in the nation's economy and displaced people who could trace their American lineage back to the early years of the republic.

As the process accelerated, the reaction to it intensified, as evidenced most notably for our purposes in the impassioned defenses by American political spokesmen of "traditional" America. Among these defenders were Father Charles E. Coughlin, Charles A. Lindbergh, Huey Long, and Gerald L. K. Smith, all talking of a conspiracy, typically "foreign," against what was essentially American. The agrarian base of America, its Christian religious foundation, and even its basic economic system—small farmers and small, enterprising merchants—were all threatened by "manipulators," "operators," urban-bred Easterners with no commitment whatsoever to the homely virtues that had made the nation strong. At one extreme this reaction led to a desperate and wholly fantastic anti-Semitism, to "100 per cent Americanism," and to the adulation of all that was "simple," "decent," and "pure" in the American experience. "American" in this case usually meant that segment of the middle class composed largely of independent farmers and businessmen, the people who could most plausibly blame their problems on the twin forces of big business above them and the industrial working class below them.[4] Both forces were seen as remote, ingeniously powerful, and massively alien.

In exploring Pound's career, therefore, we should keep in mind

[4] See Victor Ferkiss, "Populist Influences on American Fascism," *Western Political Quarterly*, 10 (1957): 359-67.

that his family would presumably have been quite vulnerable to some of the appeals first of the Populists and later of their more demagogic followers. If the elder Pounds were anxious about their economic position, alarmed about "foreigners," and reduced to what they might have considered a marginal social status, one can assume that their anxieties were, in some measure, reflected in their son. Pound was always closely loyal to his parents' beliefs; they in turn doted on him and encouraged many of his attitudes.[5]

It is from this perspective, among others, that we should view Pound's praise of Jefferson and of Jefferson's nativist, agrarian bias; Pound's belief that the Constitution had been inexorably corrupted by individuals loyal to causes other than the original American dreams; his feeling that all "higher finance" is conspiratorial and malign; his rejection of liberal democracy as "useless"; his contempt for the working masses. From such a perspective, Pound's climactic rage against Jews during the war years seems merely the culmination of long-held prejudices and fears. Just as the original nativist reaction developed into the Populist movement, and that degenerated, in some cases, into hysterical anti-Semitism and into an American version of fascism, so Pound's politics developed, his political career paralleling a general historical development.

Lest this kind of development be thought unique to Pound, it might be worthwhile to suggest Pound's similarity to another American who passed through a period of rabid anti-Semitism, who also felt he had panaceas for the nation's ills, and who was clearly as distinguished in his field of innovation as Pound was in his: Henry Ford.[6] Ford had by the early 1920's so impressed the

---

[5] Stock recounts an instance in Rapallo when Pound and his father were visiting Max Beerbohm. Pound, who had been talking fervently of history and monetary reform, momentarily left the room. The father turned to Beerbohm and said in awe, "You know, Mr. Beerbohm, there isn't a darn thing that boy of mine don't know." Stock, *The Life of Ezra Pound*, p. 3.

[6] For the best history of Ford's career, including the presidential boom and the maladroit adventure into anti-Semitism, see Allan Nevins and Frank Ernest Hill, *Ford*, vol. 2, *Expansion and Challenge, 1915-1933* (New York: Scribner's, 1957).

American mind and imagination that many people thought of him as a presidential prospect. He was seen, quite correctly, as a great leader in technological creativity. His philanthropic activities were admired. He was considered a genius for whom no problem, be it waterpower in Nebraska, the American railroads, the fluctuations of the stock market, or international peace-keeping, was without solution. The presidential boomlet lasted only from the autumn of 1922 until December 20, 1923, when Ford announced that he would support Calvin Coolidge. But the episode had shown how genuinely popular he was with some in the nation, people who liked him, as his biographers have put it, because "he was one of themselves and a good deal more."

So, indeed, he was. He came of simple, sturdy farming people whose lives had been devoted to the soil. He cherished older, rural ways. Believing, as he himself grew successful, that the nation had somehow defaulted on its original promise and had gone the way of urban degeneration, he sought a return to the values he had known as a child. His beliefs were made known in a series of some ninety articles published in his magazine, the *Dearborn Independent*. Beginning in May 1920 and abruptly halted under great pressure from national leaders in early 1922, the articles were rabidly anti-Semitic, laying the blame for virtually all problems on the Jews. The corruption of American baseball, the sensuousness of jazz music, bolshevism, Tammany Hall crookedness, bootlegging, Benedict Arnold's treason, and, of course, America's monetary problems, were all seen as the result of a nefarious Jewish conspiracy. Wherever one looked, the cancer of "the Jews" was to be found.

When Ford ended his anti-Semitic spasm and apologized to one and all, he had learned a bitter lesson about the extent of his own competence in political matters, but his tirade had not appreciably harmed him in the eyes of those who thought him a great American institution. They still admired him for the way he had transformed American industry. The Ford machine was still the marvel of the age, and, as his biographers point out, its inventor "had to be accepted as extraordinary in faults as in virtues."

As we trace Pound's career and note the degree to which he was increasingly preoccupied with breathtakingly simple ways to obliterate wrong and put right in its place; as we note his burgeoning reliance on essentially mechanical schemes of adjusting the relation between monetary life and cultural life, his kinship with Ford emerges. Both had a nostalgic reverence for a lost American purity; both advocated particular answers to enormously complex problems; both saw the world as a machine; both had affinities with the Populist movement in America; and both, like some others acquainted with Populism, found themselves at last in the desperate, hot-house world of anti-Semitism.

In the spring of 1920 appeared the first of Pound's articles praising the thought of Major Clifford Hugh Douglas, former Westinghouse engineer in India and author of numerous publications on economic reorganization. Pound had by then known Douglas for about two years, having met him through A. R. Orage, editor of the *New Age* and an ardent proponent of guild socialism. The *New Age* had been for some time a headquarters for people concerned with economic reform, and its atmosphere was no doubt the proximate source of Pound's earliest considerations on the related questions of currency, credit, and interest. This first article reveals no readiness to embrace all of Social Credit thinking. Pound in fact ignores the subtleties of Douglas's theories, and concentrates on his effectiveness in combating the idea of "man as a social unit." In furnishing an antidote to this Fabian socialist "poison," Douglas has restored the possibilities of humanism and set in motion an unmistakably new force in economic thought. With Douglas, says Pound, "one has at least honest thinking, no festoons of ecclesiastical verbiage, no weak arguments covered with sentimentalism."[7]

Pound makes one point with great force: Douglas has acknowledged the absurdity of war and its wastage of human possibility; for this he is to be acclaimed. Here is a significant change. The poet who once luxuriated in the prospect of violence now rages

[7] Review of *Economic Democracy*, by Major C. H. Douglas, *Little Review*, 6 (April 1920): 40, 42.

against war and against the socialists caught up by doctrines of "mass-men." The war just ended had taken from him certain precious individuals, among them the sculptor Henri Gaudier-Brzeska and the young philosopher T. E. Hulme, men so fine and rare no socialist's gross calculations could encompass them, much less do them honor.

The war, moreover, had created an economic and diplomatic crisis that was to issue ultimately in still another war; it had revealed the true foundations on which civilization, with its flimsy "culture," had so creakily rested. *Hugh Selwyn Mauberley*, published soon after the war, articulates, as we know, the anger, disillusionment, and sense of irrecoverable loss that had overcome Pound:

> Died some, pro patria
>   non "dulce" non "et decor" . . .
> walked eye-deep in hell
> believing in old men's lies, then unbelieving
> came home, home to a lie,
> home to many deceits,
> home to old lies and new infamy;
> usury age-old and age-thick
> and liars in public places.
> Daring as never before, wastage as never before.
> Young blood and high blood,
> fair cheeks and fine bodies;
> . . .
>
> There died a myriad,
> And of the best, among them,
> For an old bitch gone in the teeth,
> For a botched civilization,
> Charm, smiling at the good mouth,
> Quick eyes gone under earth's lid,
> For two gross of broken statues,
> For a few thousand battered books.

The deaths of Gaudier-Brzeska and T. E. Hulme are specifically memorialized in the sixteenth of Pound's cantos:

> And Henri Gaudier went to it,
>   and they killed him,

And killed a good deal of sculpture,
And ole T.E.H. he went to it,
With a lot of books from the library,
London Library, and a shell buried 'em in a dug-out,
And the Library expressed its annoyance.
                    And a bullet hit him on the elbow
...gone through the fellow in front of him,
And he read Kant in the hospital, in Wimbledon,
in the original,
And the hospital staff didn't like it.

About killing, about war, he was later to say in a snippet of autobiography: "1918 began investigation of causes of war, to oppose same."[8] The shattering impact of the World War, especially its actual grim cost in friends and comrades forever gone, added a note of sobriety to the thinking of the pre-war *enfant terrible* who had dominated the outsize pages of *Blast*. Now, with a practical bent of mind, surrounded by those of like ambition and curiosity in Orage's office, he sought to discover why wars were apparently so inevitable, so much the final product of laws and pressures beyond individual control.

It would be difficult to show that Pound ever accepted all the principles of Social Credit.[9] But it is not difficult to show how receptive he was emotionally to some of its central notions. Social Credit offered such an astonishingly straightforward explanation of so many of the world's ills, including its propensity to make wars and to smash young promise, that Pound was captivated by it. It supported, moreover, several of his own early assumptions in "Patria Mia" and elsewhere: the limitless bounty of nature and the alien forces standing ready to corrupt a nation's strength. It also supported, in fact stands as a neglected monument to, the idea that cultural maladies have specific and concrete solutions.

"Real Credit," for example, should replace "Financial Credit."

---

[8] Ezra Pound, *Selected Poems* (New York: New Directions, 1949), p. viii.

[9] Certainly, in his later years, he made a point of describing his departure from Social Credit. See, for instance, *A Visiting Card* (London: Peter Russell, 1952), p. 13: "I am not going back to Social Credit. The latter was the doorway through which I came to economic curiosity." But even with his later deviation into the doctrines of Frederick Soddy and Silvio Gesell, Pound remained essentially a Douglasite.

Real Credit, as Douglas defined it, is the rate at which a community can deliver goods and services as demanded. Pound describes it rather more poetically in, for example, Canto 43:

> there first was the fruit of nature
> there was the whole will of the people

He also has it in mind when he so often quotes Thomas Jefferson: "The earth belongs to the living." Financial Credit, by contrast, is an artificial creation of bankers and other manipulators of money. Such manipulators, the alien force, have gained a stranglehold on the wealth of the land and, by elaborate maneuvers of currency and interest, are siphoning it off, then hoarding it.

Pound's analysis of the situation, even with Douglas's tutelage, can as yet go no further than this. He understands European and American civilization in the year 1920 as the product of a wholly nefarious interaction. Bankers have created a system, he says, that has as its inevitable consequences:

(1) the paralysis of commerce and the immobilization of goods, in other words, "poverty amidst plenty";

(2) the centralization of power in a few hands;

(3) the exploitation of the debt-ridden worker;

(4) the end of independent governments and the beginning of the domination of finance;

(5) the creation of wars by competing nations demanding foreign outlets for their immobilized goods.

Social Credit entertains distinctions far more subtle than these. Douglas himself refined upon the basic theory as it was originally outlined in *Economic Democracy* (his first book, 1920) and was for many years to busy himself in constructing arguments of the most intricate sort to ward off the challenges of those many traditional economists who sought to demolish his theory.[10] But Pound was satisfied for quite some time with the essentials. He

---

[10] An excellent account of Douglas and Social Credit is provided by Margaret G. Myers, *Monetary Proposals for Social Reform* (New York: Columbia University Press, 1940), pp. 106-46. She is extremely critical of the entire movement. For very sympathetic accounts, see Philip Mairet, comp., *The Douglas Manual* (London: Stanley Nott, 1934) and E. S. Holter, *The ABC of Social Credit* (New York: Coward-McCann, 1934).

repeatedly endorsed Douglas's *A-plus-B* Theorem, the purpose of which was to show that capitalist production, by its very nature, inevitably works to create goods for which there cannot be sufficient purchasing power. Pound sets out the workings of the Theorem at length in Canto 38:

> A factory
> has also another aspect, which we call the financial aspect
> It gives people the power to buy (wages, dividends
> which are power to buy) but it is also the cause of prices
> or values, financial, I mean financial values
> It pays workers, and pays *for* material.
> What it pays in wages and dividends
> stays fluid, as power to buy, and this power is less,
> per forza, damn blast your intellex, is less
> than the total payments made by the factory
> (as wages, dividends AND payments for raw material
> bank charges etcetera[)]
> and all, that is the whole, that is the total
> of these is added into the total of prices
> caused by that factory, any damn factory
> and there is and must be therefore a clog
> and the power to purchase can never
> (under the present system) catch up with
> prices at large,
>   and the light became so bright and so blindin'
> in this layer of paradise
>   that the mind of man was bewildered.

The *A-plus-B* Theorem lies at the heart of all of Douglas's arguments. Wages, profits, and production costs, including costs resulting from loans, are added together. This total is then divided into two parts, the first being payments (such as wages and dividends) made to individuals and the second being payments (such as raw-material costs, bank charges, and other external costs) made to other entities. The price of a commodity would logically, then, be the sum of these two parts, or *A* plus *B*. But, Douglas argued, it never is. Somewhere along the line, money is taken out of circulation and the entire system, off balance, is thrust toward collapse. Purchasing power slowly dies. Men cannot buy all that men have made. A "clog" develops that benefits the controllers of wealth but oppresses everyone else.[11]

If we look at the organization of this crucial passage in the *Cantos* (written in 1933), we note the amazing suppleness with which Pound moves from theoretical summary to breathless astonishment.

The distance between economic chaos and economic paradise is, according to the poet, a short one. Paradise can be reached merely by grasping the meaning of the *A-plus-B* Theorem. Understanding Pound ultimately means understanding the dependence of his thinking on abrupt turns of this kind: from visions of ruination and collapse to visions of salvation, from visions of impenetrable economic ignorance to visions of that "bright and blindin' " light. Understanding him also means appreciating the simplicity of his basic analysis of reality. To solve a social problem, he tells us, is to use the proper instrument at the proper time. The desired result will then automatically issue forth. He who wills not to use the proper instrument has therefore done, in Pound's estimation, all the evil a man can do. He has not *been* evil (the poet accepts no arguments about the inherently evil or fallen nature of man)[12] but he has, in his stupidity, contaminated the health of society. He has subordinated society to the satisfaction of his own desires. When Pound imagines a hell, as he does in Canto 14, it includes many such people. Their sin is dullness of mind, not conscious malevolence (*"dummheit,* not *bosheit"* as he was later to say in *Guide to Kulchur*):

> The slough of unamiable liars,
> bog of stupidities,
> malevolent stupidities, and stupidities,
> the soil living pus, full of vermin,
> dead maggots begetting live maggots,
> slum owners,

---

[11] Earle Davis, in *Vision Fugitive, Ezra Pound and Economics* (Lawrence: University Press of Kansas, 1968), is helpful on Pound and Douglas (pp. 23-24).

[12] George Dekker includes a discussion of the limitations of Pound's conception of human evil in *Sailing After Knowledge, The Cantos of Ezra Pound* (London: Routledge, 1963), pp. 8-14.

usurers squeezing crab-lice, pandars to authority,
pets-de-loup, sitting on piles of stone books,
obscuring the texts with philology,
          hiding them under their persons,
the air without refuge of silence
          the drift of lice, teething,
and above it the mouthing of orators,
          the arse-belching of preachers.
          And Invidia,
the corruptio, fœtor, fungus,
liquid animals, melted ossifications,
slow rot, fœtid combustion,
          chewed cigar-butts, without dignity, without tragedy,
. . . . .m Episcopus, waving a condom full of black-beetles,
monopolists, obstructors of knowledge.
          obstructors of distribution.

The objection to be registered against this version of hell, based on Pound's final judgment of London before leaving it for France in 1920, is that it is, as Eliot later said, "vaporous" and "trivial." Eliot found difficulty in taking it seriously because he felt it did not distinguish "between essential Evil and social accidents."[13] Many readers can sympathize with Eliot's criticism. To make a distinction between such evil and such accidents, or even to recognize anything *essential* about evil, lies beyond Pound's thinking. Men make mistakes or fail to think well; these mistakes and failures can be corrected. Any of the imponderable questions about why human beings have behaved so deplorably for such a very long time are made to seem inconsequential by Pound's procedures. Only the "efficient cause" of error is worth investigating, and further analysis is not necessary.

This way of thinking, it should be noted, is compatible with Pound's later dedication to the doctrines of Mussolini and Italian fascism. Mussolini seemed to Pound to be alone among politicians of his time in understanding the nature of error and in being ready to thrust ideas into action. Abjuring metaphysical subtleties and profundities with as much annoyance as Pound, he came to be an

---

[13] *After Strange Gods: A Primer of Modern Heresy* (London: Faber and Faber, 1934), p. 47.

appropriate hero for a poet who saw metaphysics as a smoke-screen. That poet, unlike his friend Eliot, divorced himself from the spiritually abstruse and celebrated, as fascism itself was preparing to do, "the priority of action over doctrine."[14] The years would soon spell out other differences between the two Americans.

In the period immediately following the First World War, however, Pound's political attitudes were not yet representative of any clearly identifiable "side." He had not yet made up his mind, but his style hides that fact from us. Then, as always, it was a style of absolute confidence. He never spoke but as the autocrat, and if we are to understand his position, we must not allow his style to obscure our vision.

Looking beneath the autocratic style, we can see equivocation, for example, in Pound's attitudes toward ideologies of the left. Once he had announced that he would be interested in supporting those who defined a good state as "one which impinges least upon the peripheries of its citizens,"[15] he had to decide what ideology would most likely encourage the creation of that state. He had also to decide to what extent he could support any ideology. Perhaps Douglas and Mussolini did not yet appear to add up to the total answer, for it is with a mixture of caution and curiosity that he wrote in 1927 that "both Fascio and the Russian revolution are interesting phenomena; beyond which there is historic perspective."[16] At this date, "Fascio" was only five years old, having begun with the 1922 March on Rome; the Russian Revolution only ten. Between the attractions of the two, Pound's mind then moved. He questioned the workings of capitalism and Wall Street finance, and wrote, for example, to the young Mike Gold, editor of *The New Masses*, congratulating him on the appearance of his

[14] The phrase is from Ernst Nolte, *Three Faces of Fascism*, trans. by Leila Vennewitz (New York: Holt, Rinehart, 1966), p. 250.

[15] "Definitions etc.," *Der Querschnitt*, 1 (Jan. 1925): 54, as quoted in Noel Stock, ed., *Impact: Essays on Ignorance and the Decline of American Civilization* by Ezra Pound (Chicago: Regnery, 1960), p. 218.

[16] "The Exile [I]," *Exile*, 1 (Spring 1927): 88-92. Reprinted in *Impact*, p. 219.

magazine and requesting copies of "John Reed's *Ten Days that Shook the World*, Nearing's *Dollar Diplomacy*, or whatever you think most necessary for my education."[17]

The relationship Pound maintained with Gold and the *New Masses* was to continue, precariously, for a number of years. It can be traced, in much of its fascination and resistance, in the Pound *Letters* and elsewhere. Pound probably first recognized the importance of Marx and of the Bolshevik revolution when he attended a lecture by the muckraking journalist Lincoln Steffens sometime in 1924. He was moved by the talk.[18] Steffens appears in Canto 19, published in 1925, as does the first mention of Marx in the poem. But the relationship was, in a certain sense, doomed from the start. As strong as the poet's enthusiasm for Gold's personal blend of revolution and individuality might have been, he was constrained from traveling very far left with him. And Gold, for his part, obviously could have no taste for Pound's later venture into hero-worship.

The relationship finally unraveled in the pages of the *New Masses* in 1930, when Gold came down hard on Pound: "Do not be misled by ideology, Ezra. When J. P. Morgan tells you that he is an art-lover, and has lived only for Art and Antiques, you know he is only trying to shield something; piracy, for instance. Mussolini's original program was to kill Workers and destroy their organizations. The Fascist philosophy came years later. . . . Search to the roots. The roots are in economics, as ever. Capitalism is still enthroned in Italy."[19] The connection between Pound and the American left had been made, nonetheless, and is now part of the record. The poet was by his own acknowledgment a revolutionary. Indeed, as our evidence here has shown, he had felt in his early years as artist and aesthetic campaigner that revolution was what art was all about. Vorticism, *Blast*, his whirlwind fundraising plans for fellow writers, his unremitting injunction to "make it new"—all issued from his belief that art and ceaseless

---

[17] "Pound Joins the Revolution!" *New Masses*, 2 (Dec. 1926): 3.
[18] Stock, *The Life of Ezra Pound*, p. 256.
[19] "Notes of the Month," *New Masses*, 6 (Oct. 1930): 4.

change were inseparable, indeed that the one was continually creating the other.

But Pound's implicit understanding of the kind of dialectic involved in such change and causation could hardly be hammered into anything resembling a Marxist dialectic. The fundamental Marxist proposition in the Preface to *The Critique of Political Economy* could never be his: "The mode of production of material life conditions the social, political and intellectual life process in general. It is not the consciousness of men that determines their being, but, on the contrary, their social being that determines their consciousness."[20] Believing in his own fervent and oracular way that consciousness does determine being, he simply carried to an extreme, as he was to carry many other things, a notion implicit in the thinking of most artists whose cultures place a premium on individual enterprise. Those artists want to see history as a collection of isolated biographies (Carlyle), and they pooh-pooh the very existence of general forces, social and political, more powerful than individual men themselves. Pound's Promethean expressions of self-confidence ("Artists are the antennae of the race") must be seen as kindred, for instance, to Emerson's description of poets in general: "They are free, and they make free." Revolution is generated, idealistically, within the mind, particularly within the mind of the avant-garde artist, and is not the result, the inevitable product, of divisions deep within society.

If this were all to be said of Pound's politics at this moment in his life, there would be little to distinguish him from a great many other artists whose celebration of their own powers is rapturous and whose relationship to large social and historical forces is, by their own choice, either haughtily dismissive or proudly anarchistic. But Pound's strong anarchistic tendencies, endemic among artists who are convinced that they are "above politics," conflicted sharply with other urges, equally strong, compelling him to be political and to develop theories that made sense of the reality he knew lay behind events. Ergo Douglas.

Douglas agrees with Marx in several interesting and essential

[20] Karl Marx and Friedrich Engels, *Selected Works* (Moscow, 1968), p. 182.

ways. Both men stressed the degree to which the "substructure" of
organized life, the commercial, financial, and trading affairs of
men who are members of antagonistic or exploitative groups, determines the well-being or malaise of their respective societies—in
other words the degree to which economic developments condition all the rest of life. Pound, agreeing with Douglas, expressed
the idea most clearly some ten years after this postwar period of
cultural rethinking on his part in his classic formulation, Canto 45:

> with usura the line grows thick
> with usura is no clear demarcation
> and no man can find site for his dwelling.
> Stone cutter is kept from his stone
> weaver is kept from his loom
> WITH USURA
> wool comes not to market
> sheep bringeth no gain with usura

A second point of agreement is rooted in the belief that one
part of society fattens itself on the labor of another. Marx had
demonstrated quite clearly how surplus value is generated and
how its generation depends on an exploitative process. He had
pointed out that the value of a commodity is always more than
the value of a worker's labor power and the constant capital used
up in production; that "more" is surplus value. Douglas (solely
concerned, let us remember, with monetary rather than larger
economic issues) had shown, as I have said, how a gap is created
between the purchasing power of the people and the selling price
of a commodity, and how that gap widens in time as the difference
between purchasing power and selling price is drained off into
bank vaults, unspent dividends, savings, etc.

The equivalent of surplus value in Douglas's system is the resulting "clog" that benefits the controllers of wealth. There are,
of course, essential differences between the two thinkers. Marx
would have considered Douglas's monetary reforms mere tinker-
ing with machinery that was about to collapse. And they differ in
their proposed solutions to what they saw as the economic crisis
of their day, a crisis characterized by commercial paralysis, im-

mobilization of goods, competition between nations desperately looking for new markets, and centralization of power in a few hands. For Marx the solution would come, by a process of dialectical change, with the overthrow of the bourgeoisie. Douglas, who thought capitalism the best of all systems, proposed (as did J. M. Keynes) governmental control of credit in order that the gap between selling and purchasing power be closed. Marx was convinced that the entire capitalistic system was soon utterly to be transformed through class struggle and that only in the eventually classless society to follow would exploitative relationships end. Douglas, on the other hand, was concerned not with classes, in whose reality he seemed hardly to believe, but with individuals, predominantly monopolistic financiers, whose private activities were an infection within the system.

Herein at last lies the crucial difference, for our purposes, between the two versions of economic reality. Pound was intuitively drawn to Douglas's version, and at last repelled by Marx's. In his search for the mainsprings of war and international conflict, he settled upon an analysis that allowed him to blame specific people —Mayer Amschel Rothschild, Edward Vickers, Sir Basil Zaharoff, J. P. Morgan, and the other great financiers of the period—for the bloodshed and horror he had seen, and people of their ilk for comparable horrors throughout history. He confined himself, then, to pointed attacks on such people, and ignored the question of class conflict. Marx saw the problem as pandemic and fatal; Pound (and Douglas) saw it as endemic and curable. Pound, an "Imagist of politics," eschewed the generalities that Marx's mind embraced. To the poet, all generalities were vague and useless. The task was once again, and now with greater fervor, to search for and isolate the particular.

Why was Pound so reluctant to extend his critical analysis beyond the confines of particular culprits: money-men, politicians supporting the bankers, newspapers supporting the status quo, and that bugbear of early-twentieth-century pacifists and Shavians, the munitions-makers? The reason, I think, is that such an extended analysis would have propelled him directly into an irreconcilable contradiction with some of his own preconceptions. In other words, Pound was in no way prepared in the mid-1920's to launch an attack on capitalism. He was prepared to attack only its misuse, because capitalism was the system most congenial to his sense of himself as a free individual whose entrepreneurial literary energies could help transform the consciousness of his nation. It was the "free" and adventure-questing man he had always praised. No greater hero than Odysseus existed for him. Nor could he attack social hierarchy, for he had already found it proper and fitting to praise such hierarchy ("It takes about 600 people to make a civilization"; "No use waiting for masses to develop a finer taste, they aren't moving that way"). Since the contradictions were irreconcilable—stemming as they did from what it means to participate in the making of culture within a class structure—it must have seemed better to avoid them. Becoming the kind of poet he became and the kind of social reformer he became allowed him to do just that.

In sum, Pound was subjected both then and later, as we will see, to two great and conflicting pressures. The prevailing literary standards, which had much to say about the way a poet might feel about himself and his position within society, exerted one pressure. The material demands of Pound's society, issuing from war, economic confusion, and maldistribution, exerted another. As a man of extraordinary energy but rather limited powers of formal thought, he responded as fully as he could to both. Intuitively accepting Douglas, Pound established a *modus vivendi* between the pressures. Had he gone beyond Douglas into a more radical economics, he would have lost his vision of himself as one who changes the mental life of his countrymen. Thus his ultimate rejection of what he conceived of as violent ideological revolution:

As to our "joining revolutions" etc. It is unlikely. The artist is concerned with producing something that will be enjoyable even after a successful revolution. So far as we know even the most violent bolchevik has never abolished electric light globes merely because they were invented under another regime, and by a man intent rather on his own job than on particular propaganda.[21]

21 "The Exile [I]," *Exile*, 1 (Spring 1927): 88-92; repr. in *Impact*, pp. 219-20.

To see art thus, as a residual force outlasting all political and social change, might be thought oddly contradictory in a man who had for some years been consumed in revolutionary campaigns, among them one to "Make it New." These campaigns had aimed to change society in the most profound of ways: to give it "new eyes," new ways of creating forms by which to live. The same inconsistency, we may go on to say, lies at the heart of Pound's greatest achievement, the *Cantos*. In that poem, he urges upon us with one gesture the idea that forms of art are important in altering the shape and direction of civilization to come; with another gesture, pointing to the futility of any such alterations, he suggests that works of art are mere artifacts prevailing amid the collapse of civilization. The contradiction is nicely shown by two statements from 1928:

Quite simply: I want a new civilization.

As briefly as possible. I am not a revolutionist, if by that term one means a man who believes a complete smash of the existing order is necessary before one can get improvement.[22]

Very much an advocate of change, he could nevertheless endorse no united or mass efforts. Such efforts were vulgar. Poetry and other artistic expression were not vulgar, but they might be weak. Weak as they might be, however, they alone were certain good. Thus, each of his buoyant apostrophes to the salutary influences of art was eventually dragged down by the dark suspicions he harbored about those who were to be influenced. The baser inclinations of such people, the depressing spectacle they created *en masse*, their propensity to do the stupid thing preyed on Pound's mind. In coming to terms with them, he found himself in almost complete agreement with his friend Eliot: the general run of people is bad; grossness retains the upper hand in history; Gresham's Law influences ethical and intellectual qualities as well as everything else.

Hence his social crusades did not issue from any truly egalitarian sympathies for the common lot of mankind. Rather, they

---

[22] "The Exile [III]," *Exile*, 3 (Spring 1928): 102-7, reprinted in *Impact*, p. 222; "The Damn Fool Bureaukrats," *New Masses*, 4 (June 1928): 15.

issued from a belief that if only the correct ministrations were applied, all would be well and society could be left in peace forevermore, the better for art to prosper, the better for unruly men to be taught the pleasures of art. And what better ministrations to offer than, first, Social Credit and, later, fascism?

It has been said of Douglas in retrospect that he gives the impression of being more of a skillful politician than a humanitarian or an earnest truth-seeker or a man truly concerned with righting the injustices of society. Pound sometimes seems separated in the same way from his announced social concerns. True, he praises Henry James's struggles against petty social injustices; true, he dooms many to a hell of his own imagining for enriching themselves at the expense of their fellowmen. He is passionately against war and deeply wary of Marx. But Ezra Pound, on the eve both of his most active years as a political spokesman and of a great economic depression, was still toying with being a politician of the arts, not of society at large. Not yet quite ready to take on all of society on its own terms, he had a parochial message: society must maintain order so that the arts may be sustained.

CHAPTER THREE

The Components of Order

The single greatest difficulty in Pound's work is one of order, not of allusion. The reader who falters in reading the *Cantos* or the prose does so either because what is before his eyes is ordered by a principle inaccessible to him or because it possesses no real order at all. This difficulty has not been completely solved, though it has been mitigated, by the explications Kenner, Davie, Dekker, Pearlman, Schneidau, and others have provided. Even most of these critics have admitted that Pound's work possesses nothing like perfect coherence. (The *Annotated Index* is of some help in reading the *Cantos*, to be sure, but often it provides only an immense vista of uselessly scattered information.) Pound himself has not been entirely helpful about this situation. He seems to have been of two minds about the logical order, or lack of it, discoverable in his writings. At times he assured everyone that all was in good order or, in the case of the *Cantos*, soon would be. At other times, he spoke contemptuously of efforts to discern coherence where coherence was of minor importance.

Schneidau provides, I think, the most convincing analysis of the poetics of the *Cantos*, and his conclusion is far from consoling for those who seek order. By emphasizing the degree to which "real" poetry consists of precisely shaped "gists" and "piths," and by relying so strongly on Imagistic methods, Pound indirectly deprived himself of a unifying principle that might have framed his crystalline fragments. As Schneidau puts it, "If the texture is made smooth, the details cannot stand out sharply."[1] Since throughout

[1] Herbert Schneidau, *Ezra Pound, The Image and the Real* (Baton Rouge: Louisiana State University Press, 1969), p. 140.

the writing of the *Cantos* Pound remained an Imagist, a poet for whom sharp details were a matter of fundamental importance, the surface of the poem is broken. Any synthesizing theme he might have introduced would have beclouded his poem's "jagged clarity."

Moreover, Pound left open the option of including relevant notes and explanatory material in later revisions of the *Cantos*. Schneidau observes that the only appropriate defense of this disconcerting method is the one Pound himself supplies in defending the alleged formlessness of William Carlos Williams's work. Pound says (LE 394) that "it can do us no harm to stop an hour or so and consider the number of very important chunks of world-literature in which form, major form, is remarkable mainly for absence." Pound had in mind such examples as the *Iliad*, Aeschylus's *Prometheus*, Montaigne, Rabelais, Flaubert's *Bouvard et Pécuchet*. As Homer, Aeschylus, Montaigne, Rabelais, Flaubert, and Williams, so Pound.

An obvious problem arises from such a comparison, however, for Pound's poem has a more didactic function than most of the other works he cites. The *Cantos*, that is, are in part a poem written against error; they aim to set forth historical and economic truth; they are to cleanse the age and to disinfect consciousness. They have, in short, a will to action. But does the *Iliad*? Was Rabelais's ambition so pointed?

The fact is, as Schneidau nowhere states but often suggests, that Pound's matter is often ill served by his form. Pound is akin to the teacher too busy to teach; to the informant who speaks an unknown language; to the leader whose esoteric proclamations baffle his followers. Caught between his desire to alert the reading masses to what he had learned and his grave suspicion that such readers were too lumpish to appreciate his message, Pound was for years involved in writing a massively informative poem from a posture of *épater le lecteur*. Such a contradiction bewilders even the most sympathetic of scholarly readers.

Still another problem must be faced by readers of the *Cantos*. It is fairly easy to see in retrospect that the mature Ezra Pound was aesthetically and philosophically prejudiced in favor of the

Mediterranean world. He was absorbed by Mediterranean qualities of light and color; he celebrated the success of Mediterranean culture in holding in luminous synthesis beliefs and traditions and visionary possibilities that the analytical Northern cultures had segregated. The fecund mysticism that nurtured the belief in Roman divinities, some of them half divine and half human; the Ovidian mentality that visualized the living spirit transformed into a variety of shapes, both beastly and human; the fertile residue of religions and cults much older than Christianity—all this in the culture fascinated Pound. So far, so good. And Pound could argue with considerable rhetorical effect that such a culture possessed an equilibrium and sanity not elsewhere to be found. But he was wont to go further and portray other cultures as crazed, partial, or distorted by comparison. Mediterranean culture, in other words, provided Pound with one more weapon against things he had learned not to like. Perhaps the clearest expression of his tendency to use this weapon is to be found in his 1928 essay on Guido Cavalcanti (LE 154):

We appear to have lost the radiant world where one thought cuts through another with clean edge, a world of moving energies *"mezzo oscuro rade,"* *"risplende in sè perpetuale effecto,"* magnetisms that take form, that are seen, or that border the visible, the matter of Dante's *paradiso,* the glass under water, the form that seems a form seen in a mirror, these realities perceptible to the sense, interacting, *"a lui si tiri"* untouched by the two maladies, the Hebrew disease, the Hindoo disease, fanaticisms and excess that produce Savonarola, asceticisms that produce fakirs, St. Clement of Alexandria, with his prohibition of bathing by women. . . . Between those diseases, existed the Mediterranean sanity. The *"section d'or,"* if that is what it meant, that gave the churches like St. Hilaire, San Zeno, the Duomo di Modena, the clear lines and proportions. Not the pagan worship of strength, nor the Greek perception of visual non-animate plastic, or plastic in which the being animate was not the main or principal quality, but this "harmony in the sentience" or harmony *of* the sentient, where the thought has its demarcation, the substance its *virtu,* where stupid men have not reduced all "energy" to unbounded undistinguished abstraction.

Thus the richness of "Mediterranean sanity," which can somehow embrace both thought and substance, reality and abstraction, and can do so in such a way that the integrity of each is respected while the essential unity of all is preserved. This praise of sanity contains, however, a neat thrust against two "diseases"—the Hebrew and the Hindoo. They are in turn associated with other fanaticisms and excesses, some of which are Christian. According to Pound, each of these maladies makes impossible the wholeness of vision, of felt experience and thought, of sensibility, that he so highly valued. Having once defended poetic formlessness, he now exalts cultural coherence. For it is precisely that elusive thing known as the "unified sensibility" which he has in mind here.

Eliot had sought the same thing. Eliot's adoption in this same year (1928) of a position incorporating Anglo-Catholicism, royalism, and classicism was a practical and personal step toward the harmony he felt his age had long since abandoned. Eliot, however, sought to gather into one precisely delimited central attitude the strands, unraveled during the past three centuries, that alone could give proper direction to English life and to his own; whereas Pound, more inclusive than Eliot and more respectful of contrariety and multiplicity, did not seek to recover isolated strands, but rather to achieve an awareness that could harmonize the plenitude of all things and all thought. Whatever divided or separated was suspect. Thus he was fiercely hostile to any monotheistic religion or indeed any religious philosophy encouraging either the violation by one person of the integrity of another or the separation of any person from the rich variety of life around him. At almost the same time as his remarks on Mediterranean sanity appeared, he was also saying that evil consisted of interfering with the affairs of others: "Against this principle of evil no adequate precaution is taken by Christianity, Moslemism, Judaism, nor, so far as I know, by *any* monotheistic religion. Many 'mystics' do not even aim at the principle of good; they seek merely establishment of a parasitic relationship with the unknown."[2]

The good, in Pound's mind at this time, was a code of ethical conduct that would, like Confucianism, stress the establishment of order within oneself (" 'If a man have not order within him / He can not spread order about him; / And if a man have not order

---

[2] "Prolegomena," *Exile*, 2 (Autumn 1927): 35.

within him / His family will not act with due order; / And if the prince have not order within him / He can not put order in his dominions.' / And Kung gave the words 'order' / and 'brotherly deference' / And said nothing of the 'life after death' " [Canto 13]). That code would also stress the unlimited apprehension of the world in all its "sentient harmony."

To recapitulate, creating such an ideal structure ("held in the mind entire" as he was to say of another vision), which was to bridge certain great splits and fissures in modern sensibility, was also to attack divisive monotheisms like Judaism. Sentient harmony is gained, but what is lost? Perhaps that easy tolerance of ideas and notions, and the people holding them, which Pound characterized as "liberalism" and which he could never accept.

Perhaps it is in this light, a light that must probe beneath a complex series of aesthetic and philosophical assumptions, that Pound's later, and coarser, expressions of anti-Semitic feeling must be understood. It is plausible, as I have argued, that such anti-Semitism is an indigenous American product, that Pound had absorbed and was merely to repeat the conventional prejudices of the class and time into which he had been born. But it is equally plausible that the biographical circumstances set in motion a complex train of philosophical alternatives Pound could then entertain, their only common bond being their hostility to notions somehow connected with Judaism and with Jews. Thus the connection between Pound's background and the attitudes of his later years is not crudely deterministic, but flexible, allowing for much but always limiting what is possible. He had what might be called a predisposition toward anti-Semitism—of the same sort that can be found in Eliot.

For more than three decades of his life, Pound repeatedly used anti-Semitism, sometimes highly abstract and sometimes stridently vulgar, as a means of making known his position on various issues. The "Semite" tried to make life and nature less than they were, saw them narrowly and reductively. Perhaps it should be noted here that he need not even be a Jew. Witness Pound's lifelong admiration for the poet Louis Zukofsky (a Jew) and his fierce antipathy to Franklin Delano Roosevelt (whom Pound referred to as Jewish). Hebraic monotheism, like its successor, Christian monotheism, could be no proper witness to the splendor of ever-bountiful nature, which is always productive beyond man's poor capacity to describe. Monotheistic theology has an impoverished mythology, driven by logic and legalism, and fixated on proper conduct. It strives to use rational analysis where awe and praise are clearly required.

Canto 30, written during the late 1920's and early 1930's, attacks an evil born of rationality, the evil of linear time. The protagonist exhumes his lady-love's body and forces her murderers to venerate it. In morbid delight, he has "reversed" or frozen time. Instead of involving himself in the manifold rhythm of nature, he has sought to halt it. But by no means whatsoever can this be done. As Daniel Pearlman (to whose book *The Barb of Time* I am here much indebted) has put it, "cyclical" time or "natural" time must always triumph over linear time,[3] the time imposed upon life by rationalists and by those dedicated to the proposition that the world is proceeding in some upward or forward direction. A rigid hold on linear time leads only to a rigid spirit: "Time is the evil. Evil."

Pity can also be evil, according to Canto 30. Time forces nature into patterns supposedly congenial to forward-directed Western man. Pity attempts to make nature less than it is: less cruel, less pure, less austerely balanced by its own internal ecological symmetries. As Pearlman points out, the pity Pound presumably has in mind is a Christian pity, a pity defined by medieval love-poetry in which love arises from pity and not from manliness. Moreover, no Christian can appreciate the full flourishing of nature because he has been taught to believe nature essentially rank because originally fallen. Thus the Christian view is directly opposed to the mythological one. As Pearlman puts it, "the forces of order and disorder come into conflict in terms of two opposed views of time, mechanical time versus organic time, and complementarily in

---

[3] *The Barb of Time: On the Unity of Pound's* Cantos (New York: Oxford University Press, 1969), pp. 21-22.

terms of two opposed world-cultural views, the dualistic Christian as against the holistic Greek."[4]

> Compleynt, compleynt I hearde upon a day,
> Artemis singing, Artemis, Artemis
> Agaynst Pity lifted her wail:
> Pity causeth the forests to fail,
> Pity slayeth my nymphs,
> Pity spareth so many an evil thing.
> Pity befouleth April,
> Pity is the root and the spring.
> Now if no fayre creature followeth me
> It is on account of Pity,
> It is on account that Pity forbideth them slaye.

At the root, then, at the most profound reaches of Pound's imagination, is his devotion to the mythological and the Mediterranean. It is perhaps surprising that a poet so given to precise techniques of versification and image-making, so concerned with the particular at the expense of the general, would be absorbed in holistic myth. But once the initial holistic assumptions had been made, the particular reasserted itself. Thus Pound's distrust of monotheism immediately became distrust, even hatred, of one particular form of monotheism, the Judaic. These sudden leaps from axiom to finding, from principle to prejudice, are to be found throughout Pound's work. They are, of course, not logical in any ordinary sense. But for a certain kind of poet they are clearly more useful than logic could ever be. It is just such thrusts and abrupt departures, such descents from abiding code to local skirmish, that create the sense of speed and acceleration felt in the *Cantos*. The poem, after all, is not to be read as a proof. It sets out to persuade, not by logic, but by the brilliance of the poet's mind suddenly registered on the page, by truth yielded up in curious divagations, by the dexterity with which even the cumbersome interstices of syllogism are broken through and conclusions made directly apparent.

The same technique marks the *ABC of Economics* (1933). The

[4] *Ibid.*, p. 123.

title of this work promises the reader a sound, elementary understanding of economics, and the opening sentence promises him or her a logical or systematic treatment of the subject (ABC 13): "I shall have no peace until I get the subject off my chest, and there is no other way of protecting myself against charges of unsystematized, uncorrelated thought, dilettantism, idle eclecticism, etc., than to write a brief formal treatise." But soon, to our regret, Pound confesses (ABC 27), "Very well, I am not proceeding according to Aristotelian logic but according to the ideogramic method of first heaping together the necessary components of thought."

What this "ideogramic" method supplies are notions that, examined separately, reveal not only the latest axioms of Pound's political, social, and economic thinking, but also the direction in which he would necessarily be moving as the years went on. Among these notions, most of them traceable to Douglas, are the habitual overproduction of nature (and here Pound begins to cite Thomas Jefferson, whose wisdom in such matters he has recently discovered), the mysterious evil of banking houses ("hung with deep purple curtains"), the need for a national dividend that would circulate a country's wealth to all its citizens, and confidence in the *A*-plus-*B* Theorem as a solution to all problems.

There is also a darker side to this work, which may be considered to mark the beginning of Pound's long public affair with Italian fascism.[5] The *ABC of Economics* is signed and dated according to the calendar based on Mussolini's March on Rome ("E. P. *Feb. 12 anno XI dell' era Fascista*"), and is laced with remarks cheerfully favorable to Mussolini. Pound's willingness to entertain the idea of a dictatorship apparently arose from the great contempt he felt for the masses at this time, a contempt expressed in the *ABC*. Lacking both perception and a basic curiosity about the workings of the world, the masses could only subside into "abuleia" (*abulia*, loss of will power or power to act or decide; his specific complaint is that they are "too demnition stupid and too ig-

[5] Settled in Rapallo since 1925, Pound had been praising Mussolini privately to his many correspondents for some time.

norant to acquire so rudimentary a perception of cause and effect" as would allow them to understand Social Credit [ABC 37]). Earlier in the work Pound had already gone so far as to say that "in proportion as people are without intellectual interests they approach the criminal classes, and approach criminal psychology" (ABC 25).

It is clear from the intensity of this denunciation that Pound's rage against the ignorance and listlessness of mankind had been churning beneath the surface for some time before 1933. From his complaints about the neglect into which he thought poetry and the other arts had fallen in England and elsewhere despite his heroic efforts over the years to gain patronage for them, it is also clear that this rage is to be seen in part as a reaction to the bleak artistic situation he observed around him. "All the arts," says Pound, "have been unemployed in my time" (ABC 36). Even with Frost, Eliot, and Joyce in print (thanks, in part, to his Promethean energies), Pound could sense decay setting in. The years of those great discoveries were now past; the present was rotting.

What is noteworthy for our purposes here is that Pound's reaction to the situation was an outspokenly anti-Marxist one. No longer could he encourage the likes of Mike Gold. No longer was Marxist thought worthy of serious attention. The Russian Revolution was a freak, and Marxist economics contained a serious logical error: it failed to take individual free will into account. Marx, as Pound wrote (ABC 26), "knew, but forgot or at any rate failed to make clear, the limits of his economics. That is to say, Marxian economics deals with goods for sale, goods in the shop. The minute I cook my own dinner or nail four boards together into a chair, I escape from the whole cycle of Marxian economics."

The choice of this rather naive example, and of the theory it supports, is all the more remarkable when one considers the time in which it was formulated: a time of enormous economic turbulence and social fear. The Great Depression had effects noticeable almost everywhere in Europe. Experts were ransacking their statistics for solutions to problems that had seized everyone's attention. Nothing in Pound's thinking here seems sufficient to explain, for instance, the ultimate source of either the food for the meal or the nails and lumber for the chair. The failure of the *ABC* to deal seriously with Marx's economics—or anyone else's—is consistent with Pound's lifelong unwillingness to submit to any cycle or to any formal system. Attempting to liberate himself from what he envisions as the straightjacket of Marxist determinism, Pound declares the power of will to be all-important. He shall have nothing to do with constraint (ABC 27): "The science of economics will not get very far until it grants the existence of will as a component; *i.e.* will toward order, will toward 'justice' or fairness, desire for civilization, amenities included. The intensity of that will is definitely a component in any solution."

It was this worship of will that had earlier attracted Pound to the great romantic activist and writer *extraordinaire*, Gabriele d'Annunzio, and was now attracting him to Benito Mussolini. D'Annunzio, a man of extravagant will and deed, represented a courageous and ebullient use of freedom. Mussolini represented "the intensity of that will" in all its rhetorical and physical excitement. Pound even saw in him the figure of an heroic artist. As an artist creates, so, he implied, Mussolini governs. Pound exulted in the vigor with which Mussolini asserted himself, the bravura of his attempts to force himself upon the consciousness of Italy and the world at large. Pound the political thinker is at this moment united with Pound the aesthete, for both are fascinated by the *impress* of the man's endeavor.[6] The Imagist-Vorticist-volitionist in Pound wants that impress to be deep, firm, and everlasting upon the retina or the mind. The politician wants the same indelibility, but in the social sphere. And when Mussolini denounces—as many have denounced before him—the weakness of the "middle" position, the cloudiness of images, the anemic abstractions of thought, the compromises of language, "liberalism" in all its pro-

---

[6] It is this attraction for Pound of the more extreme and dramatic manifestations of will—although obviously not this union of politics and aesthetics —that William Carlos Williams had in mind when he said, "It is still a Lenin striking through the mass, whipping it about that engages his attention. That is the force Pound believes in." "Excerpts from a Critical Sketch: The XXX Cantos of Ezra Pound," *Symposium*, 2 (Apr. 1931): 262.

tean manifestations, Pound the poet, Pound the politician, and Pound the American patriot can all speak at once in echoing him (ABC 39):

> The point is that NO ONE in any society has the right to blame his troubles on any one else. Liberals and liberal thought so-called have been a mess of mush because of this unacknowledged assumption, and a tendency to breed this state of mind.
>
> The law of nature is that the animal must either adapt itself to environment or overcome that environment—soft life and decadence.
>
> Decline of the American type, often bewailed! First the pioneer, then the boob and the soft-head! Flooding of peasant type, without peasant perseverance and peasant patience in face of low return!

Although Ezra Pound left the American frontier before he was two years old, he often found his frontier origins rhetorically useful. He could set himself against the "peasant type," i.e. the immigrant, by pointing to his ruggedly superior will. As one who had overcome the odds of his hostile environment, he could castigate those who had instead gone under. Later in his career he would use an increasingly bizarre American slang against the "decadence" of the immigrants, who were involved in the "decline" of the American "type." Still later, blaming them for at least part of his own troubles despite statements like the one just cited, he would improve upon castigation as a means to deal with them; would, in fact, play dangerously with notions of eugenics as a way of reestablishing American racial purity. In retrospect it seems clear that the germ of these eugenic notions is evident as early as this book, a work that declares itself an ABC, a text, but is actually a journal, as are so many of his works, a record of intellectual growth and development.[7]

Thus, the *ABC of Economics* does not dispassionately introduce a subject, but praises a certain kind of political individual and condemns a certain way of thinking. Mussolini's devotion to will is one attempt to loosen, through sheer ego, the shackles of Marx-

---

[7] Daniel Pearlman makes the same point about the *Cantos*, saying that their "main purpose is to record the growth of the poet's consciousness—not as it appears to the poet upon afterthought, 'recollected in tranquility,' but as it actually occurs, *in statu nascendi*" (*Barb of Time*, p. 91).

ism. Since will and ego are the very forces upon which any serious artist must depend if he is to break free from the deadly conjunction of logic, determinism, and personal apathy, Pound's admiration for Mussolini can be seen as partly aesthetic, based on a credo of artistic energy and spontaneity. But this credo, certainly shared by most artists, was to lead Pound alone among American artists into the camp of a political regime that did little more during its short life than cultivate the ugly flowers of personal despotism and public confusion. For Pound, who believed that the arts carry society, also believed that no differences existed between the "essentially aesthetic" and the "essentially political." Poetic principles, he thought, could be pursued with little or no alteration into the political arena.

Pound's identification with Mussolini was, in other words, perfectly consistent with aesthetic and political ideas he had promoted for some years. These ideas are also evident in the stylistic and organizational oddities of the *ABC*. It would have been contradictory for Pound to have written the book in any other way. Anti-logician that he was, he presented ideas without making use of argument. Fascism likewise eschewed argument, and relied on faculties and forces other than the rational.

CHAPTER FOUR

Mussolini: The New Synthesis, the Totalitarian

In Canto 21, published in 1928, Pound begins an extensive quotation from Thomas Jefferson with the lines, " 'Could you', wrote Mr. Jefferson, / 'Find me a gardener / Who can play the french horn?' " The letter referred to (written from Williamsburg to Giovanni Fabbroni on June 8, 1778) does not actually include that memorably phrased request, but does say something like it and does illustrate Jefferson's great intellectual energy. In America, Jefferson was deprived of good music; he hoped Fabbroni would send good musicians to him:

> The bounds of American fortune
> Will not admit the indulgence of a domestic band of
> Musicians, yet I have thought that a passion for music
> Might be reconciled with that economy which we are
> Obliged to observe. . . .

Pound's biographer tells us that in the early 1920's Eliot had presented his friend Pound with the Memorial edition of Jefferson's works. We also know that Pound's "Paris Letter" to the *Dial* of June 1922 includes a laudatory reference to Jefferson as one who would have recognized, as would Caesar or Machiavelli or Napoleon, the "utility" of accurate language. Throughout the 1920's, Pound's admiration for Jefferson grew steadily.[1] It flashed out with greatest ardor in three cantos (31-33) published in *Pagany*

---

[1] Just as John Dos Passos's admiration for Jefferson grew. Dos Passos had once toyed with the Marxist prospect, but had rejected it. In his later passionate defense of American free enterprise and individualism, he, like Pound, saw Jefferson as a congenial figure.

in 1931. The first of those cantos begins with the four words in-
scribed on the tomb of Isotta degli Atti in the Tempio Malates-
tiano, words that might well have been Pound's own at that
moment: "Tempus loquendi, / Tempus tacendi." For it is now
Pound's turn to be silent—to bring to a momentary halt the synthesis of Artemis, Aphrodite, the themes of pity and of time, the
story of Pedro and Ignez da Castro, which he had begun in Canto
30—while Jefferson speaks.

These three cantos are, in fact, centos. They afford some of the
purest instances in Pound's poem of montage, of quotation connected by quotation to quotation. The burden of it all is Jefferson's intelligence, his range of curiosity, his profoundly good sense
in matters civic, moral, and philosophical. In but a few years, Jefferson and Mussolini would be yoked together in favorable comparison by Pound. Mussolini's policies would be seen as Jeffersonian principles in action. Here, however, Jefferson is the focus.
It is his achievements and his tireless curiosity that are examined.
The magisterial background presence of John Adams speaks in
grave and sober judgment of the world: "Take away appetite, and
the present generation would not / Live a month, and no future
generation would exist; / and thus the exalted dignity of human
nature, etc. ....." (Canto 31). Such a presence serves to highlight
Jefferson's intellectual vivacity and his pride in the American
people, in their "human nature":

> I can further say with safety there is not a crowned head
> in Europe whose talents or merits would entitle him
> to be elected a vestryman by any American parish.
>   T. J. to General Washington, May 2. '88.

Of the three cantos, 33 is most directly suited to our purposes.
Castiglione once asked what makes for good and stable government, how a sensible leader should think, and how he should manage the affairs of his state. Now Pound, employing Jefferson as his
example, asks the same questions, questions to which he often
returns. The canto opens with Adams speaking to Jefferson in
1815, and ends with the quoted fulminations of a more recent
American political spokesman, Senator Smith Wildman Brookhart

(Republican from Iowa, 1928-32), a champion of farming interests and an enemy of what he saw as a malign conglomerate of railroads, the Federal Reserve System, and Wall Street. From Adams-Jefferson to Brookhart, then, is stretched a line of quotations figuring forth both the good and the bad in leadership.

One phrase of the canto reads: ".... was in the minds of the people, and this was effected from / 1760 to 1775 in the course of fifteen years..before Lexington....." The words are Adams's. The subject cryptically missing from the phrase is *revolution*. It was revolution, Adams wanted Jefferson to know, that was in the minds of the people. It was there a full fifteen years before the battle of Lexington. Revolution is thus seen as a cerebral act, not a physical one. It exists less when blood is being spilled than when men, prior to the act, think of changing their lives. Once thought has been transformed into action, once the physical revolution has occurred, postrevolutionary confusion sets in. The good leader must resolve the confusion, mediating between revolutionary dream and practical possibility. At this kind of negotiation, Jefferson and Adams were masters. It is within the context provided by revolution, in fact, both its possibility and its results, that the two men are seen. Juxtaposed with them are such apparently unrelated things as British industrialism in the nineteenth century, the methods of Soviet diplomacy, the records of the Federal Reserve Board, and the loan policies of the Armour Packing Company.

Jefferson and Adams were somehow able to transform revolutionary and wartime disorder into civic order; Jefferson was able to attend to even the most vexing of daily circumstances, such as the proper maintenance of a single prisoner-of-war commissary. Against such solicitude and wisdom is placed the example of British industrialism, particularly as seen through the eyes of one very attentive scholar: Karl Marx. This canto contains the most extensive quotation of Marx anywhere in Pound's work. In the first volume of *Capital* Marx was fascinated, and succeeded in fascinating Pound, with the blindness evident at every turn in Parliament's deliberations on labor conditions—particularly child labor—in British factories.

During the very early 1930's, when this canto was written, the United States and most of Europe were experiencing the profound shocks of economic depression. Overnight the intellectual landscape was altered by the emergence of a legion of amateur economists where before had stood only intellectuals and men of letters uninterested in the workings of higher finance. Pound, of course, had long been interested, mostly through Douglas, in the dysfunctions of capitalism in general and of credit in particular. But the tremors of this new time jostled him into more extensive reading. New titles began to appear in his essays: Fenner Brockway's *The Bloody Traffic*, Corbaccio's *Mercanti di Cannoni*, René Crevel's *Les Pieds dans le Plat*, and *L'Abominable Venalité de la Presse*.

But it is his old stalking-horse, Marx, that serves Pound in Canto 33 as a source of evidence about another, possibly prerevolutionary, historical moment. Nineteenth-century British leaders had failed to understand the conditions surrounding them; would contemporary Britain fare any better?

> ... (Das Kapital) denounced in 1842 still continue (today 1864) report of '42 was merely chucked into the archives and remained there while these boys were ruined and became fathers of this generation...for workshops remained a dead letter down to 1871 when was taken from control of municipal...and placed in hands of the factory inspectors, to whose body they added eight (8) assistants to deal with over one hundred thousand workshops and over 300 tile yards.
>
> . . .
>
> They (the owners) denounced the inspectors as a species of revolutionary commissar pitilessly sacrificing the unfortunate labourers to their humanitarian fantasies (re/ the law of 1848).

Pound's sources in *Capital*[2] have all been slightly reworked in the interests of providing a sharper poetic impact. Their point, however, is retained. Insofar as time has its echoes, the stupidity

---

[2] Well into the first volume (Part IV, "The Production of Relative Surplus Value") Pound locates a discussion of a Parliamentary commission on child labor. An 1842 report from that commission disclosed a "frightful picture of

of 1842, 1848, 1867, and 1871 might well be the stupidity of 1931. Were people not to heed Douglas, recognize the brilliant leadership of Mussolini, and transform, as Jefferson and Adams had once done, the inchoate swirl of postrevolutionary conditions into the harmony of civil order, all good would be surrendered.

An excellent example of the mishandling of a postrevolutionary situation was, to Pound's mind, the Soviet Union under Josef Stalin. Pound was perhaps guided to that example by Grigory Bessedovsky's *Revelations of a Soviet Diplomat*. The book, appearing in 1931, the same year as the canto, details some of the difficulties encountered by Soviet diplomats after 1917 (Bessedovsky himself represented the Soviet Union in Poland, Japan, and France). Thus the lines following Pound's hurried glance at British industrial life, and beginning with "avénement révolution allemande posait des problèmes nouveaux" are taken directly from

---

avarice, selfishness and cruelty." A later commentator, quoted by Marx, says that "a pamphlet published by Hardwicke about 2 years ago states that the abuses complained of in 1842, are in full bloom at the present day. It is a strange proof of the general neglect of the morals and health of the children of the working class, that this report lay unnoticed for 20 years, during which the children 'bred up without the remotest signs of comprehension as to what is meant by the term morals, who had neither knowledge, nor religion, nor natural affection,' were allowed to become the parents of the present generation" (*Capital: A Critique of Political Economy*, vol. 1, *The Process of Capital Production*, trans. by Samuel Moore and Edward Aveling [Chicago: Charles H. Kerr and Co., 1906], p. 539). Pound then alludes to the Workshops' Regulation Act of 1867, which, Marx wrote, "wretched in all its details, remained a dead letter in the hands of the municipal and local authorities who were charged with its execution. When, in 1871, Parliament withdrew from them this power, in order to confer it on the Factory Inspectors, to whose province it thus added by a single stroke more than one hundred thousand workshops, and three hundred brickworks, care was taken at the same time not to add more than eight assistants to their already undermanned staff" (*ibid.*, p. 541).

The passage about the factory owners is based on Marx's comments earlier in the volume about certain manufacturers who had resisted the Factory Act of 1848: "They denounced the Factory Inspectors as a kind of revolutionary commissioners like those of the French National Convention ruthlessly sacrificing the unhappy factory workers to their humanitarian crotchet" (*ibid.*, p. 312).

Bessedovsky's book, or, apparently, from a French translation of it.[3] One phrase in the canto reads:

> for ten years our (Russian) ambassadors have enquired what
> theories are in fashion in Moscow and have reported their
> facts to fit. (idem)

Given the emphatic premise that the revolution would expand and would everywhere be successful, Soviet ambassadors who questioned that inevitability found themselves out of favor. Bessedovsky's words are:

> an Ambassador who told the truth would be suspected of corruption and would be recalled at once. If the facts do not coincide with the theories prognosticated at Moscow, so much the worse for the facts! For six years the Ambassadors have inquired at Moscow what was the theory in vogue, and composed their reports accordingly.[4]

The problems of maintaining the revolution do not stop there. In London, as elsewhere, Bessedovsky says, the Soviet Union stood an excellent chance of being cheated by its own financial agents working in collusion with British banks. Soviet bills were simply discounted at a much higher rate than the standard offered by the Midland Bank ("Bills discounted at exorbitant rates, four times or three times / those offered by the Midland...."). The annual loss due to usurious discounting was "150 millions." Thus, according to the canto's elliptical coverage of the matter, does the revolution fall on the hard days of the postrevolution. Where Jefferson and Adams once cannily managed things, the Soviet Union apparently fails.

Pound concludes Canto 33 by turning back to the United States and to the speech of Senator Brookhart in the Senate on February 25, 1931. Brookhart had risen to oppose the confirmation of Eu-

---

[3] I have been helped by the preliminary work done on this canto by James P. Shannon. His notes on it are included in the "Annotations of the Pound Cantos" prepared by students in the graduate seminar directed by Norman Holmes Pearson at Yale in 1953.

[4] *Revelations of a Soviet Diplomat* (London: Williams and Norgate, 1931), p. 228. Bessedovsky says six years; Pound says ten. Shannon speculates that Pound, using a French translation, confused "dix" with "six."

gene Meyer for membership on the Federal Reserve Board. Long a foe of the Board, and of higher finance as controlled by Wall Street, Brookhart exemplified a kind of Populism dear to Pound's heart. Pound, in fact, wrote to Brookhart from Rapallo immediately after reading the speech, proclaiming parts of it "the most important historical document of the period I have come upon."[5] For that reason, it goes into the canto by bits and pieces. Brookhart's point was that in 1920, after actively encouraging inflation during the immediately preceding period by urging member banks to lend more money, the Federal Reserve Board (and the Interstate Commerce Commission at the request of the Federal Reserve Board) manipulated interest rates, availability of loans, and railroad rates to achieve a deflation of the economy—and achieved a depression instead. But perhaps worst of all, they kept their deliberations secret from everyone except certain important industrialists and financiers (bankers linked to such firms as Armour and Company, Swift and Company, and Sinclair Oil, for example, sat on the Reserve Board), who took economic advantage of their advance information to protect themselves against the coming depression—to get large loans before the interest rates went up, and the like. Small businessmen, unaware of what was going on, had their existing loans called in and had to sell at losses to pay them, could not get new loans, and were presumably, though Brookhart does not spell this out, harder pressed than the large businesses to pay the new railroad rates.

Thus, monopolists of both money and knowledge obstruct the little man and his enterprise. In a country originally dedicated to the glory of the individual, whose rights were championed by Jefferson, such latter-day machinations are particularly repellent.

On this note the canto ends. Although it may fairly be thought of as a cento, it is no hodge-podge. It is given coherent design by its message. Clearly preferring a government that does not bleed its people, is not enamored of metaphysical speculations, and lets

[5] Noel Stock, ed., *Impact: Essays on Ignorance and the Decline of American Civilization by Ezra Pound* (Chicago: Regnery, 1960), p. 269. For Brookhart's speech see *Congressional Record (Senate)*, Feb. 25, 1931, pp. 5922-23.

authority reside in small indigenous bodies rather than in large centralized sovereignties, Pound advocates his own kind of Jeffersonian democracy. Having established, moreover, a presiding concern for the canto—revolution—he allows himself no deviation into idle speculation, but fixes on prerevolutionary and postrevolutionary historical instances. Examples are proffered; inferences are left to be drawn. Thus is poetic method brought into alignment with political philosophy. Neither is friendly to abstractions; both let practical examples speak in place of generalities; both assume that authority, whether governmental or aesthetic, grows out of specific results in specific situations.

This is not to say that Pound has here solved the age-old aesthetic problem of the correspondence between *style* and *belief* in a writer's work. Within the narrow confines of his example, however, the correspondence is there, as Pound wanted it to be. The stringent compressions have destroyed neither. Indeed, the practical and cogent efficiency of such telegraphic abbreviation is part of the message and the bias. Revealing Pound's set of mind in the early 1930's, the years of Rapallo and economic depression, the years of the so-called "American history" cantos, Canto 33 demonstrates both the aesthetic and the instructional uses to which certain episodes in American, British, and Soviet history could be put. Thus, although the canto presents difficulties, Pound's original claim for his epic, as a poem "with a will to action," is validated there: aesthetic form and didactic intent are united.

The *ABC of Economics*, as we have noted, is an early indication that the theoretical Douglas will be asked to share Pound's attentions with the more practical Mussolini, whose achievements are praised in Canto 41:

Having drained off the muck by Vada
From the marshes, by Circeo, where no one else wd. have
  drained it.
Waited 2000 years, ate grain from the marshes;
Water supply for ten million, another one million *"vani"*
that is rooms for people to live in.
  XI of our era.

Pound continues in the mid-1930's to link the two men together after his fashion. *Jefferson and/or Mussolini* and *Social Credit: An Impact*, both published in mid-1935, praise Douglas as the major theorist and Mussolini as the major leader of the century, without attempting in any way to explain how an attachment to Douglas is to be reconciled with an attachment to Mussolini. (Just as he once praised Lenin while being anti-Marxist, he could now praise both Douglas and Mussolini.) Nor do they explain how political theory is, in general, to be reconciled with political practice. This lacuna can be discovered in all of Pound's writings from the mid-1930's onward. Pound was at that very moment moving directly into practical politics, and doing so without the kind of theoretical justification that would have given coherence to his activities. "The disease of the last century and a half," he once said, "has been 'abstraction.' "

A guiding principle, if not a theory, to which both those small but important pamphlets subscribe is one first enunciated by Jefferson: "The earth belongs to the living." This principle gives rise to two classic Poundian formulations (SC 4):

Increment of association: Advantage men get from working together instead of each on his own, e.g., crew that can work a ship whereas the men separately couldn't sail ships each on his own.

Cultural heritage: Increment of association with all past inventiveness, e.g., thus, crops from improved seed; American wheat after Carleton's researches; a few men hoisting a locomotive with machinery.

Both the increment of association and the cultural heritage permit men to rely, without being parasitical, upon their fellowmen. (And although Pound does not admit it, the collectivism of both is at odds with the individualism he celebrates.) Both make available the achievements of the past. Both derive from everlasting natural bounty, crimes against which can all be termed usury. "Usury and sodomy," Pound says in one of the pamphlets, "the Church condemned as a pair, to one hell, the same for one reason, namely that they are both against natural increase. Dante knew this and said it. It is registered in *The Merchant of Venice*, where

Shylock wants no mere shinbone or elbow, but wants to end An-
tonio's natural increase" (SC 6).

To combat usury, Pound goes on to say, is an admirable but
rare activity among men. The institutions that have fought it are
few; chief among them is the Monte dei Paschi. Two kinds of
banks have existed, he says: "the MONTE DEI PASCHI and the devils"
(SC 8). Characteristically, he finds the one good bank. It is described at some length in Canto 42:

> They had been ten years proposing such a Monte,
> That is a species of bank—damn good bank, in Siena
> A mount, a bank, a fund a bottom an
> institution of credit
> a place to send cheques in and out of
> and not yet a banco di giro. . . .
>   . . . the Magistrate
> give his chief care that the specie
> be lent to whomso can best use it USE IT
> (*id est, più utilmente*)
> to the good of their houses, to benefit of their business
> as of weaving, the wool trade, the silk trade

This unusual bank, founded as an experiment in 1624 by Cosimo I of Tuscany, and backed by the public lands and pastures
of Siena, wins Pound's admiration because its strength as an institution rests "*in ultimate* on the ABUNDANCE OF NATURE, on
the growing grass that can nourish the living sheep" (SC 8). Pound
tells us that Cosimo underwrote the capital of the bank to the
tune of 200,000 ducats, and that money was lent at five and
one-half percent. The shareholders of the bank ("the people of
Siena") were to realize a return of five percent on the original
capital. Overhead and salaries were to be kept at a minimum. All
excess profits were to go to hospitals and other good works. "That
was in the first years of the 17th century," wrote Pound, "and that
bank is open today. It outlasted Napoleon. You can open an account there tomorrow" (SC 8).[6] His moral is the obvious one:

---

[6] These words, written in 1935, were adumbrated in 1934 in Canto 41 ("To
pay 5% on its stock, Monte dei Paschi / and to lend at 5 and ½ / Overplus of
all profit, to relief works / and the administration on moderate pay . . / That

that it is good to found a public institution, not for individual profit, but for the purpose of extending life to all the people of a city.

During this period of Pound's career, he gave considerable attention to the "devil" banks, particularly to the Bank of England. In one of the Bank's public circulars soliciting investments, Pound discovered a statement that he thought the very quintessence of evil: "the bank hath benefit of the interest on all moneys which it creates out of nothing."[7] Just as nature abhors a vacuum, so Pound abhors all adventitious creation. Most forms of credit, like most abstractions, violate the flinty, unyielding empiricism that became Pound's only defense against the crazed flux which he believed characterized his age. Despite his genuine mystical respect for the divine multiplicity and surprising bounty of the world around him, he seems at times the most reductive of scientific positivists, a modern Thomas Gradgrind. It is good to remember when reading him that his mind can be split into at least two parts. One part functions religiously, enriching itself and its products with visions almost Ovidian in their spellbound praise of fructifying life and limitless possibility. The other functions mechanically and with the narrowest view of causality. Pound as Ariel is often to be seen in the company of Pound as "rude mechanical."

Important among the individuals who have fought usury, according to Pound, is the eighth President of the United States, Martin Van Buren (1782-1862), a man whose virtues have gone largely unrecognized in our own time[8] and were hardly a matter of consensus in his own. Van Buren figures prominently in Canto

---

stood even after Napoleon"). The bank does exist today. For further details, and description of present assets, see *The Italian Banking System* (Rome: Banco di Roma, 1960), p. 36.

[7] Mentioned in *A Visiting Card* (London: Peter Russell, 1952), p. 9, and quoted in Canto 46 as "*Hath benefit of interest on all / the moneys which it, the bank, creates out of nothing.*"

[8] Donald Davie has gone so far as to call Van Buren "a product of tasteless demagoguery," and argues that Pound allowed himself to be a victim of bad taste in celebrating Van Buren's achievements (*Ezra Pound: Poet as Sculptor* [New York: Oxford University Press, 1964], pp. 137-38).

37, published in 1934, where his *Autobiography*[9] is paraphrased
in extended allusions to the struggle between the United States
Government and the Second National Bank over the power of that
Bank and whether it was to serve all the American people or only
the moneyed interests of the Eastern seaboard:

> "employing means at the bank's disposal
> in deranging the country's credits, obtaining by panic
> control over public mind" said Van Buren
> "from the real committee of Bank's directors
> the government's directors have been excluded.
> Bank president controlling government's funds
> to the betrayal of the nation....
> government funds obstructing the government...
> and has sequestered the said funds of the government...
> (with chapter, date, verse and citation)
> acting in illegal secret
> pouring oil on the press
> giving nominal loans on inexistent security"
> in the eighteen hundred and thirties

Although Van Buren was Secretary of State rather than President
when this struggle was going on, Pound calls him "FISCI LIBERA-
TOR." And indeed, Van Buren's principles compelled him when
he was President, during the financial panic of 1837, to wrest certain federal moneys from the states and secure them in a central
treasury. The result was the independent National Treasury, the
single, stable fiscal authority, responsible to public representatives
and sensitive to public weal, for which Jackson had been fighting.

Except for the Monte dei Paschi, then, and the ill-remembered
documentary account of a major battle in the long struggle, the
enormous monolith of usury stands unopposed. Nothing is more
vividly presented in *Social Credit* than this monolith's malignancy.
It, and examples of diseases kindred to it, can be seen everywhere:
"agglomerates of protoplasm, listed as professors in the 'phone

---

[9] Pound complains in *Social Credit: An Impact* that this work, written in
1860, was not printed until 1920. But it should be pointed out that it was kept
in the family until about 1905, when a manuscript copy was presented to the
Library of Congress. We have, then, not a sixty-year but a fifteen-year delay.
See Noel Stock, *Reading the Cantos* (London: Routledge, 1967), p. 27.

book," "Roosevelt's entourage," "English high-gangsters," "lily-livered Bloomsbury pinks," "Chelsea pansies," "war profiteers and gun bastards." The worst scoundrel in the lot, however, is the one who had by now become Pound's *bête noire*: the leftist. On him is heaped the greatest scorn: "There is nothing less capable of mental motion than a socialist, unless it is his side-kick, the bolo" (SC 20).

Pound's increasing anti-Marxism best explains his use of the doctrines of Silvio Gesell, a monetary and banking reformer whose ideas resembled those of Douglas. Gesell's approach to economic problems was rooted in a conviction that putting an end to hoarding and speeding up the circulation of currency would solve all difficulties.[10] A plan whereby stamps had to be bought and affixed to paper money at regular intervals would ensure that nobody would want to keep his currency with him for long; thus buying and the flow of economic transactions in general would be stimulated. The sale of the stamps would be an additional source of revenue, and national debts would be eased. As a result, banks would have less opportunity to insinuate themselves into the economy. Production would be pushed higher and higher, and fewer financial middlemen would be able to find an opening in which to thrive.

Many years later in his career, Pound was able to look back with favor on the one instance in which Gesellite principles were actually put into operation. In Wörgl, Austria, in the early 1930's, work certificates were used as money, and were given a time-value by the need to affix to each of them, every month, a stamp representing one percent of the face value. This money did circulate rapidly, and the success of the experiment (increased employ-

[10] See Margaret Myers, *Monetary Proposals for Social Reform* (New York: Columbia University Press, 1940), pp. 26-70, for a critical discussion of Gesell. Ms. Myers says that Gesell "never was able to free himself from the old idea of value as something intrinsic in commodities" (p. 32). Gesell felt that although *things* could not successfully be hoarded, money could. If hoarding were stopped, an equilibrium would be established between the physical things available and the means to acquire them. In this direct contrast to Marx's belief that value inhered in the labor-time involved in producing an object, Gesell supports the Jeffersonian-Poundian doctrine of natural bounty.

ment, sales, and other business transactions, and reduced debt) attracted many interested visitors. According to at least one scholar,[11] however, the Austrian National Bank intervened through the government, and stopped the experiment. The economy of Wörgl soon thereafter declined. Pound summons up a memory of that golden moment before the decline in Canto 74:

> the state need not borrow
> as was shown by the mayor of Wörgl
> who had a milk route
> and whose wife sold shirts and short breeches
> and on whose book-shelf was the Life of Henry Ford
> and also a copy of the Divina Commedia
> and of the Gedichte of Heine
> a nice little town in the Tyrol in a wide flat-lying valley
> near Innsbruck and when a note of the
>   small town of Wörgl went over
> a counter in Innsbruck
>   and the banker saw it go over
>   all the slobs in Europe were terrified

"Two men have ended the Marxist era," says Pound (SC 13), "Douglas in conceiving the cultural heritage as the great and chief fountain of value. Gesell in seeing that 'Marx never questioned money. He just took it for granted.' "

The intensely negative tone of *Social Credit: An Impact* may be ascribed to the burden, by now familiar, of anti-Marxian sentiment that had settled upon Pound in the 1930's. Again and again he rose to declaim that value resides not in labor ("Work is not a commodity") but in the wealth naturally yielded by the land and the people upon the land. Against the splendor of images of that land, and those people toiling, is set the bitterness of Pound's prejudices: one instant, the goodly people of Wörgl "in a wide flat-lying valley"; the next instant, "all the slobs in Europe." This split vision, alive in one of the Pisan cantos, is thus alive at a much earlier, and more labile, moment in his progress as a poet. The one great prospect that could bring Pound out of anger and

---

[11] Christine Brooke-Rose, in *A ZBC of Ezra Pound* (London: Faber and Faber, 1971), p. 227.

into adulation was Mussolini. In the 1930's the promise of Il Duce was enough to overwhelm all gloom and resentment. Thus *Jefferson and/or Mussolini*.

The tone of this book, published in 1935, but written in 1933, is extraordinarily positive. Its aim in describing a paradigm of order inherent in the rule of two apparently quite dissimilar men is to force the reader to recognize a continuum of good governance transcending both time and geography. Operating in the highly selective and highly dramatic manner that has always characterized him, Pound declares (J/M 12): "The heritage of Jefferson, Quincy Adams, old John Adams, Jackson, Van Buren is HERE, NOW *in the Italian Peninsula* at the beginning of fascist second decennio, not in Massachusetts or Delaware." The excitement felt throughout *Jefferson and/or Mussolini* comes from Pound's sense of discovery, from his feeling that at last the great Marxist juggernaut has been destroyed and a new order, more responsive to individual volition, has been established (J/M 24): *"The fascist revolution is infinitely more INTERESTING than the Russian revolution because it is not a revolution according to preconceived type."* A "preconceived" revolution is one more bad result of abstract ideas, ideas that have no connection with specific needs and conditions— with real things like soil, light, and individual human desires— but only with a disembodied metaphysics. Mussolini recognizes, as Jefferson did, that man must attach himself, Antaeus-like, to the earth if he is to find reality.

The poet is also fascinated by Jefferson and Mussolini because they both appear to him as men concerned with order, with new ways to envision society. He sees them—one might almost say perversely—not as men primarily concerned with power, but as artists: "The great man is filled with a very different passion, the will toward *order*" (J/M 99). Mussolini willed the birth of an Italy cleansed of its swamps and mobilized to fight both the stranglehold of its own decadent aristocracy and the corrupt activities of international usurers and munitions-makers. Jefferson willed the birth of a nation, and he did so with "the opportunism of the artist, who has a definite aim, and creates out of the materials present" (J/M 15-16). Both men worked the way a sculptor works: to reveal the form that lives within the stone. Since Jefferson, America has slowly fallen into liberal decay and now stands no chance of regaining the strength it lost during the "cultural shock" of the Civil War. Italy is the new hope, "the only possible foundation or anchor or whatever you want to call it for the good life in Europe" (J/M 35).[12]

Pound's reliance upon the creative powers of single individuals leads quite naturally to his belief that democratic procedures are inefficient and anti-artistic. "One might speculate," he says, "as to how far any great constructive activity CAN occur save under a *de facto* one-party system" (J/M 125). The reader is reminded by such remarks that Pound composed *Jefferson and/or Mussolini* under the aegis of what he called "Volitionist Economics." Then, as always, his stress is on will, not on system. This allows him to wend his way between systems and focus on men, who actually matter. Politics for Pound was thus, as it was for Carlyle, a kind of hero-worship.

When he once again introduces Lenin's name into his discussion, this does not mean that communism, or even socialism, has suddenly risen in his favor. It simply indicates that Lenin has proved to be a sufficiently interesting invigorator of the political imagination to win a place in Pound's gallery of heroes. Lenin, like Jefferson and Mussolini, recognized the triviality of all other activities when compared to the achievement of one man, with imagination and muscle, building a state. As Pound remarks, "The rest is political 'machinery,' bureaucracy, flummydiddle" (J/M 69-70). Marxist economics is still in error; communists still cannot govern; socialism still will fail. Moreover, no collective system

---

[12] Pound was not the only American in Italy who fancied that Mussolini would reform the country and lead all of Europe to the good life. The American Ambassador to Italy from May 1921 to February 1927, Richard Washburn Child, wrote: "In our time it may be shrewdly forecast that no man will exhibit dimensions of permanent greatness equal to those of Mussolini." See his Foreword to Mussolini's *My Autobiography* (New York: Scribner's, 1928). For an account of the diversity of American reaction to Mussolini, see John P. Diggins, *Mussolini and Fascism: The View from America* (Princeton: Princeton University Press, 1972).

can have any real existence once it is separated from the individual acting at its center. Nor can any such system be recommended for the United States. None is capable or worthy of being transplanted. Therefore, although Pound makes many favorable comparisons between Jefferson and Mussolini and Lenin, he also cautions: "This is not to say that I 'advocate' fascism in and for America, or that I think fascism is possible in America without Mussolini, any more than I or any enlightened bolshevik thinks communism is possible in America without Lenin" (J/M 98).

What he does advocate is a renewal of the American promise as once set forth by Jefferson. In so doing, he once again reveals that his position with respect to politics is strangely apolitical. At the very moment of choosing between conflicting ideologies, he shrinks from the choice, presenting instead a pluralistic sampling of the three major ideologies then available to Europe and the United States: fascism, democracy, and communism. Pound's ultimate unwillingness to accord full respect to any of the three diminishes the force of *Jefferson and/or Mussolini*, and is akin to Eliot's reluctance to embrace anything so vast as an ideology.

His energies and interest in the book are directed elsewhere. He finds it especially pleasing to enumerate the deeds, of so specific a nature, characterizing a man. About Jefferson, for instance, he says (J/M 40):

As to Jefferson's interests, let us say his practical interests: he was interested in rice, he believed in feeding the people, or at least that they ought to be fed, he wasn't averse from pinching a bit of rice or at least from smuggling a sack of a particularly fine brand out of Piedmonte. With the moral aim of improving all the rice in Virginia.

Mussolini has persuaded the Italians to grow better wheat, and to produce Italian colonial bananas.

This may explain the "Dio ti benedica" scrawled on a shed where some swamps were.

Canto 31, we may recall, also deals with Jefferson:

"I remember having written you while Congress sat at Annapolis,
"on water communication between ours and the western country,
"particularly the information....of the plain between
"Big Beaver and Cayohoga, which made me hope that a canal

......navigation of Lake Erie and the Ohio. You must have had
"occasion of getting better information on this subject
"and if you have you wd. oblige me
"by a communication of it. I consider this canal,
"if practicable, as a very important work.
                        T. J. to General Washington, 1787
.....no slaves north of Maryland district....
.....flower found in Connecticut that vegetates when
    suspended in air...
...screw more effectual if placed below surface of water.

Thus the genius of the third President of the United States.

Devoid of genuine ideological content, Pound's argument is essentially anarchistic and hence is forced to concentrate upon the style of individuals. Pound exalts the one thing that appears good and scorns all else. Yet he avoids the *ad hominem* judgments to which anarchists are traditionally prone, by maintaining that personal style corresponds indirectly to the style or character of the surrounding society. To judge Jefferson or Mussolini, therefore, is ultimately to judge the society to which he belongs. Analyses of style become analyses of something greater. Pound, in the spirit of John Ruskin and William Morris, believes in the kinship of aesthetic, moral, and social judgments.[13] As he says in *Jefferson and/or Mussolini*: "I can 'cure' the whole trouble simply by criticism of style. Oh, can I? Yes. I have been saying so for some time" (p. 17).

If by style all else can be measured, it follows that by examining the style of art in a given time and society, the quality of that time and society can be discovered. The *locus classicus* of Pound's political and economic thought, Canto 45, appearing in 1936, thus has a great deal to say about art—and about *usura*, the cause of its decay:

> With *Usura*
> With usura hath no man a house of good stone
> each block cut smooth and well fitting
> that design might cover their face,

---

[13] See Raymond Williams, *Culture and Society* (chap. 7, "Art and Society") for a brief but most helpful discussion of how, with Ruskin, Morris, and A. W. Pugin, this belief took hold and made itself felt in the mid-nineteenth century and thereafter.

. . .

no picture is made to endure nor to live with
but it is made to sell and to sell quickly

. . .

with usura the line grows thick
with usura is no clear demarcation

. . .

Duccio came not by usura
nor Pier della Francesca; Zuan Bellin' not by usura

. . .

Usura rusteth the chisel
It rusteth the craft and the craftsman
It gnaweth the thread in the loom

. . .

Usura slayeth the child in the womb
It stayeth the young man's courting
It hath brought palsey to bed, lyeth
between the young bride and her bridegroom
                    CONTRA NATURAM

The undeniable effectiveness of this canto is in part to be explained by its incantatory power. It is also to be explained by the
astonishingly forceful way in which the poem simplifies a problem
as complicated as the relationship of art, life, and society. There
is something captivating about such repudiation of complex issues. Pound severs all the Gordian knots he finds by boldly assert-
ing that "BAD economics are complicated. Good economics are
simple."[14] We are again made to recognize that from the pursuit
of the simple his mind gains its sustenance.

Nor should we forget this when we come to consider the meaning of "usura." Kenner is in error when he talks of "the separation
of wealth from living processes for which [Pound's] synecdoche
is usura."[15] To see Pound's "usura" as a synecdoche, or as figura-
tive language for some indescribable evil, is to ignore the truly

[14] "Ezra's Easy Economics," a letter to the *Chicago Tribune*, Paris (Apr. 2,
1934), p. 2.
[15] "The Broken Mirrors and The Mirror of Memory," in Lewis Leary, ed.,
Motive and Method in the Cantos of Ezra Pound (New York: Columbia University Press, 1961), p. 22.

radical and mechanical nature of his beliefs. It is to mitigate his unqualified and unmistakable contention that the charging of excessive interest is at the very root of all cultural collapse. Pound's poetry does not gain its power through the manipulation of connotative elements. It is entirely of the surface; it speaks and does not suggest. "When I say CAT, I mean CAT." This fact, not readily appreciated by readers exploring Pound for the first time, is in harmony with his belief that poetry has too long been used as an idle entertainment and not as a medium of important information: "The intelligentsia, or a part of it, delayed Marxian, [supposes] that writing is a commodity, and not a system of communication; failing to recognize that the value of a printed page depends not on the amount of its verbiage, but on its efficiency as communication" (SC 12). He makes his feelings even clearer when he speaks of poets who have used symbol and metaphor:

> and no man learned anything from them
> for their speaking in figures.[16]

The unrelenting explicitness of Pound's writing and of his political attitude becomes more and more a force to reckon with in the works that follow *Social Credit: An Impact* and *Jefferson and/or Mussolini*. That force is surely appropriate to one who believed he had a message of crucial importance to deliver to men and to their misdirected governments. Any reader will notice how besetting Pound's economic and political interests become as his career moves into the late 1930's. Hayden Carruth's analysis of the way the *Cantos* were developing during that period is worth quoting in this connection:

The earlier cantos, roughly the first fifty, are a "detective story," in which the poet has searched through history to find out what was wrong and to turn up, if possible, the usable remnants of cultural value from

---

16 These lines are from a fragment first published as "Canto Proceeding (72 Circa)" in *Vice Versa*, 1 (Jan. 1942): 1-2. The fragment has since been reprinted, with some minor changes, in the latest collected edition of the *Cantos* (1972) as "Addendum for Canto C." Why it should be an "addendum" to a canto composed and first published much later (*Yale Literary Magazine*, 126 [Dec. 1958]: 45-50) is not clear.

past epochs; the later cantos are recurrent and reiterative, variations on the earlier themes, to "hammer home" the truth of Pound's multifaceted insight into the cultural and historical processes.[17]

This hammering home contributed to the ever-widening division of Pound's readers into two camps: believers and skeptics.

To study Pound during the late 1930's is to study his movement toward concentration on those few elements of the world that he thought sufficient to explain each and every event. Settling on usura as the central factor in the evolution of Western history, he excluded from his mind many other factors that, to the dismay of some readers but to the satisfaction of others and of his own metaphysical severities, had to be deemed irrelevant. Wielding Occam's razor with a zeal few writers have been able to match, Pound eventually became an aesthetic tyrant. This tyranny, a logical consequence of his belief that interest inheres in things because he has studied them and that the world takes its shape from the way he looks at it, is exemplified by his conclusion to Canto 62. There, comparing Alexander Hamilton and John Adams, he says:

> and as for Hamilton
> we may take it (my authority, ego scriptor cantilenae)
> that he was the Prime snot in ALL American history
> (11th Jan. 1938, from Rapallo)
> But for the clearest head in the congress
> 1774 and thereafter
> pater patriae
> the man who at certain points
> made us
> at certain points
> saved us
> by fairness, honesty and straight moving
> ARRIBA ADAMS

The historical and political judgment turns here most crucially upon "my authority, ego scriptor cantilenae"—"I, the author of the canto." It is a kind of judgment, relying on personal conviction and almost nothing else, with which we shall become familiar as we follow Pound's career into the years before and during the

---

[17] "The Poetry of Ezra Pound," *Perspectives USA*, 16 (Summer 1956): 145.

Second World War. In turning his back on that which had for so long passed as art and was, in his opinion, only ornamentation, and in seeing true art manifested in the clean harmonious motion of certain men in the creation of social order, Pound put further behind him the infirm hold of poetry—the poetry Eliot had been writing, the poetry of all the poets in his time—and walked forward into the muscular embrace of politics.

If this was confusion, as now seems obvious to us, Pound was hardly the first writer to be besieged with doubts about the efficacy of his chosen art in a time of social conflict, preparation for war, and evidence of malfeasance in high places. His response, however, was not to fall into gloom and despair, but to advance the cause of the likeliest leader he could find—Mussolini—and to attach himself, in whatever way he could (a radio program was made available) to him. Pound's exuberance was never diminished. Noel Stock tells us that Pound's interview with Mussolini at the Palazzo Venezia in Rome on January 30, 1933, matched his highest expectations.[18] During the meeting, Mussolini looked here and there in *A Draft of XXX Cantos* (published three years earlier). Commenting that he found the volume of poetry "divertente" (amusing), Mussolini gave all the pleasure and confirmation the poet could ever want. For here was a leader who truly could lead, could see what mere artists could not see, and could appreciate the degree to which Ezra Pound had made poetry meant for men of action (Canto 41):

> "MA QVESTO,"
> said the Boss, "è divertente."
> catching the point before the aesthetes had got there.

[18] *Life of Ezra Pound* (New York: Pantheon Books, 1970), p. 306.

CHAPTER FIVE

A Guide to Culture: Anti-Semitism

And if you will say that this tale teaches...
a lesson, or that the Reverend Eliot
has found a more natural language...you who think you will
get through hell in a hurry...

These words open Canto 46. Written in late 1935 or early 1936, the canto is at once a short review of Pound's beliefs up to that time and an announcement that the modern Inferno in which he as a poet has dwelt has not yet ended. The grasp of history is strong. The test of a man is his ability to endure the contemporary hell contrived by usurers and, moreover, to so describe its shape and feel that the preciseness of his description will serve the struggle of all others so imprisoned.[1] The Odyssean travail will at last become success if sanity and knowledge are preserved. As Pound puts it in Canto 47:

Who even dead, yet hath his mind entire!
This sound came in the dark
First must thou go the road
               to hell
And to the bower of Ceres' daughter Proserpine,
Through overhanging dark, to see Tiresias,
Eyeless that was, a shade, that is in hell

[1] The black poet LeRoi Jones (Imamu Amiri Baraka), a writer artistically indebted to Pound, has said of the black artist: "His role is to report and reflect so precisely the nature of the society, and of himself in that society, that other men will be moved by the exactness of his rendering and, if they are black men, grow strong through this moving, having seen their own strength, and weakness." *Home, Social Essays* (New York: Morrow, 1966), p. 251.

So full of knowing that the beefy men know less than he,
Ere thou come to thy road's end.
        Knowledge the shade of a shade,
    Yet must thou sail after knowledge

The road's end is knowledge, the means is fortitude. There are,
we also see, shortcuts through hell, but they are all avenues cheaply
taken. They would make less of Pound's "tale," his *Cantos*, by
thinking of them as a poem yielding no more than a "lesson," a
schoolboy's homily. The *Cantos* are instead, we infer, a means of
educing from the vastness of history an ideal culture, a total configuration of the mind against which the detritus that is modern
"civilization" may be judged. In these terms the struggle of men
like Mussolini may be evaluated and, in the course of things,
praised. To scant that most useful configuration would indeed
be to speed through hell, for the main task of a man trapped in
the contemporary turmoil we know surrounds us would thereby
be avoided.

Another way to scant hell is to believe that T. S. Eliot "has
found a more natural language." Pound's ire in this canto seems
directed not so much at his former ally in matters aesthetic and
poetic, but at those who were discovering in the Eliot of the mid-
1930's what they believed was a means of transcending history.
Perhaps, they thought, religious affirmation could lift one out of
the imprisonment of time and into a station secure beyond flux.
The degree to which Eliot was himself exploring such a possibility is indicated by "Burnt Norton" (see pp. 192-93 below)
and by some of his discussion in *After Strange Gods* (1934; see
pp. 159-64 below). But Eliot's answers are no answers at all to
the Odyssean man, says Pound. Moreover, those who believe that
Eliot had found a more natural language are just as wrong as those
who believe that Pound's long poem can be dismissed as a homi-
letic lesson. It is he himself, in fact, who employs the more natural
language, for he is sensitive, as Eliot is not, to the demand that
poetic language in their day be a language of rage, of bitterness,
of arousal to complete transformation. Whereas Eliot seeks stasis,

Pound seeks indictment and change. He condemns pandemic usury and advocates a society inspired by Jefferson, modulated by Confucian precepts, and heedful of the changes Mussolini had already brought into being in one country.

Canto 46 can be seen as a review of Pound's beliefs and of his activities, along with those of others, in gathering evidence for his indictment and promoting change:

> ... nineteen
> Years on this case, CRIME
> Ov two CENturies, 5 millions bein' killed off
> to 1919, and before that
> Debts of the South to New York, that is to the
> banks of the city, two hundred million,
> war, I don't think (or have it your own way...)
> about slavery?
> ...
>   Seventeen years on the case; here
> Gents, is/are the confession.
>   "Can we take this into court?
>   "Will any jury convict on this evidence?
> 1694 anno domini, on through the ages of usury
> On, right on, into hair-cloth, right on into rotten building,
> Right on into London houses, ground rents, foetid brick work,
> Will any jury convict 'um? The Foundation of Regius Professors
> Was made to spread lies and teach Whiggery, will any
>   JURY convict 'um?
> The Macmillan Commission about two hundred and forty years
>   LATE
> with great difficulty got back to Paterson's
> The bank makes it *ex nihil*
> Denied by five thousand professors, will any
> Jury convict 'um? This case, and with it
> The first part, draws to a conclusion[2]

---

[2] This canto is one of the few dealt with at any length by Pound in his radio broadcasts from Rome. He apparently thought seriously enough of it to give it his undivided attention during the broadcast of February 12, 1942 (see transcript available at the Library of Congress). For some six years, then, it had held his attention.

Before concluding the case, however, Pound first criticizes Marx for not knowing, as he should have, what Pound now knows. Pound implies that it is to the credit of his system of ideogrammic analysis, an analysis unencumbered by theoretical consistency, that it can detect the one crucial element in economics, the cancer of usury. Pound then lashes out at Great Britain's and America's failure during the Depression with a rhetoric many Marxists would gladly have employed:

> . . . Mr Marx, Karl, did not
> foresee this conclusion, you have seen a good deal of
> the evidence, not knowing it evidence, is monumentum
> look about you, look, if you can, at St Peter's
> Look at the Manchester slums, look at Brazilian coffee
> or Chilean nitrates. . . .
>
> . . .
>
> Hic Geryon est. Hic hyperusura.
> FIVE million youths without jobs
> FOUR million adult illiterates
> 15 million 'vocational misfits', that is with small chance for jobs
> NINE million persons annual, injured in preventable industrial
> accidents
> One hundred thousand violent crimes. The Eunited States ov
> America
> 3rd year of the reign of F. Roosevelt, signed F. Delano, his uncle.
> CASE for the prosecution.

This, then, is Pound's "case," circa 1936, against the net of usury hemming him in. The case was still being prosecuted in *Guide to Kulchur* (1938),[3] the prose complement of the *Cantos*, sharing with the poem the problems of apparently random juxtaposition as a method. Its fascinations and difficulties are, in part, those of the *Cantos*.

It provides one of the best introductions to Pound and to the landscape of his mind. That landscape is dense with good civilizations and bad, good art and usury-ravaged art, good men and

---

[3] (Norfolk, Conn.: New Directions, 1952). Originally published in 1938 by Faber and Faber and New Directions, this work was to have been called *"Kulch," or Ez' Guide to Kulchur*.

bankers, proper and improper ways of nourishing society. The *Guide* includes the Poundian secularized equivalents of heaven and hell, and it delineates as clearly as anything he wrote those forces of justice and injustice that for a quarter-century defined his conception of politics. The *Guide* also reveals Pound taking his favorite stance, that of the teacher whose learning, delivered up like so much hard-grained buckshot, invites the student either to stand aside or to join the attack upon the myriad enemies of "straight-thinking." Disagreement is out of the question. His manner is not only informal, abrupt, and at times strangely avuncular; it is also the manner of a man who confidently assumes that his answers to the problems of the world will have a validity denied to mere experts.[4] In an age of experts, his casual presumptions have the charm of rarity, and partially explain why the *Guide*, with all its faults, is an engaging work. The spectacle of a man speaking out his whole mind on every imaginable issue, with no regard for the enabling apparatus of formal learning, is worth looking at.

It incorporates, helter-skelter, most of the elements to be found in Pound's earlier work: belief in nature's bounty, concern with the obligations of the serious artist, dedication to monetary reform, anti-leftist attitudes, loyalty to Mussolini, and beliefs about the relationship of usury to bad art. Devoted to what it calls "The New Learning," it is unified by being composed, as Pound himself says, of "notes toward a totalitarian treatise" (GK 27). It also benefits from tension between old, acquired stubbornnesses and fresh visions, a desire to achieve a new alertness and reappraise old judgments ("Renovate, dod gast you, renovate," as he said on another occasion). Much of that tension is lost, of course, on readers who have not followed Pound through his previous attempts to back politics into a corner. Such readers may write off the *Guide* as freakish and opaque. But other readers may note that it shows both zeal (in its frank authoritarianism and its virulence

---

[4] Or, as Gertrude Stein once rather frivolously said of Pound, quoting herself in *The Autobiography of Alice B. Toklas*, "he was a village explainer, excellent if you were a village, but if you were not, not."

against "demo-liberal ideology") and modesty, referring to its author as a "fanatic," a "credit-crank," and as someone whose writing has already suffered from being "coloured" by his convictions (GK 93, 182, 195).

Moreover, Pound's aesthetic approach to totalitarianism is original and intrinsically interesting. Describing his own plight as a mature artist who is disengaged from the culture surrounding him, Pound explains that such a condition occurs only in cultures that have not yet realized the obvious advantages of an authoritarian melding of individual and milieu. He argues that true culture begins, not with mere knowledge, but with knowledge perfectly integrated with deed and sensibility. It begins, he says, "when one HAS 'forgotten-what-book' " (GK 134) and can go about one's business without conscious reference to the cultural environment. The marooned artist, forced to create his own entirely personal and idiosyncratic world, is proof positive that his society has malfunctioned. To illustrate the difference between the artist who must flee or wage war against his society and the artist embraced by his society, Pound contrasts Béla Bartók (and himself) on the one hand and Luigi Boccherini on the other. The efforts of the first are marred by "the defects inherent in a record of struggle," while in the achievements of the other "no trace of effort remained" (GK 135). As Davie has suggested, Pound believes that art in a totalitarian society will be "simple and transparent,"[5] qualities issuing naturally from a situation in which the artist will always be able to find a clean, well-lighted place.

The artist will no longer be a pariah; his work will gain respect among a people in whom a sense of future possibility will urge the acceptance of every man's skills. As in almost every utopia, however, the idle, the trivial, and the merely elegant will be offered no room. As Pound applies these criteria, Plato and Aristotle, the other Athenian Greeks, "the Hebrews," most Protestants, most economists, and all Englishmen would be excluded.

[5] Donald Davie, *Ezra Pound, Poet as Sculptor* (New York: Oxford University Press, 1964), p. 147.

Pound's enmity toward Plato, whom he calls a "purple swine," and Aristotle, whom he calls a "dhirty greek" (GK 327), is based on his conviction that these men, although usually considered good "professors of philosophy," are in essence dilettantes or faddists. In contrast to Confucius, who presides god-like over much of Pound's thinking,[6] they are not basically concerned with the good of the whole society, nor do they consider how right thought can issue in right action, embracing with one clear motion the interlocking duties of man, family, and state. And neither philosopher, of course, had thought sufficiently about money and interest. Dwelling on the sublime and outlining in the air an elegant but irrelevant dream (*The Republic*), Plato forgot man. Full of "imbecilities" and "yatter" (*The Nichomachean Ethics*), Aristotle left little worth saving and, with his many abstractions, brought more trouble than relief. "The greek philosophers," Pound states, "did not feel communal responsibilities. . . . The sense of coordination, of the individual in a milieu is not in them" (GK 38). Heir to the Enlightenment and to Confucian anti-transcendentalism,[7] Pound sees nothing but danger in the "fantasies" of Plato and in the "academic" systems of Aristotle. His sole criticism of Mussolini in the *Guide* is that his mind contains "an Aristotelic residuum" (GK 309).

Aristotelian flaw or no, Mussolini is precisely the kind of political figure that must be admired by anyone interested in the translation of thought into action and in the virtues of orderly form: "Mussolini a great man, demonstrably in his effects on event, unadvertisedly so in the swiftness of mind, in the speed with which his real emotion is shown in his face" (GK 105). De-

---

[6] Pound's "Pentagon" of most-admired works consisted of the *Odes* of Confucius, the Homeric "Epos," Ovid's *Metamorphoses*, the *Divine Comedy*, and Shakespeare's plays. By extension, the societies that sustained these works are also admirable.

[7] George Dekker refers to H. G. Creel's *Confucius: The Man and the Myth* (London, 1951), pp. 276-301, as "a scholarly account of the connections between Confucian, French Enlightenment, and early American political thought." *Sailing After Knowledge, The Cantos of Ezra Pound* (London: Routledge, 1963), p. 181n.

votion to form is a quality of mind also characteristic of Hitler, and it is in the tone of one connoisseur praising another that Pound refers to the *coup d'éclat* of his old friend Wyndham Lewis (GK 134): "Form-sense 1910 to 1914. 15 or so years later Lewis discovered Hitler. I hand it to him as a superior perception. Superior in relation to my own 'discovery' of Mussolini."

The appreciation is an aesthetic one. Pound fixes his attention, not on the uses of power, or on the results of these uses, but on what he calls "the *forma*, the immortal *concetto*, the concept, the dynamic form which is like the rose pattern driven into the dead iron-filings by the magnet" (GK 152). Mussolini's concept of a new Italy is seen as a beautiful rose, an image that ignores the force required to impose this concept on the country. From here it is not far to Mussolini's son remarking the beauty rather than the death in bombs exploding over Ethiopia, and we are reminded that true barbarity may issue as easily from order as from disorder. Horror begins when aesthetic order is separated from its human content.

These reflections may color but should not obscure our view of Pound here. In contrast to Mussolini, a force liberating new thought and the previously dormant energies of Italy, stand "those who petrify thought, that is KILL it, as the Marxists have tried to in our time, and as countless other fools and fanatics have tried to in all times" (GK 277). One way to kill thought is to trample on subtle distinctions, to smear differences. That is what usury does—it is antithetical to sense discriminations and thus, in discouraging the development of the perceptive faculties, encourages ignorance. Protestantism (or puritanism) has offended as grossly in this way as has usury or Marxism, and is equally scorned (GK 185):

The puritan is a pervert, the whole of his sense of mental corruption is squirted down a single groove of sex. The scale and proportion of evil, as delimited in Dante's hell (or the catholic hell) was obliterated by the Calvinist and Lutheran churches. I don't mean to say that these heretics cut off their ideas of damnation all at once, suddenly or consciously, I mean that the effect of Protestantism has been semiticly to obliterate values, to efface grades and graduations.

Here we can see that just as feelings against usury or Marxism lead Pound immediately to feelings against Protestants, so feelings against Protestants lead him immediately to feelings against those who behave "semiticly." Pound's anti-Semitism has thus apparently developed since *Patria Mia*, wherein the Jew is portrayed simply as one who adheres to the values of the "nickel-plated cash register." Here, many years later, the Jew ("the Hebrew") is cited specifically as something much worse, as the chief obstacle to clear thinking. The entire history of the Jews has been inimical to rational values (GK 330): "Nothing cd. be less civil, or more hostile to any degree of polite civilization than the tribal records of the hebrews. There is not a trace of civilization from the first lies of Genesis up to the excised account of Holophernes." This variety of anti-Semitism[8] comports most appropriately with the kind of anti-communism prompted by Father Charles Coughlin, who is mentioned favorably several times in the *Guide*. "Communism," says Pound, "with its dictatorship of the proletariat is merely barbarous and Hebrew, and it is on a level with primitive theocracies" (GK 270-71).

Some further discussion of the precise nature of Pound's anti-Semitism is in order here. At times it seems merely that Pound is enraged at a certain general mode of thought and behavior but must, in accordance with his habitual procedures, give it a specific designation—here "Hebrew." It is as if Pound, suddenly realizing that he, adamant against abstractions, was using abstractions, decided to obscure that fact by a sudden infusion of intemperance.[9] At other times, and within this same work, Pound can suddenly relent and even speak decisively against racial prejudice. It is, he says, a "red herring. The tool of the man defeated intel-

---

[8] "All the Jew part of the Bible is black evil." Pound in a letter to Henry Swabey, May 9, 1940. See Pound's *Letters*, ed. by D. D. Paige (New York: Harcourt, Brace, 1950), p. 345.

[9] Regarding this paradox, Stephen Spender has said that Pound "allowed his scrupulous poet's rhetoric of the study of 'minute particulars' to be overwhelmed by his secret yearning for a heroic public rhetoric. Sensibility has surrendered to will." "Writers and Politics," *Partisan Review*, 34 (Summer 1967): 377.

lectually, and of the cheap politician. No one will deny that the jews have racial characteristics, better and worse ones. . . . It is nonsense for the anglo-saxon to revile the jew for beating him at his own game" (GK 242-43).

This same ambivalence appears in Cantos 35 and 52:

> this is Mitteleuropa
> and Tsievitz
> has explained to me the warmth of affections,
> the intramural, the almost intravaginal warmth of
> hebrew affections, in the family, and nearly everything else....
> pointing out that Mr Lewinesholme has suffered by deprivation
> of same and exposure to American snobbery..."I am a product,"
> said the young lady, "of Mitteleuropa,"
> but she seemed to have been able to mobilize
> and the fine thing was that the family did not
> wire about papa's death for fear of disturbing the concert
> which might seem to contradict the general indefinite wobble.
> It must be rather like some internal organ,
> some communal life of the pancreas....sensitivity
> without direction...this is...

> Remarked Ben: better keep out the jews
> or yr/ grand children will curse you
> jews, real jews, chazims, and *neschek*
> also super-neschek or the international racket

The first of these passages is primarily a view of the exotic, an evocation of the atmosphere of intriguing situations. If it attacks anything, it attacks "the general indefinite wobble," loosely translatable as ambiguity, something Pound had been hammering away at for many years. Pound's hatred for the wobble, as his many diatribes indicate, cuts across all racial lines.

The passage from Canto 52 is an altogether different matter. There Pound has, to borrow one of his own disturbing phrases, "localized the infection," and he abandons accurate description in favor of fierce denunciation. Making use of the anti-Semitism spuriously attributed to Benjamin Franklin, he indulges his baroque penchant for name-calling—the "big jews," the "chazims" (probably his distortion of the Hebrew word "hazirim," meaning "pigs")—in an unmistakably direct attack.

Repelled as even the initiated reader of Pound must be by such a passage, and certain as he may be that it jars hopelessly with the quiet grace of the rest of the canto,[10] he can scarcely be surprised. Blaming the Jews for all the ills of civilization is not only already familiar from Pound's earlier works, but perfectly consistent with his predilection for single and specific causes. In order to sidestep what he calls "the pimps' paradise of indefinite verbiage" (GK 324), and in order to institute the new synthesis, the totalitarian, Pound directed the enormous fund of his eccentric learning and research through the strait gates of anti-Semitism. As he says, "some kind of line to hang one's facts on is better than no line at all" (GK 221). If the line gives him a means of explaining, without reference to anything so indeterminate as "human frailty" or so intangible as "original sin," the unending maladies of civilization, then it has served its purpose well. As Pound says in the *Guide to Kulchur* (p. 189), "there is no use in blaming the mass of humanity." It is quite sufficient, and far more efficacious, to blame the Jews.

All this is not to say that his anti-Semitic remarks are arbitrarily made to advance his argument. His strategies are never contrived or duplicitous; we cannot doubt the sincerity of his feelings against Jews. We are obliged, however, to note that Pound's anti-Semitism and the literary uses to which he repeatedly puts it may be evaluated most productively as an altogether logical corollary to his philosophical and aesthetic principles, not as an inexplicable divergence from them.

The decisive tone of the *Guide*, in perfect keeping with the authoritarian philosophies Pound favored at the time, falters at several crucial points. Interestingly enough, they are all in passages dealing with religious sentiments. We know how often and with what fervor he could refer to "the unquenchable splendour and indestructible delicacy of nature" (GK 282). But his praise of nature, his devotion to her bounty, his apostrophes to the world as made possible by Demeter, Aphrodite, and Artemis, were never

---

[10] The rest of Canto 52 is a reworking into English of the *Li Ki* or "Record of Rites," one of the Five Classics upon which Confucianism is partially built, and contains lines like "Toward summer when the sun is in Hyades / Sovran is Lord of the Fire / to this month are birds."

meant to be understood as mere materialism. For all of Pound's affinity for "the real" as he saw it, and for all of his scorn of foggy mental life, he harbored religious feelings that buoy up even some of his crassest political judgments.

Occasionally these feelings appear to be no more than a form of pragmatism: "Without gods, no culture. Without gods, something is lacking. Some Stoics must have known this, and considered logic a mere shell outside the egg." Occasionally those feelings appear to be something else, something higher: "I repeat: this view repudiates materialism. It is volitionism." And occasionally Pound toys with the overwhelming prospect of the Catholic Church: "Again I repeat: I cd. be quite a 'good catholic' IF they wd. let me pick my own saints and theologians" (GK 126, 189). But these circumnavigations of a problem that must have been in the forefront of his mind are, late in *Guide to Kulchur*, abruptly abandoned in favor of a more direct attack, when, in reviewing the legacy of Victorian belief, he comments that the Victorians "bred a generation of experimenters, my generation, which was unable to work out a code for action. We believed and disbelieved 'everything,' or to put it another way we believed in the individual case."

The best of us accepted every conceivable "dogma" as a truth for *a* situation, as the truth for a particular crux, crisis or temperament.

And a few serious survivors of war grew into tolerance of the "new synthesis" (GK 291).

Pound, of course, immediately places himself among those "best." And among those "few serious survivors of war," he had since 1918 seen that his task was to construct that "new synthesis." At times that synthesis might seem entirely made up of C. H. Douglas, Wörgl, Mussolini, anti-Semitism, and praise for the Monte dei Paschi. But at other times (GK 295-99) he reveals there is more. After discussing Victorians, he admits that:

the foregoing pp. are as obscure as anything in my poetry. I mean or imply that certain truth exists. Certain colours exist in nature though great painters have striven vainly, and though the colour film is not yet perfected. Truth is not untrue'd by reason of our failings to fix it on paper. . . . I assert that the Gods exist.

That the gods do exist, that a poet may fail of describing them; that certain truth also exists yet may never wholly be apprehended; and that a new religious sensibility must comprehend a world beyond individual cases—on these foundations stand Pound's religious convictions. *Guide to Kulchur* moves too brutally fast for those convictions to be understood clearly. And perhaps Pound found the confessional, or inspirational, mode in which his attitudes would have to be described too embarrassing to stay with for very long. Those attitudes are nevertheless there.

In their idiosyncrasy, they explain the temper that flares against Eliot in *Guide to Kulchur*. It is precisely Eliot's religion, or his religiosity, that angers Pound. It is not simply that Eliot's church is an English church, and that England is hypocritical and stultifying. It is also that Eliot allows his religious feelings to "thrive" in an atmosphere poisonous to any true mental or spiritual invention. No new synthesis could ever issue from England, much less from its church: "no intellectual curiosity in any anglican publication" (GK 301). In the patronizing tone that was increasingly to characterize Pound's comments about Eliot as the 1930's progressed, Pound says, "*Thoughts After Lambeth* one of Eliot's most creditable essays. I wonder who suggested it? But J. H.'s criticism 'lot of dead cod about a dead god' quite just as describing a good deal of T. S. E.'s activity" (*Ibid.*).

Only one year after the appearance of *Guide to Kulchur*, Pound condemned Eliot's somewhat racist *After Strange Gods*, about which he stated, *mirabile dictu*: "Eliot, in this book, has not come through uncontaminated by the Jewish poison."[11] This kind of anti-Semitism grew cruder, and more compulsive, as Europe sank into the barbarism of World War II. The war years were, of course, the years of Pound's broadcasts on shortwave Rome Radio.[12] On the basis of these broadcasts, he was indicted for treason

[11] *A Visiting Card* (London: Peter Russell, 1952), p. 22.

[12] Appendix B contains a complete transcript of one broadcast, that of March 15, 1942. It is as "comprehensive" as any of the others, and it is more clearly argued than most. It returns, vituperatively, to one of Pound's favorite subjects, England. To read it is to get a fairly good sense of the broadcasts as a whole.

by the United States government; more severe than the government, his peers and their heirs indict him still. Pound's poetic reputation may never exist independently. Nor, I think, should it so exist.

It is difficult to be objective about those broadcasts, but they can be considered a demotic expression of what Pound had been saying for years. The subjects remain the same. The opinions are the old opinions. Pound sees old-fashioned "Yankee" independence and craftsmanship everywhere on the wane (broadcasts of April 30 and May 9, 1942):

Why did our Colonial architecture, what is called our Colonial architecture[,] go to pot? Wood carving, Colonial cabinet making, I mean furniture making, not digging holes and knots, why did that go to pot? American [silversmiths'] technique, why did it peter out? Why do such things synchronize with other phenomena, such as usury tolerance[,] tolerance of usury?

No second rating cooking ever heated my face, till I got to eating in restaurants when going to college. And even then, God damn it, an oyster stew was an oyster stew. I mean as [to] cooking, we were second to no man and to no woman of any nation. French chefs were more fancy, but ice cream made of cream, all cream and peaches, solid peaches, were not surpassed by Theodore; it was not distinctive of Europe.

Certain specific references, however, are new: those to "the Jewspapers and worse than Jewspapers," to "Franklin Finklestein Roosevelt," to "kikes," "sheenies," and "the oily people." Also new are Pound's commendation of *The Protocols of the Elders of Zion* (the most notorious of contemporary tracts purportedly revealing a Jewish or Zionist plot against the foundations of Western civilization) and his remarks that history is "keenly analyzed" in *Mein Kampf*.

Pound implied, as have many anti-Semites, that Jews are a "rootless" people: "The Jew is a savage, his psychology is . . . may the stink of your camp drive you onward—herders—having no care but to let their . . . herds grouse and move onward when the pasture is exhausted" (May 11, 1943). He spoke against America's involvement in the war on May 28, 1942:

And every hour that you go on with this war is an hour lost to you and to your children. And every sane act you commit is committed in [homage] to Mussolini and Hitler. Every reform, every lurch towards the just price, toward the control of a market is an act of [homage] to Mussolini and Hitler.

About the killing of Jews, he had this to say on March 30, 1942:

Don't start a pogrom. That is[,] not an old style killing of small Jews. That system is no good, whatever. Of course, if some man had a stroke of genius, and could start a [pogrom] up at the top, I repeat that, if some man had a stroke of genius, and could start a pogrom up at the top, there might be something to say for it. But on the whole, legal measures are preferable. The 60 kikes who started this war might be sent to St. Helena, as a measure of world [prophylaxis], and some hyper-kikes or non-Jewish kikes along with them.

There is perhaps only a clinical explanation for such utterances. They issue from an anger gone far beyond reason, from a desperation grown extreme. Pound's daughter writes of his condition then:

He was losing ground, I now see, losing grip on what most specifically he should have been able to control, his own *words*.
lord of his work and master of utterance[13]—
— he was that no longer. And perhaps he sensed it and the more strongly clung to the utterances of Confucius, because his own tongue was tricking him, running away with him, leading him into excess, away from his pivot, into blind spots.[14]

Yet neither this explanation nor the fact that American varieties of anti-Semitism increased substantially in general during World War II[15] has helped Pound's reputation. His words have for once had the power he always maintained they had, haunting him until his death and even beyond.

[13] From Canto 74.
[14] Mary de Rachewiltz, *Discretions* (Boston: Little, Brown, 1971), p. 173.
[15] See Morton Keller, "Jews and the Character of American Life since 1930," in Charles H. Stember, ed., *Jews in the Mind of America* (New York: Basic Books, 1966), p. 265.

CHAPTER SIX

The 'Pisan Cantos': "Paradise"

Our awareness of a religious impulse in Pound's mind[1] serves to counteract our suspicions that he can only curse the evil surrounding him and can praise nothing. True enough, much of his energy is consumed by political hatred. Cantos 14 and 15 are early adumbrations of the nightmare vision into which his mind, and that of his readers, would be forced as his long poem continued. One does not so much read the *Cantos* as undergo them. Once Pound's basic assumptions are assented to by the reader, then "must thou go the road / to hell . . . ere thou come to thy road's end." Central among these assumptions is that usury "slayeth the child in the womb," "stayeth the young man's courting," and "gnaweth the thread in the loom."

The road to hell is long, as long as history written and interpreted by Pound, but the growing nightmarishness of the journey is broken by visions of a kind of earthly heaven (Canto 49):

> Autumn moon; hills rise about lakes
> against sunset
> Evening is like a curtain of cloud,
> a blurr above ripples; and through it
> sharp long spikes of the cinnamon,
> a cold tune amid reeds.

[1] Donald Davie has discussed Pound's religious aspirations; see *Ezra Pound, Poet as Sculptor* (New York: Oxford University Press, 1964), p. 152. See also Ronald Duncan, "Religio," *Agenda*, 4 (Oct.-Nov. 1965): 56; Noel Stock, *Poet in Exile: Ezra Pound* (Manchester: Manchester University Press, 1964), pp. 15-28.

Behind hill the monk's bell
borne on the wind.
Sail passed here in April; may return in October
Boat fades in silver; slowly;
Sun blaze alone on the river.

When Pound turns in this way toward nature, his recriminations are abandoned. Paradisal visions arise. There are, after all, things in this world good enough to praise, things whose perfections demand to be understood.[2]

It is to these things that he would return, but he is fascinated by the foul evil of the world, and driven to snuff up its noxious elements. Some of the turbulence in Pound's writings is traceable to an extreme tension between moments of rage and moments of mystical stillness. "We find two forces in history," he wrote in 1942, "one that divides, shatters, and kills, and one that contemplates the unity of the mystery."[3] It is the latter, one slowly comes to recognize, with which Pound would be in harmony if he could.

The positive force is not manifested solely in nature, but also in the wise leadership of a great man. Thus, for instance, Napoleon and Leopold II in Canto 44. Napoleon attracts Pound because he created a superb code of law and civil procedure. Leopold was Holy Roman Emperor from 1790 to 1792; as Leopold I of Tuscany (1765-90) he had advocated many governmental reforms. Pound sees in such men one version of goodness and he praises them, in turn, accordingly:

. . . law code remains.
monumento di civile sapienza
dried swamps, grew cotton, brought in merinos
mortgage system improved
. . .

And before him had been Pietro Leopoldo
that wished state debt brought to an end;
that put the guilds under common tribunal;
that left names only as vestige of feudal chain;

[2] Pound is fond of quoting Spinoza in this connection: "The intellectual love of a thing consists in understanding its perfections."

[3] *A Visiting Card* (London: Peter Russell, 1952), p. 7.

> that lightened mortmain that princes and church be under tax
> as were others; that ended the gaolings for debt;
> that said thou shalt not sell public offices;
> that suppressed so many *gabelle*;
> that freed the printers of surveillance
>   and wiped out the crime of lèse majesty;
> that abolished death as a penalty and all tortures in prisons
> which he held were for segregation;
> that split common property among tillers;
> roads, trees, and the wool trade,
> the silk trade, and a set price, lower, for salt

For Pound, then, goodness arises from particular realities—and dies with them. Nothing can outlive the manifestation in which it is figured forth. Thus, the demise of the Leopoldine influence in Tuscany and the defeat of Napoleon (by the Rothschilds, Pound believed) shattered the goodness Pound saw in these two men and in their influence. As Brooks Adams declared and as Pound thenceforth apparently believed, "Probably Waterloo marked the opening of the new era, for after Waterloo the bankers met with no serious defeat."[4] Hell spewed forth contagion again (Canto 50):

> and that son of a dog, Rospigliosi,
> came into Tuscany to make serfs of old Tuscans.
> S..t on the throne of England, s..t on the Austrian sofa
> In their soul was usura and in their minds darkness
> and blankness, greased fat were four Georges
> Pus was in Spain, Wellington was a jew's pimp
> and lacked mind to know what he effected.
> 'Leave the Duke, Go for gold!'
> In their souls was usura and in their hearts cowardice
> In their minds was stink and corruption
> Two sores ran together,
> and hell pissed up Metternich
> Filth stank, as in our day

From Count Rospigliosi, the Austrian regent in early-nineteenth-century Tuscany, then, to the Georges ruling England from 1714 to 1830, and to Prince Klemens Metternich, Austria's foreign minister, the evidence of an infernal conquest of Europe is clear. With

---

[4] *The Law of Civilization and Decay* (New York: Macmillan, 1896), p. 330.

Napoleon defeated, and the Congress of Vienna (September 1814-
June 1815) convened, with the Duke of Wellington a British representative, to settle the economic and diplomatic destiny of the
various European states, the machinations of the usurers were to
become everywhere successful. Aristocratic control was preserved
against the claims of the Jacobin middle classes. Austria emerged
as a stronger power, appropriating Lombardy-Venetia, Dalmatia,
Carniola, Salzburg, and Galicia, and even exercising a certain
power over Italy. Moreover, a vast system of international diplomacy was established, based on Metternich's doctrine of the balance of power, that lasted throughout the nineteenth century and
into the twentieth. This consolidation of influence meant that
the usurers could attack one centralized body rather than many
disparate entities. After Waterloo, according to Adams and Pound,
that is exactly what they did.[5]

The chief usurer was the British banker Samuel Loyd, condemned by Pound in 1942:[6]

Certainly [Loyd] understood as few men, even of later generations, have
understood, the mighty engine of the single standard. He comprehended
that, with expanding trade, an inelastic currency must rise in value; he

---

[5] Pound might also have been influenced in his view of post-Napoleonic
European economic history by Jeffrey Mark's *The Modern Idolatry, being An
Analysis of Usury & the Pathology of Debt* (Bombay: Shree Laxmi Naryan
Press, n.d. [1934]). Mark, mentioned quite favorably by Pound in his radio
broadcast of April 5, 1943, was clearly in the Douglas-Soddy-Arthur Kitson
tradition of economists opposed to usury and usurers. A paragraph that Pound
might have studied with great attention reads (p. 52):
But the money lenders['] rise to respectability and power was definitely achieved
at the end of the eighteenth and the beginning of the nineteenth centuries, when
the banking-house of Rothschild controlled the destinies of Europe and the profound issues which devolved from the French Revolution much more absolutely, if a good deal less spectacularly, than did Napoleon. Their position thus
acquired was firmly consolidated by their close co-operation with Metternich
in his subsequent determination of European policy and the "balance of
power." Since then, they have been universally accepted by Church and State
through the silent assertion of their money authority; and the sinister nature of
their origin has been entirely forgotten.
[6] *A Visiting Card*, p. 9. The words are those of Brooks Adams in *The Law
of Civilization and Decay*, p. 337.

saw that, with sufficient resources at its command, his class might be able to establish such a rise, almost at pleasure; certainly that they could manipulate it when it came, by taking advantage of foreign exchange. He perceived moreover that, once established, a contraction of the currency might be forced to an extreme, and that when money rose beyond price, as in 1825, debtors would have to surrender their property on such terms as creditors might dictate.

After thus quoting Brooks Adams, Pound admits that the passage might "seem obscure to the average man of letters." And indeed the critic who can grasp Pound's specialized kind of economic history is typically not the man who can appreciate his poetry. Knowing this, Pound took by 1942 an extremely bleak view of things. He saw all lines of intellectual commerce broken: "Our culture lies shattered in fragments, and with the monetology of the usurocracy our economic culture has become a closed book to the aesthetes."[7]

Pound had, of course, seen this split many years before, believing always that men of letters spoke a language foreign to men of affairs. (The existence of writers like E. M. Forster, C. Day Lewis, or W. H. Auden, for whom economic culture was not exactly a closed book, made no difference to Pound. He had shut out many things before; he could just as easily shut them out.) Some "dissociation of sensibility" always bothered him, although he had dated it differently at different times. What is new in the mid-1940's is the desperate and apocalyptic note he sounds. Whereas before he had rather enjoyed the prospect of attempting some bridge-building between those two worlds, while maintaining mastery of both, Pound now sees little hope from either. Men of affairs have become everywhere powerful, Jewish, and obscenely vulgar; the poets, knowing nothing, have revealed a willingness to succumb to any crude tyranny. Pound's sense of the world surrounding him is quite similar to that of Brooks Adams: "The ecstatic dream, which some twelfth-century monk cut into the stones of the sanctuary hallowed by the presence of his God, is reproduced to bedizen a warehouse; or the plan of an abbey,

[7] *Ibid.*, p. 10.

which Saint Hugh may have consecrated, is adapted to a railway station."[8]

What Pound means when he says "our culture lies shattered in fragments" may be given a fairly precise historical context. On July 25, 1943, a coup led by King Victor Emmanuel and Marshal Badoglio forced Mussolini to resign. Imprisoned, he was rescued by German parachutists and established the Salò Republic in German-occupied northern Italy. But on April 28, 1945, he was shot on the shore of Lake Como by Italian partisans. His corpse and that of his mistress Clara Petacci were taken to the Piazzale Loreto in Milan and defiled. The end of a great hope for Pound, a leader who could combine boldness of action, originality of conception, and artistic *éclat*, dictates the weary and elegaic opening of Canto 74:

> The enormous tragedy of the dream in the peasant's bent
> shoulders
> Manes! Manes was tanned and stuffed,
> Thus Ben and la Clara *a Milano*
> by the heels at Milano
> That maggots shd/ eat the dead bullock
> DIGENES, διγενές, but the twice crucified
> where in history will you find it?
> yet say this to the Possum: a bang, not a whimper,
> with a bang not with a whimper,
> To build the city of Dioce whose terraces are the colour
> of stars.

The manner of Mussolini's death is also taken up in Canto 78:

> but was hang'd dead by the heels before his thought in proposito
> came into action efficiently

Pound's regret and loss—revealing once again the degree to which his politics should be seen as hero-worship—are the abiding spirit of the *Pisan Cantos*, published in July 1948, some three years after his forced return to the United States to stand trial for treason.

In these cantos, wave follows on wave of learning. The poet's

[8] This is the conclusion of *The Law of Civilization and Decay*, p. 383.

experiences, stretching back some fifty years and viewed from the position of one who had lost everything save his memory, are summoned up in a vast and shattered panorama. Amid such profusion, he nevertheless asserts, with characteristic bravado, that "with one day's reading a man may have the key in his hands" (Canto 74). This statement shows how consistent his attitudes had remained, war and imprisonment notwithstanding. He had during the war maintained (quoting his old friend Hulme): "All a man ever *thought* would go onto a half sheet of notepaper. The rest is application and elaboration."[9] After the war, at least in these particular cantos, application and elaboration are virtually abandoned. In a highly compressed style, Pound once again sets down his ideas about credit, history, nature, paradise and hell.

Nothing has happened to change his convictions—nothing, that is, except the end of the world as he knew it and had hoped to change it—and Canto 74, in many ways the fullest of these cantos, sets the tone for the rest:

> a man on whom the sun has gone down
> nor shall diamond die in the avalanche
> > be it torn from its setting
> . . .
>
> Lordly men are to earth o'ergiven
> > these the companions:
> Fordie that wrote of giants
> > and William who dreamed of nobility
> > > and Jim the comedian singing:
> > > > "Blarrney castle me darlin'
> > > > you're nothing now but a StOWne"
> and Plarr talking of mathematics
> > or Jepson lover of jade
> Maurie who wrote historical novels
> > > and Newbolt who looked twice bathed
> > > > are to earth o'ergiven
> . . .
>
> dry friable earth going from dust to more dust
> > grass worn from its root-hold

[9] *A Visiting Card*, p. 30.

> is it blacker? was it blacker? Νύξ animae?
> is there a blacker or was it merely San Juan with a belly ache
>   writing ad posteros
> in short shall we look for a deeper or is this the bottom?
> . . .
>
> "I believe in the resurrection of Italy   quia impossibile est

The poet of the *Pisan Cantos* had been overwhelmed by events. He was without prospects, without companions. He was buffeted by the free-floating debris that was Western Europe at war's end. The association between himself and the ruined West is everywhere evident (Canto 76):

> As a lone ant from a broken ant-hill
> from the wreckage of Europe, ego scriptor.

The collapse of history, which Pound felt had already happened, becomes in turn the abiding spectre of his poem. If Pound had followed his own hopeful program ("to write an epic poem which begins 'In the Dark Forest,' crosses the Purgatory of human error, and ends in the light, 'fra i maestri di color che sanno' "), he might now have turned to the establishment of a triumphant vision in which the steady accumulation of historical fact and historical error, the evidence drawn from so many sources as an overwhelming indictment of a certain kind of ignorance, would be transcended, and a new order of understanding would be achieved. But the cruel fact is that by 1948 error was still stronger than order. Paradise was darkened. The assemblage of knowledge, feelings, and experience was left largely untransformed. No mere contrivance of the mind could impose form where none, by itself, now existed (Canto 74):

> Le Paradis n'est pas artificiel
> but spezzato apparently
> it exists only in fragments unexpected excellent sausage,
>   the smell of mint, for example,
>   Ladro the night cat

Form was to be imposed by memory and by love (Canto 76, Canto 81):

                    nothing matters but the quality
of the affection——
in the end——that has carved the trace in the mind
dove sta memoria

    What thou lovest well remains,
                      the rest is dross
    What thou lov'st well shall not be reft from thee
    What thou lov'st well is thy true heritage

Thus Pound concentrates his attention on the effects and casualties of time, cherishing them because he has once known them.[10] But although time has given him all he knows, it has also revealed the distance between what so dismayingly is and what might have been. In its guise of history, it relentlessly measures the failures of men, and records the way in which real possibilities have not been exhausted. It silently chronicles the unused good. Pound, so interested in the fullest development of potentials within nature, was both fascinated and profoundly distressed by this ruthlessness. We recall that the tyranny of time has long been a theme of the cantos (Canto 42):

              wave falls and the hand falls
    Thou shalt not always walk in the sun
        or see weed sprout over cornice
    Thy work in set space of years, not over an hundred.

[10] The critic Georg Lukács, in speaking of "the Romanticism of disillusionment" and of the nineteenth-century novels pervaded by that spirit, remarks that once the sense of an "abstract *a priori* condition" characterizing social life has been lost, and a "purely interior reality" has been established, a new kind of novel comes into being. "In the type of novel which we are considering," he says, "all the relationships have ceased to exist from the start." With the disappearance of social relationships, subjectivity asserts itself and holds sway everywhere in the novel. Yet, interestingly enough, the outside world is not ignored or forgotten, but engaged in a new way. As Lukács puts it, subjectivity "proceeds as an arbitrary conqueror, it snatches fragments out of the atomised chaos which is the outside world and melts them down—causing all origins to be forgotten—into a newly created, lyrical cosmos of pure interiority." The basic similarities between the nineteenth-century novels Lukács has in mind (*Salammbô*, *Oblomov*, those by C. F. Meyer) and the *Pisan Cantos* are clear, even if their historical connections are obscure. In these cantos, just as in those novels, fragments are snatched out of chaos and reduced to a "lyrical cosmos of pure interiority." In Pound's case, the process is mediated

The political and economic implications of this view of time are somewhat indirect,[11] but if a man has no more than his "set space of years" in which to realize his own nature, his "bounty," these years should be unencumbered by systems of government likely to interfere with that realization—which for Pound meant systems vulnerable to the usurers or even actually controlled by them.

Were inexorable time alone his enemy as he stares out at the world from his American-Army-built prison-cage, Pound would at least be confronting a known and understandable adversary, even if it was, as Dr. Johnson once said, "not subject to casualty." The Pisan cantos are written, however, with the recognition that even time has come to a stop and that, with Il Duce dead, a stasis has been reached. To be freed from stasis, to make things move forward once again, the poet looks hopefully to what he terms "the process," the generative dynamic that controls nature.

Daniel Pearlman seems absolutely right when he suggests that a form of nonchronological time, a time made up of memory, love, and the rhythms of nature, helps establish this generative dynamic and provides Pound with the possibility, at least, of escaping the static burden of history.[12] Not historic time, but "cyclical or organic time," can perhaps be one answer to his plight. Pound thus tries to breathe life into his past by infusing with affection his memories of friends and places long gone. He also turns to ob-

---

by the deep affection he invokes and the despair he wishes constantly to drive away. (All quotations here are from *The Theory of the Novel*, trans. Anna Bostock [Cambridge, Mass.: M.I.T. Press, 1971], p. 114.)

[11] Lukács can again be helpful. In speaking of novels possessed by "the romanticism of disillusionment," he reveals that Pound's situation is not without precedent and that the poet of our time is faced with a situation repeatedly confronted by writers whose connections with "the outside world" have been obliterated. For the nineteenth-century novelists Lukács mentions, "meaning is separated from life, and hence the essential from the temporal; we might almost say that the entire inner action of the novel is nothing but a struggle against the power of time. In the Romanticism of disillusionment, time is the corrupting principle: poetry, the essential, must die, and time is ultimately responsible for its passing. That is why in such novels all value is on the side of the defeated protagonist" (*The Theory of the Novel*, pp. 122-23).

[12] *The Barb of Time* (New York: Oxford University Press, 1969), pp. 21-22.

serve the way the smallest of animate things take root and flourish. With his mind partially on the past and its broken artifacts, he beholds the process in miniature (Canto 83):

> and in the warmth after chill sunrise
> an infant, green as new grass,
> has stuck its head or tip
> out of Madame La Vespa's bottle
> mint springs up again
>   in spite of Jones' rodents
> as had the clover by the gorilla cage
>   with a four-leaf
> When the mind swings by a grass-blade
>   an ant's forefoot shall save you
> the clover leaf smells and tastes as its flower

A little later in the same canto, he brings out of the past a delightful reverie on friendship, in this case with William Butler Yeats:

> so that I recalled the noise in the chimney
> as it were the wind in the chimney
>   but was in reality Uncle William
> downstairs composing
> that had made a great Peeeeacock
>   in the proide ov his oiye
>   had made a great peeeeeeecock in the...
> made a great peacock
>   in the proide of his oyyee
> proide ov his oy-ee
> as indeed he had, and perdurable
> a great peacock aere perennius
>   or as in the advice to the young man to
> breed and get married (or not)
>   as you choose to regard it
> at Stone Cottage in Sussex by the waste moor
> (or whatever) and the holly bush
>   who would not eat ham for dinner
> because peasants eat ham for dinner
>   despite the excellent quality
> and the pleasure of having it hot
> well those days are gone forever

The poet would will himself into paradise, into the full consciousness of past and present in such a way that time would once again be tripped into motion. Occasionally certain syntheses are created out of memory and close attention paid to fundamental nature, but it is difficult to argue, as Pearlman does, that "spiritual synthesis always manages to reassert itself again against the pressure of the quotidian."[13] The poet is simply not so triumphant. He cannot release himself from the sinewy hold of so much historical knowledge, so much confirmation of evil, so much evidence that the usurers' poison has become fatally toxic. The quotidian is indeed powerful. Canto 77, for instance, cryptically reaffirms his findings of so many years before:

>   . . . the state *can* lend money
>   as proved at Salamis
>   and for notes on monopoly
>   Thales;   and credit, Siena;
>   both for the trust and the mistrust;
>   "the earth belongs to the living"
>   interest on all it creates out of nothing
>   the buggering bank has;   pure iniquity
>   and to change the value of money, of the unit of
>   money
>   METATHEMENON
>   we are not yet out of *that* chapter
>   Le Paradis n'est pas artificiel

These fragments have proved enduring enough to be locked forever in Pound's memory ("certain images be formed in the mind / to remain there / *formato locho*" [Canto 74]). For us, they may need some elucidation. Salamis, the island near which the Greeks vanquished the Persians in 480 B.C., had always reminded Pound that the state need not resort to parasitical private banks to support military activities. If the state retained credit-granting powers, wars would be few. Wars were the doing of profiteers who stood to gain from conflict and carnage.

Pound next mentions Thales, from Book I, Chapter 11, of

---

[13] *Ibid.*, p. 237.

Aristotle's *Politics*. Thales, a philosopher, wished to demonstrate that philosophers could become wealthy. He did so quickly by deducing from the stars when there would be a good crop of olives, hiring all the oil presses in Miletus and Chios, and then renting them out at exorbitant fees when the demand for them suddenly rose. Adding something to Aristotle's wisdom, Pound might say that the problem of our time has been caused by such clever men (some of whom he could name), who, in situations less homely than that in which Thales figured, commit financial treachery. There is no question here of ideological currents, for we know that Pound supported no ideology as an explanatory tool in the affairs of men. He had no need to. Politics, as he chose to see it, is a bad man doing that which is bad, and, occasionally, a good man doing good.

Siena (home of the Monte dei Paschi), mentioned next, we recognize from our discussion of Canto 42. Jefferson's statement ("The earth belongs to the living") has been discussed above, as well. We have also discussed the statement that William Paterson, seventeenth-century founder of the Bank of England, once made in a shareholders' prospectus: "the bank hath benefit of the interest of all moneys which it creates out of nothing." Pound had used the statement in Canto 46 and in *A Visiting Card*, one of the wartime money pamphlets. Its repetition here indicates the zeal with which he could still throw himself into the question of unearned increment.

METATHEMENON is another reference to Aristotle's *Politics*. Pound has in mind a passage (Book I, Chapter 9) distinguishing in ethical terms between the proper and improper functions of currency. The Greek word refers to a phrase ("μεταθεμένων τε τῶν χρωμένων," or "if those who use a currency give it up in favor of another") which Pound repeatedly uses as a talisman to suggest the profoundly ethical character of good economic policy. Merely to alter a currency system is to change the vehicle of money-making. But money-making is not wealth. True wealth is in accordance with nature and is itself productive.

He ends the passage by warning us that "we are not yet out of *that* chapter." We were warned the same way in Canto 46: "you who think / you will / get through hell in a hurry." The "chapter" is "hell"; the familiar hell of financial inequities. And his warning is appropriate. That chapter, we may be sure, has no real end so far as Pound is concerned. It will extend as far as the cantos extend. As long as Pound traces down the root sources of error, he will find them in economic dysfunctions, and as long as he finds them, he will continue to absorb them. That is why he rephrases Baudelaire to say, "Le Paradis n'est pas artificiel." No contrivance of the mind, or of pharmacology, can be worth considering as long as brute fact, the "quotidian," keeps drawing our gaze back to the real spectacle of men harming other men by usurious means. Real paradise will come, if at all, when that spectacle no longer exists.

In the meantime, as these cantos point out, man deludes himself. He is surrounded, as was Pound without books at Pisa, by an endless bleakness; all of his dreams of escape are idle. He is thrown back upon himself. Yet his dreams are desperately needed (Canto 74):

> I don't know how humanity stands it
> > with a painted paradise at the end of it
> > without a painted paradise at the end of it

Pound rejects both the bleakness and the idle dreams, settling in, instead, for the infinite duration of usury and fixing his vision, in the *Pisan Cantos* and thereafter, on the innumerable examples of its ugly power. Thus does content determine one aspect of the poem's form: its endlessness. Which is another way of saying that Pound's politics determine that form. The cantos could never have the end Pound originally projected for them, and are perhaps intrinsically endless (although they had ceased even before Pound's death), because neither he nor any man of his convictions could ever mine the immense historical deposit of bad government, bad men, evil banks, and unearned increment, much less transcend it.

Visions of paradise would always be eclipsed by the poet's awareness of the darker powers. "It is difficult to write a paradiso,"
wrote Pound, "when all the superficial indications are that you
ought to write an apocalypse."[14]

He is perhaps most poignantly aware of these darker powers
when he allows his thinking to stray back to England. He had
loved England, particularly London, as a young man starting his
life as a writer, as an ambitious man of letters; but he had come
to detest it because of its stuffiness, its recalcitrance toward new
literary ideas. In Canto 80, England emerges again as something
of a possibility. In 1945, Winston Churchill had just been defeated
as prime minister of the coalition government. Perhaps money
might be free again, if the original charter for the Bank of London
were remembered and repealed. This playful echo of Browning
shows the kind of affection Pound now wishes to sustain.

> Oh to be in England now that Winston's out
>   Now that there's room for doubt
>   And the bank may be the nation's
>   And the long years of patience
>   And labour's vacillations
> May have let the bacon come home,
>   To watch how they'll slip and slide
>   watch how they'll try to hide
>   the real portent
>   To watch a while from the tower
>   where dead flies lie thick over the old charter
>   forgotten, oh quite forgotten
>   but confirming John's first one,[15]
> and still there if you climb over attic rafters;
> to look at the fields; are they tilled?
> is the old terrace alive as it might be
> with a whole colony
>   if money be free again?
> Chesterton's England of has-been and why-not,
> or is it all rust, ruin, death duties and mortgages
> and the great carriage yard empty
>   and more pictures gone to pay taxes

---

[14] *Paris Review*, no. 28 (Summer-Fall 1962), p. 47.
[15] The Magna Carta, signed by John Lackland, King of England, in 1215.

. . .

> and the Serpentine will look just the same
> and the gulls be as neat on the pond
> and the sunken garden unchanged
> and God knows what else is left of our London
>   my London, your London

This reverie confirms no happy possibilities; it merely opens them. The suspicion that the old terrace might not be so lively as it could be, that money might not be wholly free again, and that much of London might have changed irrevocably in the years of Pound's absence, weighs heavily over these fragile lyric lines. The poet does seek to oppose the force of such suspicions, does seek a means "to build the city of Dioce whose terraces are the colour of stars," a place to forget the smashup of history. Thus he turns to the neo-Platonic philosophers of light and of perfectly ordered knowledge, such as Johannes Scotus Erigena (Canto 74):

> Light tensile immaculata
>   the sun's cord unspotted
> "sunt lumina" said the Oirishman to King Carolus,
>   "OMNIA,
> all things that are are lights"

Or he turns to nature made divine by the presence of Maenads and of Aphrodite herself (Canto 79):

> Lynx, keep watch on this orchard
>   That is named Melagrana
> or the Pomegranate field
>   The sea is not clearer in azure
>   Nor the Heliads bringing light
> Here are lynxes   Here are lynxes
> Is there a sound in the forest
>   of pard or of bassarid
>   or crotale   or of leaves moving?
>   Cythera, here are lynxes
> Will the scrub-oak burst into flower?
>   There is a rose vine in this underbrush
> Red? white? No, but a colour between them
>   When the pomegranate is open and the light falls
> half thru it

Or he turns simply to a kind of magic, to a kind of reification whereby the impossible is suddenly made possible by an act of sheer will: "bricks thought into being ex nihil" or "in Tangier I saw from dead straw ignition" (Canto 74). In order to save his mind, he would create something from nothing. But doubts creep in as Pound thinks back on his literary companion of the 1920's, Ralph Cheever Dunning, and on certain elegant restaurants in London, New York, and Paris. He now permits himself one more excursion into a golden past. Such moments are few for him (Cavalcanti's Mediterranean sanity, Siena, Jefferson's America, and Wörgl among them). Now the itinerary is his own early literary life (Canto 76):

> we recall him
> > and who's dead, and who isn't
> > and will the world ever take up its course again?
> very confidentially I ask you: Will it?
> > with Dieudonné dead and buried
> not even a wall, or Mouquin, or Voisin or the cake shops
> > in the Nevsky

But Dunning is gone, as is the Restaurant Mouquin. Many things, things that had once nourished his mind, are gone. "Beauty is difficult," as Pound, quoting Aubrey Beardsley again and again in these late cantos, reminds us. No artificial paradise is here legitimate.

And yet, despite the remoteness of true paradise, the poet is unyielding in his attachment to the world that is now to be found only in his mind, held there inviolate (Canto 74):

> I surrender neither the empire nor the temples
> > > > plural
> > nor the constitution nor yet the city of Dioce

Pound's steadfast insistence on a world beyond this one, partaking of this world's grace and beauty but not of its poisons, has roots in circumstances that are more than individual and psychological. Once before, we may recall, Pound's poetic life had been changed by war and its aftermath. In 1914-18, senseless destruction had taken from him several close friends and had left him with the sense of cultural wastage explored in *Hugh Selwyn Mauberley*. The second wave of senseless destruction, with its climax in 1945, had an even greater impact on him than the first. Whereas the First World War had had a largely personal and artistic effect, the Second had an effect that may be described as both political and philosophical: the "saving remnant" of artists, which he had declared some twenty years earlier to be crucial in the preservation of culture—including a proper government—was now reduced to a single individual, Pound himself. Only he ("ego scriptor") retained enough historical knowledge, enough understanding of the root sources of error, and enough solicitude for the "process" through which life comes into being, to be considered anything like a savior. Separated from the rest of society, he nevertheless served it in a special way. The Pisan cantos unmistakably assert Pound's belief that it is his own painstaking and energetic ministrations to the world, in both its smallest natural configurations and its largest political ones, that will lend it life. As he (once called "A Man in Love With the Past" by Wyndham Lewis) remembers it, so the world of the past takes shape. As he lovingly scrutinizes it, so the world of nature is understood and inspirited. As he announces them, so solutions to problems can be thought plausible.

One may recall in this connection Pound's early pronouncements about the serious artist, statements that, with the energy of youth and the unencumbered verve of Shelley, asserted the uniquely vital creative and social responsibilities of anyone who would call himself a writer. These pronouncements reflected a great deal of the self-importance, and only a small part of the self-mockery, of Flaubert's contention about the War of 1870: "If they had read my *Education Sentimentale*, this sort of thing wouldn't have happened." As the years went on, in fact, Pound was to turn more and more often to himself as the court of first and last resort. Even when his wide-ranging interests had led him to confront issues of the most unwieldy sort, he felt he could rely on his own sensibility to handle them.

Arthur Griffith, the founder of Sinn Fein, had once warned him, friend to friend, that a poet "can't move 'em with a cold thing like economics" (ABC 26). That bit of advice is now preserved in Canto 78. So, of course, is the complex product of Pound's rejection of it. With Griffith's warning ignored, the poet felt free to use as material the most apparently intractable stuff available to him. His voice was to bring life to the "unpoetic"; his mind was to make all things cohere. Such is the rare energy that for years enlivened Pound's writing. That energy provides much of the pleasure to be had in reading him. Here at last, one may feel, is a poet and poetry free of any provinciality, free from the constraints born of traditional procedure, or of coterie, or even of plain modesty.

One may apprehend that sense of energy and freedom in some of Pound's writing composed decades earlier than the Pisan cantos. He steadfastly maintained certain convictions for almost all of his creative life. One was that Marx and communism, despite their enormously appealing call to political liberation in a society and a century given over to greed and wars, are alien to the power of will and order great artists must possess. What had momentarily tempted him was discovered to be the worst of the modern Circes.

Another assumption, maintained with equal fervor, concerned the degree to which the strong individual poet, and not the "massman," is the true voice of feeling and health in any culture. As a corollary, the strong poet looks with admiration to the strong leader. The muse is quickened as much by authority as by beauty. Pound became bold enough, in time, to conclude that as much beauty inhered in the transformation of the world through totalitarianism as through imagination. To the Ezra Pound who idolized Mussolini, an imagination disengaged from politics was a derelict agency of the mind. It was embarrassingly feeble in comparison to the massive energies seeking to recreate a country, a people, perhaps a whole world. When Pound attached himself first to a loose amalgam of reactionary ideas and at last to Mussolini, he did so in the belief that he was acceding to a creative power as yet untapped by men of letters. He could thus rise above such men and what he saw as their trivial pursuits. The compulsion to be superior asserted its terrible power once more.

The Pisan cantos and the cantos thereafter are a record, however, of what inevitably had to happen when, with Mussolini's death, with the disappearance of Social Credit as a monetary possibility for any great number of people, and with the postwar splintering of the avant-garde Pound had led, his own world came to an end. The connection to totalitarianism was broken and he was faced with the vast rubble of politics and history, now wholly out of his control and piling up around him. He thus became not so much a creator as one who would salvage from the rubble that which was largely lost, not so much a poet as a stunned observer. He at last fully entered a world he had for years been building, a world at once lyrical, decomposed, and solipsistic.

PART TWO

T. S. ELIOT

I am not sure . . . that we can judge and enjoy a
man's poetry while leaving wholly out of account
all of the things for which he cared deeply, and
on behalf of which he turned his poetry to account.
—*T. S. Eliot, "Shelley and Keats"*

CHAPTER SEVEN

Suprapolitical Man

In 1960, in a foreword to Wyndham Lewis's reissue of the poem *One-Way Song*, T. S. Eliot referred to the charge leveled at his friend for his political attitudes during the 1930's: " 'Fascist!'—a term falsely applied to Lewis, but flung by the *massenmensch* at some who, like Lewis, choose to walk alone."[1] This remark can serve as well as many another to begin a discussion of Eliot's political identity. Casually delivered though it may have been, it conveys an immediate sense of the separation Eliot felt between artists, including himself, and the barbarous public. Concerned though he was with the reality of political forces, Eliot felt compelled to transcend those forces, to walk alone, to be suprapolitical. The difficulty in coming to terms with Eliot's political position is that these terms are not entirely political, or entirely stable.

There is not even the same sure kind of help with Eliot as with Pound in studying the American background. For although one may assume that Eliot absorbed roughly the same basic predilections and prejudices from his genteelly declining, New England-connected family as Pound did from his, Eliot rejected his American origins so thoroughly in later life that it seems presumptuous to try to make much of them.

Moreover, Eliot's political and social ideas exist for the most part in uncollected form, never organized and never synthesized, as notions and suggestions put forward with characteristic diffidence and obliqueness during some forty years. They were offered as apparently avocational reflections by one whose reputa-

[1] London: Methuen, 1960, p. 10.

tion as poet, literary critic, editor, and Anglo-Catholic was fully covered. His tact, or perhaps his cunning ("Ol' Possum," Pound called him), eschewed the direct, unqualified statement (save that which is chiefly remarkable for its innuendoes, such as his comment on Shelley's "Ode to a Skylark": "I do not understand it"). Before beginning one of his literary studies, for example, he confided: "I hope that these three papers may in spite of and partly because of their defects preserve in cryptogram certain notions which, if expressed directly, would be destined to immediate obloquy, followed by perpetual oblivion."[2]

However cryptic their expression, however, Eliot's feelings were strong: "I have felt obscurely," he wrote when bringing his magazine *Criterion* to an end in 1939, "the grave dangers to this country which might result from the lack of any vital political philosophy, either explicit or implicit. . . ."[3] And elsewhere he was to say, "Politics has become too serious a matter to be left to politicians."[4] How, then, is one to judge attitudes at once political and impracticable, intensely partisan and vaporously utopian? How is one to judge feelings at once so indirect and so integral a part of the man?

To talk about Eliot at all is to talk about his political identity, but to talk about that identity soon involves one in extraordinarily delicate questions of "sides," "parties," and "sympathies." Eliot was clearly on the political right. He was not inclined to speak charitably of those on the left. Beyond this superficial classification, however, matters become difficult. Was he a fascist? Did he support Mussolini or Hitler? Did his anti-Semitic tendencies go so far as to make him sympathetic to the violent persecution of Jews? Again and again people return to these questions, but to ask them is immediately to reveal their inadequacy in making sense of him. If Eliot committed himself to stands on central political questions of his time, those stands were compromised by their complexity and abstruseness.

If one thinks of politics in its usual sense—voting, organizing,

<hr/>

[2] *Homage to John Dryden* (London: Hogarth Press, 1924), p. 9.
[3] [A Commentary] "Last Words," *Criterion*, 18 (Jan. 1939): 272.
[4] "A Commentary," *Criterion*, 6 (Nov. 1927): 386.

running for office, leading marches, or affecting elections—Eliot will hardly be seen as political. He *disposed* himself in political situations. To understand this political disposition, one must also understand his religious disposition. The "royalist" is also the "Anglo-Catholic." At times, however, his political and religious sympathies seem to exist harmoniously only in his own mind, or, to use F. H. Bradley's phrase, as "a non-relational unity of many in one." But his diverse and contrary attachments, political and religious, must all be gathered up if he is to be comprehended.

One currently comfortable way of treating Eliot's political identity is to misunderstand it as an ancillary support to his poetic theory. The poetry and his poetic innovations, it is argued, are of primary concern; all else, including politics, is subordinate, simply a disposable scaffolding by which to ascend to the poetry. Stephen Spender writes, "What seems wrong about the Sweeney poems [and here Spender discusses their anti-Semitism] is not that they are reactionary-political but that they use a tawdry view of a conspiratorial capitalism to construct a rather cardboard background to the poetry."[5] This passes over the question of what is cardboard and what is not, of what is scaffolding for what. Spender wants to understand Eliot nominally, as a *poet*, and to see the literary criticism as an extension of the poetry, the political criticism as an extension of the literary criticism. This line of reasoning comes, I think, as a result of two things: the benumbing power of the title "poet," and the desire to guide attention away from what might prove distasteful upon close scrutiny. But it is invalidated by the fact that Eliot himself did not treat his political concerns as ancillary. Again and again, with greater frequency as he grew older, he involved himself deeply in political questions. The truth seems to be that, particularly in *After Strange Gods*, *The Idea of a Christian Society*, and *Notes towards the Definition of Culture*, he saw himself in a role inadequately described by "poet."

Certain other obvious problems present themselves in studying Eliot's ideas on politics and society. One must, for instance, choose a path between the aggressive crudities of political labeling (during

---

[5] "Writers and Politics," *Partisan Review*, 34 (Summer, 1967): 375.

the Stalinist Wroclaw Congress of Intellectuals in the forties, he
was, for example, decried as a "Fascist Jacktail"), and the evasive
delicacy that overlooks his political beliefs as secondary effects.
Spender is generous to a fault; the Stalinists simply obliterate distinctions; neither deals with Eliot's extreme subtlety.

A well-reasoned approach is that of John Harrison, who tries
to see Eliot as a man holding an elitist view of culture as a prerogative of the few—by extension an elitist political position—that is,
as he puts it, "not untenable." Says Harrison, "Eliot's is a legitimate view, and can only be attacked, as it was formed, from preconceived notions of the relationship between literature and society."[6] Yet Mr. Harrison, who proceeds from preconceived notions of his own, would have one understand that Eliot carried
the banner of "Society for art's sake" and that such a position, so
ultimately romantic, was maintained in simple ignorance of what
anyone of real common sense or good will, such as Mr. Harrison,
can all too easily see. He argues that Eliot apparently did not understand the complex structure of modern society, and that he
failed to see that there can be no going back.

The approaches taken by two other recent critics, John D. Margolis and Roger Kojecký,[7] who read Eliot very closely, and with
great attention to detail and nuance, are also flawed. The first uses
Eliot's review *Criterion* (1922-39) as "a valuable chronicle of the
evolution of his interests." Mr. Margolis performs his task with
intelligence and impartiality; he makes no judgments, however,
and shrinks from the controversies that form the very heart of his
study. Mr. Kojecký seeks "to explore the defensibility of Eliot's
positions" and engages more directly the controversial aspects of
the poet's achievement. He thinks Eliot's record as a social critic
is better than his reputation, and suggests that "two or three
phrases" from the poet's work have been used, unfairly, to be-
smirch that reputation. He rests his argument, however, at a point

---

6 *The Reactionaries* (London: Gollancz, 1966), p. 160.
7 John D. Margolis, *T. S. Eliot's Intellectual Development, 1922-1939* (Chicago: The University of Chicago Press, 1972); Roger Kojecký, *T. S. Eliot's
Social Criticism* (London: Faber and Faber, 1971).

beyond argument: "in the long run any opinion of Eliot's social criticism, as such, will depend largely on individual attitudes towards Conservatism." The issue, however, is not Eliot's, or the reader's, personal political sympathies; to say that it is, is a way of trivializing the matter. Nor is it two or three unfortunate phrases in Eliot's works. The issue is a superlative poet who, over the course of a whole life, attempted uneasily to grapple with the crucial questions of his age and, by his example, alerted us to dangers and difficulties that may plague writers and critics of a later generation.

CHAPTER EIGHT

Eliot and the "New Attitude of Mind"

Eliot's first public announcement on political affairs rings of the manifesto, the grand style of Wyndham Lewis's *Blast*, Pound's strident "Make It New," and the manic energies of both Futurism and Vorticism. Writing in the seventh number (April 1924) of his new magazine *Criterion*, Eliot declared that the late "militarist by faith" T. E. Hulme "appears as the forerunner of a new attitude of mind, which should be the twentieth-century mind, if the twentieth century is to have a mind of its own. Hulme is classical, reactionary, and revolutionary; he is the antipodes of the eclectic, tolerant, and democratic mind of the end of the last century."[1]

Hulme stood on the parapet and urged those loyal to his doctrines to be skeptical of the free display of emotions in literature and to censure the heretical effusions of romanticism. "Romanticism is spilt religion," he announced, leaving for posterity the kind of aphorism helpful in any such campaign. And posterity has seen to it that the aphorism has been effective; attempts to reject romanticism in our century have followed roughly Hulme's lines. Believing that without the stabilizing doctrine of Original Sin all chaos would break loose, Hulme could find solace only in a hier-

[1] Many critics have discussed Hulme's influence on Eliot. Vincent Buckley, Raymond Williams, Frank Kermode, and Herbert Schneidau have all explained how Eliot was to carry forward the tenets of Hulme's philosophical-poetical campaign. "In the critical battle against the nineteenth century," says Buckley, "the central point of attack will be the conception of personality, and emotion as the chief agent of its inflation. This emphasis passes into Eliot's work and remains relatively constant in it." *Poetry and Morality* (London: Chatto and Windus, 1959), p. 92.

atic, geometric, and tough-minded art. The dry, hard image was welcome in poetry, and Jacob Epstein, Cézanne, and Wyndham Lewis were welcome in the visual and plastic arts. All else was misconceived. As Frank Kermode has put it, Hulme's aesthetic had implications that pointed everywhere: "Romanticism was a calamity however you looked at it: politically, philosophically, aesthetically. It was the anthropocentric assumption of the Renaissance at the stage of mania, all Rousseauistic rubbish about personality, progress and freedom, all a denial of human limit and imperfection."[2]

Thus, early on, Eliot smoothly engages himself in the contrary motions of Hulme's campaign. The twentieth century, we note, is to have "a new attitude of mind"—if it has a mind at all. Moreover, the tolerant and democratic mind is to be repudiated in favor of a mind that is, amazingly enough, to be "revolutionary," yet "reactionary," and even "classical." Eliot's argument turns on a belief that only with a certain political culture may literary culture be saved. Like his ally Pound, he is at this early point in his career working to promote literature and he is not unlike the crusader for literature depicted by John Harrison. Not first and foremost as a theorist of culture, but as an artist Eliot says: "Democracy appears whenever the governors of the people lose the conviction of their right to govern: the claims of the scientists are fortified by the cowardice of men of letters."[3] And, he says, a new "state of equilibrium" will be attained "when the dogma, or *ideology*, of the critics is . . . modified by contact with creative writing."[4] This is not, we shall see, the manner of the later Eliot, the author of *After Strange Gods* or of *The Idea of a Christian Society* or of *Notes towards the Definition of Culture*. There he is the moralist, the amateur philosopher and the social planner. Here he is the young poet, the innovative critic. His social concerns arise out of his solicitude for literary enterprise—which is, after all, larger and more powerful than the surrounding culture seeking to constrain

[2] *Romantic Image* (New York: Vintage Books, 1964), pp. 125-26.
[3] "A Commentary," *Criterion*, 2 (Apr. 1924): 233.
[4] *Ibid.*, p. 232.

it. What remains of interest in this statement of 1924 is Eliot's conscious direction toward a strategy of criticism that, while not forcing him into the uncomfortable position of pretending to comprehend all he surveys, would still permit him the flexibility he would need to grasp certain literary problems at one with certain political problems.

This strategy is, in large part, what Eliot meant by the phrase, "new attitude of mind." Not to see him as a strategist is to miss him entirely. His career can be read, in fact, as a progress toward eminence during which new ground is gained, new positions taken, and the conscious deployment of talent never neglected. One clear sign of his intelligence is the sense he gave always of being a writer aware of the situation, literary and historical, surrounding him. Rarely surprised by events, and ready both to anticipate and encourage changes in cultural fashion, he progressed not *ad hoc*, but according to plan, with an eye clearly on the systematic development of his taste, authority, and reputation. Pound noticed this kind of sophistication when he first met him. Writing in September 1914 to Harriet Monroe, he reported that Eliot was

the only American I know of who has made what I can call adequate preparation for writing. He has actually trained himself *and* modernized himself *on his own*. . . . It is such a comfort to meet a man and not have to tell him to wash his face, wipe his feet, and remember the date (1914) on the calendar.[5]

By this date Eliot had completed the earliest pieces in *Prufrock and Other Observations* ("Preludes," "Portrait of a Lady," "The Love Song of J. Alfred Prufrock," and "Rhapsody on a Windy Night"). Already behind him was graduate work at both Harvard and the Sorbonne. Leaving the University of Marburg in 1914 because of the threat of war, he was settling in at Merton College, Oxford, to study Greek philosophy. During the next ten or twelve years of his life he expertly laid the foundation for his development. As both his poetry and his prose of those years show, he was working toward a philosophical and political orientation that

---

[5] D. D. Paige, ed., *The Letters of Ezra Pound 1907-1941* (New York: Harcourt, Brace, 1950), p. 40.

would sustain him through the years thereafter. Hulme was but a part, although an important part, of that "new attitude of mind."

Not all events, of course, were under the poet's control. The "new" mind was also to be marked by its awareness of the beginning of war, a war so destructive of life and promise that many writers, Eliot and Pound among them, could well wonder whether civilization possessed any stability whatsoever. Hulme himself was among those killed in the conflict. Eliot's customary reticence in his writing held even here, but the dedication to the 1917 *Prufrock* volume reads: "For Jean Verdenal, 1889-1915 / mort aux Dardanelles." And later, when thinking back in the pages of *Criterion* to the atmosphere of the prewar years in Paris, he wrote:

I am willing to admit that my own retrospect is touched by a sentimental sunset, the memory of a friend coming across the Luxembourg Gardens in the late afternoon, waving a branch of lilac, a friend who was later (so far as I could find out) to be mixed with the mud of Gallipoli.[6]

The ravages of war are at the heart of poems such as "Gerontion" and "Burbank with a Baedeker: Bleistein with a Cigar." Eliot's grave skepticism about the so-called civilized order of man produces a sense within the poem of sterility, despair, and frustration. These poems thus subsume the notes of frustration found in "Prufrock" (written 1910-11). With war, with memories of loss, the tone becomes darker, the gnawing apprehension of waste and emptiness becomes more inclusive. No longer are the tragicomic limitations of an unwholesomely fastidious Prufrock subject enough for the poet. He turns instead, in "Gerontion," to the cunning contrivances of history and, in "Burbank with a Baedeker: Bleistein with a Cigar," to the decline and sordid vulgarity of Venice, victim of neurasthenia and mercantilistic Jews.[7]

[6] "A Commentary," *Criterion*, 13 (Apr. 1934): 452. John Peter also cites these references to Verdenal. But his argument ("A New Interpretation of *The Waste Land*," *Essays in Criticism*, 2 [July 1952]) concerns intensely personal aspects of the poem that do not interest me here. However, his treatment of Eliot's desire to withdraw from, or to transcend, events interests me greatly.

[7] Robert Alter has, I think, commented helpfully on the nature of the anti-Semitism in the "Burbank" poem. Quite rightly fascinated by the apparently intense emotions involved in the poet's "vehement energy of repulsion," he

In the later poem, just as history is inhabited by malevolent mysteries, so the rented house is inhabited only by a stiffening body and the charming Venetian palace only by animals pretending to be people. Literary allusion conflates time and place: Shylock becomes Bleistein, Chicago blurs into Vienna, the ideal Venice of Canaletto and Baedeker becomes a place where rats live in the foundations. Art can no longer be appreciated, romance fails, the lovely lady stretches out her phthisic hand. Burbank is the naive idealist, ineffectual in keeping alive his dreams and yet much too weak to cope with the world as he finds it. He can contemplate the ruins of time but that is all. Those ruins, I would suggest, are also "time ruined." Not only is modern Venice a sad reminder of the city Canaletto once saw, but it is also evidence that time has come to a stop. "The smoky candle end of time / Declines."

"Gerontion" probes more fully (and less elliptically) the confusions and resultant collapse of time, and even includes a lecture on the deceptions of history. Certain Eliotic features reappear: the impossibility of heroism, the stolid possessiveness of the Jew or "jew" (he who "squats on the window sill"), and the arid hopelessness of spring. The memory of Christ's promise, most urgent in spring, can lead only to despair and to a futile wait for signs which will never come into view. May is all the more "depraved" for every false hope it inspires; moreover, it is rich with reminders of the betrayal of Judas. Indeed, once hope is evoked, and once Christian knowledge is absorbed, how bleak the time thereafter. The speaker in "Gerontion" is not unlike the Joycean victim whose curse is history, "a nightmare from which I am trying to awake." The pressure of guilt, of unanswered belief, of confusion between methods to find relief, all drive the speaker into a cul-de-sac from which fragmented meditations can alone emerge.

---

sees as the source of this vehemence Eliot's strained, even desperate, reliance on the Western cultural tradition, and suggests that the poet invokes that tradition as something "at once universal and esoteric, impenetrable to the outsider. The Jew in this regard is important to Eliot as the archetypal outsider, a European who is not a Christian, which for Eliot is a virtual self-contradiction." I am sure Alter is correct in this. ("Eliot, Lawrence and the Jews," *Commentary*, Oct. 1970, pp. 83-84.)

One such meditation, delivered pedagogically, is, as I say, on the subject of history. With echoes of *The Education of Henry Adams*, a book fascinating to Eliot at this postwar time,[8] it sees history as irrational, centerless, and inaccessible to those wishing to "join" it. Adams had written that at the end of the century the historian "entered a far vaster universe, where all the old roads ran about in every direction, overrunning, dividing, sub-dividing, stopping abruptly, vanishing slowly, with side-paths that led nowhere, and sequences that could not be proved." Centripetal energies had torn apart a former whole, its wholeness now beyond recovery. This gloomy sense of the apocalyptic, central to Adams throughout the *Education* and indeed throughout his life, appealed to Eliot, who apparently felt in 1919 that the values of the society that had reared him and of the Europe to whose cultural resources he had traveled, were suddenly empty. The past, all of whose confusions, treacheries, and ambiguities had been thrust into the present, was devoid of any quality about which one could be certain, save that it could precipitate war. Time, whether it be called past, present, or future, is deadly. It negates all attempts, and freezes all action in a *tableau non vivant* of highly stylized, very disagreeable figures known only by their freakish names: Mr. Silvero, De Bailhache, Fresca, and Mrs. Cammel. The alien presence, Jew or gentile, is everywhere.[9]

Thus did Eliot respond to the impact of war and international chaos. Just as Conrad's Kurtz (who, like Gerontion, says, "I am lying here in the dark waiting for death,") is in some way an index to the mortifying diseases of nineteenth-century imperialism, so Eliot's old man bespeaks a kind of hopelessness particular to the early twentieth century. Poems are a part of history; they do not

---

[8] He had reviewed it the same year for *Athenaeum* (4647 [May 23, 1919]), and had, in echo of Matthew Arnold's words about Shelley, termed Adams a "sceptical patrician" with "the wings of a beautiful but ineffectual conscience beating vainly in a vacuum jar."

[9] As Grover Smith has put it, "the enduring past urges no vital evolution through a creative present and instead hugs a vampirish immortality into a dead future." *T. S. Eliot's Poetry and Plays, A Study in Sources and Meanings* (Chicago: University of Chicago Press, 1956), p. 59.

transcend it. The only way they have of seeming eternal is to respond wholly to a present situation that seems itself eternal. For
Eliot that eternally present situation was the chaos of history, the
impossibility of heroic action, and the sterility of contemporary
Western society. *Heart of Darkness* is a novel of "eternal" interest
to a society for whom the repercussions of imperialism are a matter of immense concern. Just so, "Gerontion" proves interesting
to readers whose daily anxieties are prompted by the deterioration
of feeling and by the growth of something resembling *accidie.*
Facing a future without bright prospects, Eliot, and his sympathetic readers of some fifty years, reveal not that they together
share timeless verse, but that they share a common political and
historical predicament. Resisting *accidie* as well as they can, they
nevertheless feel its claim upon them. The verse grows from, and
finds readers in, a context of war and its dislocations.[10]

Much the same kind of relationship between Eliot and his readers can be felt in *The Waste Land* (1922). That poem, still the
sphinx of the age, was, as we now know, originally to have included "Gerontion" from *Ara Vos Prec* as its prelude. Pound
argued persuasively that the two be kept separate, but Eliot's feeling that the earlier poem is kindred in spirit to the later should be
acknowledged. The paralysis or impotence of the first is extended
in the second. Gerontion becomes Tiresias, and the modern landscape a vast mythological one. Particles and fragments of time
past are commingled with those of time present. The central figure,
earlier a Prufrock or a Gerontion, becomes no individual man at
all, but a presiding consciousness, omniscient and androgynous.
In one of his mysterious, snare-like notes to the poem, Eliot wrote
that Tiresias is "the most important personage in the poem, unit-
ing all the rest" and that "what Tiresias *sees,* in fact, is the substance of the poem."

[10] The presence in early-twentieth-century writing of characters such as the
desperate Kurtz, the historically oppressed Stephen Dedalus in the "Nestor"
section of *Ulysses,* and the miserable Gerontion is literary confirmation of
the statement by Marx and Engels that "in bourgeois society . . . the past
dominates the present."

This note, reliable or not, is as good a point of departure as any-thing else in a poem about which virtually everything has been an-notated and about whose qualities every position, pro or con, has been exhausted. The note, along with certain works of recent scholarship, leads us to believe that the central "personage" will be a so-called finite center resolving all experience by both under-going it and describing it; in short, the consciousness of the poem. This would all be well, if we could be sure how to disentangle the consciousness that suffers from the one that observes. Such a dis-tinction is as crucial as it is impossible. Although some readers of the poem would have us believe that consciousness is conscious-ness, as pudding is pudding, and that any consciousness is bound both to suffer and to observe, such a shaky assumption ignores the fact that suffering is of various kinds, the particular kinds largely determined by situations historical and otherwise, and that the purely objective consciousness, the Tiresias free of all partiality, is an imaginary entity put forward by those who wish to believe that partiality, characteristic of absolutely everyone, can be transcend-ed. To agree with Eliot's modest note on Tiresias is, in other words, to take a philosophical position with strong political over-tones. It is to relegate the historical and the political, those largely determining forces, to mere skin, easily torn from the poem.

Rather than embracing Eliot's Bradleyesque notions about con-sciousness, we might consider the possibility that the confusion between spectator and sufferer points to a central confusion in the poem. It is not enough to say that such confusion works to enhance or deepen our aesthetic involvement. There is no recourse, in this case, to the headier mysteries of the New Criticism. The question is one of narrative reliability. John Lucas and William Myers have, I think, written well on this point and have asked, in sum, "how do we decide whether we should assent to the speaker's words or see in them a token of his own disease?"[11] Their uncertainty is actually the uncertainty, I think, of many readers. When Lucas and Myers confess that "we cannot hold a presiding voice in focus,"

[11] *"The Waste Land Today," Essays in Criticism,* 19 (Apr. 1969): 195.

or when they say that it is unclear "whether we are listening to a witness giving evidence or to the judge summing up," they perceive that *The Waste Land* is problematic partly because it is an uneasy mixture of the purely diagnostic ("I Tiresias, old man with wrinkled dugs / Perceived the scene, and foretold the rest") and the purely pathological ("My friend, blood shaking my heart / The awful daring of a moment's surrender / Which an age of prudence can never retract / By this, and this only, we have existed"). What, indeed, is the nature of the "ruin" against which the ambiguously conceived narrator shall shore his fragments? Is the ruin his? Or is it everyone else's?

The mystery originates with "The word," in this case a pronominal one. The poem begins:

> April is the cruellest month, breeding
> Lilacs out of the dead land, mixing
> Memory and desire, stirring
> Dull roots with spring rain.
> Winter kept us warm, covering
> Earth in forgetful snow, feeding
> A little life with dried tubers.
> Summer surprised us, coming over the Starnbergersee
> With a shower of rain; we stopped in the colonnade,
> And went on in sunlight, into the Hofgarten,
> And drank coffee, and talked for an hour.
> Bin gar keine Russin, stamm' aus Litauen, echt deutsch.
> And when we were children, staying at the arch-duke's,
> My cousin's, he took me out on a sled,
> And I was frightened. He said, Marie,
> Marie, hold on tight. And down we went.
> In the mountains, there you feel free.
> I read, much of the night, and go south in the winter.

The question, at the outset, is not only who "I" happen to be, but also who "we" happen to be. That question is not an idle one. Asked at almost any moment within the poem, it will elicit an ambiguous answer. Whether "we" be all humanity, or a lone reader and traveler, or a son of man, or Stetson's friend, or son and brother to kings, or an acquaintance of the Smyrna merchant, or all of the living dead, our sense of connection with one, or with several, or with all, is not at all assured. To hint that "we," as readers, can become Tiresias, that we can assert the same "omniscience" shared by Tiresias and Eliot, is to offer knowledge and insight where almost none is justified. Let us admit that we move through the poem in virtual ignorance, and that our knowledge is not Tiresian (nor are we sure we wish it to be). We can be assured, however, that to compose a poem in which the referent of "we" is so uncertain must be to begin with an equally uncertain sense of "I."

The inability to provide personal identity, and to write out of it, the inability to provide more than an illusion of personal order through reliance on Tiresias, reveals the infirmity of Eliot's social sensibility. Alienation from one's society is well defined as an individual's blind "throbbing between two lives." The equally plaintive confession that an individual "can connect nothing with nothing" should suggest that Edmund Wilson's pioneering analysis of the poem, now almost lost in the welter of astringently apolitical discussions, is essentially correct. Wilson saw that Eliot, a product (albeit an unwilling one) of the commercial-industrial middle class of America and Europe, would naturally share the disabilities and frustrations of that class. Desolate in a world of largely meaningless labor, its members cannot even bring themselves to choose between their routinized pains and their sordid pleasures. Spiritually disenfranchised from the class to which they objectively belong, they cannot turn to any other. Wilson saw in 1922 that "In our post-War world of shattered institutions, strained nerves and bankrupt ideals, life no longer seems serious or coherent—we have no belief in the things we do and consequently we have no heart for them."[12]

Eliot himself said in 1931, "when I wrote a poem called *The Waste Land* some of the more approving critics said I had expressed 'the disillusionment of a generation,' which is nonsense. I may have expressed for them their own illusion of being disil-

[12] "The Puritan Turned Artist," as reprinted in C. B. Cox and Arnold P. Hinchcliffe, eds., *T. S. Eliot, 'The Waste Land': A Casebook* (London: Macmillan, 1968), p. 101.

lusioned, but that did not form part of my intention."[13] Later he
said that the expression of disillusionment could not have been
part of any conscious intention. Beneath his characteristically coy
diplomacy, Eliot's attitude toward this issue is stubbornly truthful.
There is little sense in speaking of an artist's intention in matters
of this sort. Still less is it sensible to speak of any conscious intention at the moment of creative inspiration. An artist is at that moment armed only with the ambiguous legacies of his own particular history.[14] He can neither escape it nor transpose himself into
a situation in which its power is mitigated. As Eliot has said, "The
great poet, in writing himself, writes his time."[15] But he does so
involuntarily. He both represents and reinforces the historical tendencies of that time. Indeed, for him to do otherwise would be
continually to improvise a poetic context and an intellectual experience, always at the mercy of whim. This, obviously, was not
Eliot's way. The times are to be felt in his lines.

Eliot defined poetic responsibility, in fact, as loyalty to a certain kind of history. This is the gist of "Tradition and the Individual Talent." Published in 1919, almost concurrently with the
poems considered here, this essay urges the poet to "procure the
consciousness of the past" and to develop it throughout his career.
It describes the artistic monuments of the past as forming an "ideal
order" whose symmetry, when violated by any new poet, immediately reforms around him, incorporating him into a new symmetry. The poet thus sacrifices himself to that order, extinguishing
himself in the process. Losing himself, he thereby gains himself.
Historical tendency is confirmed, and the status quo perpetually
maintained.

Other thinkers who would have agreed with Eliot on little else,
perhaps, can be found in essential agreement with him on this.

---

[13] "Thoughts After Lambeth," *Selected Essays* (New York: Harcourt, Brace,
1950), p. 324.

[14] Eliot's own words are: "I wonder what an 'intention' means! One wants
to get something off one's chest. One doesn't know quite what it is that one
wants to get off the chest until one's got it off." *Writers at Work, The Paris
Review Interviews*, Second Series (New York: Viking, 1965), p. 97.

[15] "Shakespeare and the Stoicism of Seneca," *Selected Essays*, p. 117.

Some seventy years before "Tradition and the Individual Talent," in an often-cited passage from the opening of the *Eighteenth Brumaire*, Karl Marx had said:

The tradition of all the dead generations weighs like a nightmare on the brain of the living. And just when they seem to be engaged in revolutionizing themselves and things, in creating something that has never yet existed, precisely in such periods of revolutionary crisis they anxiously conjure up the spirits of the past to their service and borrow from them names, battle cries and costumes in order to present the new scene of world history in this time-honored disguise and this borrowed language.

Both Eliot and Marx accord the past a great power. For Marx, the past is *mortmain*; for Eliot, it is the means whereby the sordid present may be redeemed. And yet if a poet is wholly responsive to the past, and wholly dissatisfied with the present that surrounds him, he can do nothing to escape the infirmity of social sensibility of which I have spoken. Thus he "throbs" between two worlds and desperately gropes for some escape, some transcendence, which he is at the same time always too scrupulous to take. This is Eliot's posture in *The Waste Land*, by turns censorious and pitiable.

Despite all that has been said about Eliot's (and Pound's) revolutionary impact on contemporaries, and despite the enthusiasm with which Eliot formulated his "new attitude of mind," we should understand that he made no real departure from the consciousness of his age. His fundamental attitudes, his confusions, and his anxieties arose from and were part of his social ambience. His genius as a poet, manifested most strikingly in *The Waste Land*, was to make spiritual alienation so real that even those suffering from it could marvel at the diagnosis of their disease. The victims were rightfully impressed, even stunned, by what they had theretofore only suspected. But the bringer of the devastating news was speaking partly to and for himself.

We should remember, in speaking of this formative period of achievement in Eliot's career, that his poetry was not always written in the same spirit as his prose. He himself made a distinction between the genres: "In one's prose reflexions one may be legitimately occupied with ideals, whereas in the writing of verse one can only deal with actuality" (ASG 30). This comment can help us greatly. Eliot's prose is often a medium that seeks to clarify wishes and develop ideas left implicit in the poetry. But the two do not say the same thing. Only rarely does Eliot, in his poetry, allow himself the freedom of his prose speculations. If I may make my own distinction, his poetry is one of reaction, his prose one of aspiration. From "Prufrock" on, the poems can be characterized by their passivity in the face of decay and even calamity whereas the prose persistently conveys a kind of active and inventive despair. This alternation sets the rhythm for the rest of Eliot's life. He knows that basic problems will not, cannot be solved, but he assents to the fiction that a responsible person, with a heritage of New England puritan concern behind him, must conscientiously attend to them.

In 1926, Eliot attempted to clarify his political and literary position more precisely than the phrase "new attitude of mind" would permit. He concentrated on one aspect of the attitude as Hulme defined it, the classical, investing the term "classicism" with implications rich enough to let it serve as a summary of everything he wanted. The tendency of which he spoke may be regarded as his own desire:

I have expressed my aversion to stating any programme or erecting any platform. But it might not be amiss to clarify by illustration the notion of a 'tendency'. . . . I believe that the modern tendency is toward something which, for want of a better name, we may call classicism. . . . I will mention a few books, not all very recent, which to my mind exemplify this tendency:

Réflexions sur la violence, by Georges Sorel;[16] L'Avenir de l'intelligence, by Charles Maurras; Belphégor, by Julien Benda; Speculations, by T. E. Hulme; Réflexions sur l'intelligence, by Jacques Maritain; Democracy and Leadership, by Irving Babbitt. . . .[17]

[16] The English translation of this volume was made by Hulme.
[17] "A Commentary," Criterion, 4 (Jan. 1926): 5.

Since Eliot does not make perfectly clear what is "classical" about any of these works or their writers, his examples must be used with great care. This care, however, seems justified, for here, if anywhere, is where we should look for influences on Eliot's politics. In the case of Sorel, we might imagine that Eliot would have been attracted to his distrust of parliamentary socialism, his hatred of middle-class democracy, his monarchist nationalism, and by his abstruse intellectuality. In the case of Maritain, it is perhaps important to note that the French Thomist had for some time admired Maurras and wrote, at this time (1926), "Une opinion sur Charles Maurras et le devoir des Catholiques," an attempt to reconcile the factions created within the Church by the question of the Action Française.

Such uncertainty plagues every effort to track down Eliot's "influences." No mere receptacle for other men's thoughts, he was most influenced, not by individuals, but by the pressure of a historical moment. One might even say that he first decided what he wanted and what he wanted to affirm, and then supported those desires and affirmations with a number of altogether suitable references. His inclusion of Julien Benda and his *Belphégor* as exemplars of classicism is one telling instance of this procedure.

Published in 1918, *Belphégor* is an attack on a long list of things its author felt had poisoned the age: the cults of sensation and feeling, art as mystic union with the phenomena of life, the present "hatred of intelligence," the vertiginous descent of the intellect to a world of fluidity and mobility, the "effeminacy" of thought, the disappearance of all mental distinctions. All of these malign forces had been set loose by the masses, by the pressures of democratic society. The true intellectuals, those bound to the very highest standards of cerebral discrimination, had either fallen silent or cast in their lot with the mass mind. The procedure here is the same as in Benda's later and more famous book *La Trahison des Clercs* (1927): to set a standard, abstract and pure, and then tendentiously chastise those who fall short of it. Effeminate and fluid minds fail by the test of the earlier book; intellectuals who adopt partisan politics fail by the test of the later.

The unspoken motive behind *Belphégor* is Benda's great hatred of the chaos and vulgarity of democratic political movements. The "crowd" oppresses him just as it had Matthew Arnold, just as it did Eliot. Himself a Jew, and a defender of Dreyfus, Benda is not above crudely categorizing Jews: the severely moralistic and the greedily sensationalistic, the sons of Spinoza and the sons of Bergson. Proclaiming himself above politics, he engages in the sport of finding enemies of civilization where not a few demagogues of this century have also found them: among women, Jews, and supporters of democracy. He exemplifies the avid polemicist who bids all others respect impartiality. Benda's great skill was in holding a series of strong opinions behind a façade of perfect objectivity. It was a skill not lost on Eliot.

Just three years after celebrating Benda in his 1926 "Commentary," Eliot was to say that the thinking of *La Trahison des Clercs* seemed "infected with romance."[18] Benda, once pointing toward the "classic," now gravitates toward its antithesis. How is such an apparent reversal in Eliot's thinking to be explained? By our understanding that the terms "classic" and "romantic" actually confuse more than they clarify. The real change in Benda's thought, from *Belphégor* in 1918 to *La Trahison des Clercs* in 1927, has nothing to do with classicism and romanticism as they are normally understood and everything to do, I believe, with Benda's attack on Sorel and Maurras in the later book for profaning their work with political opinions. Eliot changes his opinion of Benda, in other words, as Benda changes his mind about right-wing ideologies. That was not consistent with Eliot's own development toward reaction, so he turned it aside as "romantic."

Eliot's use of Benda illustrates what I have called his "strategy." In the postwar years, Eliot was arranging his intellectual life. He was careful to mention certain names favorably in his *Criterion* Commentaries. Those names are not to be thought of as influences so much as they are to be considered public notifications of his own course of development.

18 "The Idealism of Julien Benda," *Cambridge Review*, 49 (June 6, 1928): 485.

About the "classicism" of Maurras and Babbitt, whose views proved more harmonious over the years with Eliot's own, Eliot wrote with greater clarity and helpfulness. Maurras' *L'Avenir de l'Intelligence* offered the intelligentsia the choice of joining forces either with the cosmopolitan financial powers or with the aristocracy of blood. In devoting to this book one of the very few of his own essays he ever put into *Criterion*, Eliot revealed its importance to him. And in praising it as representative of the "classical" tendency, he demonstrated an obvious preference for the second alternative. In his later arguments against Karl Mannheim's theory of elites, he argued against elites of mere skill and talent, and maintained that Mannheim's elites, deprived as they would be of blood, aristocratic connection, and unifying religious belief, would fail because they would be too "atomic" to form a whole culture. Between a monetocracy and a blooded aristocracy, there is no doubt where Eliot's true sympathies lay.

The affinity between Maurras and Eliot, however, goes deeper than this. It is through Maurras that Eliot was to be introduced to a school of continental thinking that helped to define his entire intellectual life. Maurras was the product of a thorough classical education but was nevertheless so frustrated among mere books that as a young man he declared: "Literature led us to politics." Just as he was deeply offended by names containing *k*, *w*, or *z*, so Eliot was to form an ostensibly aesthetic distaste for names like Klipstein, Bleistein, Sir Ferdinand Klein, and Mr. Silvero. Maurras, seeing the crowds at the Olympic Games, conceived a violent dislike for the masses. Eliot, offended by these same masses, turned to the solace offered by the "aristocracy of culture." Maurras, as Eliot knew, waged a lifelong struggle against the enemies of France and culture as he saw them: individualism, les droits de l'homme, parliaments, religious liberty, democracy, and internationalism. Moreover, his explanation of his development is somewhat similar to Eliot's. He said, "I entered politics like a religion."[19] This statement can remind us of Eliot's famous announcement of 1928:

[19] As quoted in Ernst Nolte, *Three Faces of Fascism* (New York: Holt, Rinehart, 1966), p. 64.

"[My] general point of view may be described as classicist in literature, royalist in politics, and anglo-catholic in religion."[20]

There remains but one other name among those in Eliot's list of classical exemplars, his teacher at Harvard, Irving Babbitt. In 1927 Eliot wrote "The Humanism of Irving Babbitt," an essay that contained both praise and criticism. Humanism, as Eliot saw it, could never really be anything more than a substitute for religion; it was certainly not the perfect alternative Babbitt saw it as. Rather, it was a "parasitical" doctrine, "merely the state of mind of a few persons in a few places at a few times" and "auxiliary to and dependent upon the religious point of view."[21] He saw the advent of humanism as an aftermath of a truly religious period and those adopting it as people deprived of any external support for their frail beliefs. Those beliefs would soon die, for, finally, "religion is Christianity; and Christianity implies, I think," says Eliot, "the conception of the Church."[22] Moreover, the very presence of humanism revealed the extent of the world's decline: "it is doubtful whether civilization can endure without religion, and religion without a church."

What, then, makes Babbitt "classical"? It is not, we see, his humanism that earns him Eliot's commendation, but certain other qualities. If Maurras came to politics through literature, and "entered politics like a religion," Babbitt was also able to see many issues as one. Both Maurras and Babbitt saw that the twentieth century faced inseparable problems: the economic problem inextricable from the political, the political from the philosophical, and the philosophical from the religious. The political problem is the central concern of Babbitt's book and it can be defined simply as the mass versus the elite. The mass provides confusion and the seeds of chaos; the elite, or, as Babbitt calls it, "the saving remnant,"[23] provides the last means of maintaining order. Babbitt's

---

[20] For Lancelot Andrewes (London: Faber and Gwyer, 1928), p. ix.

[21] Selected Essays, pp. 421, 427.

[22] Ibid.

[23] This and the other quotations in this paragraph and the next are from

book could fairly be called *Democracy versus Leadership*, for democracy is all bad, and the genuinely strong leader all good. "Social justice," says Babbitt, "means in practice class justice, class justice means class war and class war, if we are to go by all the experience of the past and present, means hell." Thus social justice ultimately means hell.

Viewed from the perspective of such a defense of the status quo, any liberalizing or progressive social change is bound to be bad, and Babbitt goes on to say that "democracy is, in so far, incompatible with civilization." He sees modern man reduced to a choice between being a Bolshevist or being a Jesuit, and the Catholic Church as perhaps "the only institution left in the Occident that can be counted on to uphold civilized standards." In an emergency, only extremes can be acknowledged. Eliot was also soon to adopt such a tone of crisis in his arguments. Democracy is, to Babbitt, an ultimate irrelevancy, an error. Meaningful answers can come from the strong leader alone, and from his plateau Babbitt envisions the kind of leadership that would be needed: "Circumstances may arise when we may esteem ourselves fortunate if we get the American equivalent of a Mussolini; he may be needed to save us from the American equivalent of a Lenin." What links Eliot's "classical" writers together, then, is a common appeal, not to Hellas, but to Lacedaemon; democratic principles are, in one way or another, scorned; the repulsive masses are almost beyond hope; liberalism is a threat to all things civilized.

This brief review of Eliot's "classicism" should therefore show us two things: that Eliot has redefined "classical" to mean "antidemocratic" (as René Wellek has pointed out, Eliot's classicism is a matter of cultural politics rather than literary criticism[24]), and that by the mid-twenties Eliot had drawn the lines of the quiet struggle he was to wage for at least the next three decades of his

---

Irving Babbitt, *Democracy and Leadership* (Boston: Houghton Mifflin, 1924); in order of appearance, pp. 1, 308, 312, 186, 311-12.

[24] *Concepts of Criticism* (New Haven: Yale University Press, 1963), pp. 46-47, 357.

life. He knew he was not simply to be a poet, wholly an aesthete, and that his response to his surroundings would have to be, in part, a scrutiny of its politics. Like Pound's Hugh Selwyn Mauberley, Eliot saw that "The age demanded an image / Of its accelerated grimace."

The artist in the modern world, as he wrote in *Criterion*, June 1926,

is heavily hampered in ways that the public does not understand. He finds himself, if he is a man of intellect, unable to realize his art to his own satisfaction, and he may be driven to examining the elements in the situation—political, social, philosophical or religious—which frustrate his labour. In this uncomfortable pursuit he is accused of 'neglecting his art.' But it is likely that some of the strongest influences on the thought of the next generation may be those of the dispossessed artists.

Eliot's thinking here reminds us of Pound's question in 1933 (see p. 6 above): "What drives . . . a man interested almost exclusively in the arts, into social theory or into a study of the 'gross material aspects' videlicet economic aspects of the present?" Both men were dispossessed artists. Literature indeed led them to politics.

CHAPTER NINE

From Machiavelli to the Flirtation with Fascism

With "Niccolo Machiavelli," included in *For Lancelot Andrewes* (1928), and with the classicism, royalism, and Anglo-Catholicism pronouncement in that volume,[1] something of great importance was added to Eliot's political identity. The change is indicated by his new sophistication in coming to terms with "the mob." He had in 1927 spoken of "those of us who are higher than the mob"[2] and had looked queasily on the prospect of any great number of people gathering for religious worship. No good, but only harm to civilized governments, could come of it:

We are already accustomed to seeing, from time to time, immense numbers of men and women voting all together, without using their reason and without enquiry; so perhaps we have no right to complain of the same masses singing all together, without much sense of tune or much knowledge of music; we may presently see them praying and shouting hallelujahs all together, without much theology or knowledge of what they are praying about. We cannot explain it. But it should at present be suspect; it is very likely hostile to Art.[3]

In 1928 Eliot, if not any more comfortable with the mob, had found a way to quiet some of his anxieties: the realism of Machia-

---

[1] Eliot's profession of loyalty to the King should not be equated with the emotions usually involved in patriotism or in respect for the British people. In 1918 he had written that "No one can be so aware of the environment of stupidity as the Englishman; no other nationality perhaps provides so dense an environment as the English." "Tarr," *Egoist*, 5 (Sept. 1918): 105-6. Pound's antipathy toward the British was also strong at this time.

[2] "A Note on Poetry and Belief," *Enemy*, 1 (Jan. [Feb.] 1927): 17.

[3] "A Commentary," *Criterion*, 5 (June 1927): 286.

velli. Praising Machiavelli for his impersonality and innocence, and dismissing his dark reputation as the result of devil-worship, Eliot suggests that a lower order of people might be disciplined through a higher order of being. If the mob, in other words, needs discipline, it can be provided by the church. "You cannot govern people for ever against their will," says Eliot, devising his own kind of corollary to the principles of Machiavelli, "and some foreign peoples you cannot rule at all; but if you have to govern an alien and inferior people—a people inferior in the art of government— then you must use every means to make them contented and to persuade them that your government is to their interest. Liberty is good; but more important is order; and the maintenance of order justifies every means."[4]

Let us not hesitate to imagine that the "alien and inferior people" may very well be those at home; a mob, after all, is any-where still a mob. The means by which order is to be maintained, however, even at home, are perhaps less sinister than the phrase "justifies every means" suggests. "It is quite possible," he says, "that an established National Church, such as the Church of En-gland, might have seemed to Machiavelli the best establishment for a Christian commonwealth; but that a religious establishment of some kind is necessary to a nation he is quite sure. If his words were true then they are true now."[5] The Church, then, is nothing so sinister as a police force. But it does provide order; it does have great practical usefulness.

Machiavelli's words provide a way to understand at least some of the elements involved in Eliot's confirmation in the Church of England, an act that took place at almost the same time the Ma-chiavelli essay was written. That confirmation, and the deeper conections it established between Eliot's attitudes toward poli-tics, mass society, civic order, and what he was later to call "the necessity of Christianity," marks the distance traveled between

---

[4] "Niccolo Machiavelli," in *For Lancelot Andrewes* (London: Faber and Gwyer, 1928), p. 58.

[5] *Ibid.*, pp. 56-57.

what might be called two Eliots. The first is the literary critic, author of *The Sacred Wood* (1920) and *Homage to John Dryden* (1924) who, like his friend Pound, was worried lest "the cowardice of the men of letters" succumb to "the demagogy of science." Although he then sought a wider influence for the world of letters, he cautioned his readers about the "growing and alarming tendency in our time for literary criticism to be something else; to be the expression of an attitude 'toward life' or of an attitude toward religion or of an attitude toward society."[6]

The second Eliot encourages that very same "alarming tendency" and, in fact, places the emphasis of his writing not simply upon literature but upon the kind of social reordering that would be good, first and foremost, for society itself. The question, to be sure, is one of proportion: Eliot certainly continued to write literary criticism after 1927, but he organized his powers in such a way that he became more and more interested in the forces, political and religious, that form or malform society as a whole.

Another striking example of this new direction of interest is his essay "John Bramhall" (1927). It illustrates how he is able, in very short order, to bring an argument beginning in criticism of style and philosophy to rest finally upon both an indictment of the present age and a celebration of a model way of thinking. Bramhall's thought, Eliot suggests,

is a perfect example of the pursuit of the *via media*, and the *via media* is of all ways the most difficult to follow. It requires discipline and self-control, it requires both imagination and hold on reality. In a period of debility like our own, few men have the energy to follow the middle way in government; for lazy or tired minds there is only extremity or apathy: dictatorship or communism, with enthusiasm or with indifference.[7]

Bramhall exists for Eliot not simply as a historical figure, the Bishop of Derry under Charles I and Primate of Ireland under Charles II, but as a strong mind to which he can compare present weaknesses and excesses. That Bramhall is of another century is

[6] "A Commentary," *Criterion*, 11 (July 1924): 373.
[7] "John Bramhall," *Selected Essays*, 315-16.

irrelevant, for there is "a fundamental unity of thought between Bramhall, and what he represents, and ourselves."[8]

In Eliot's remonstrance against "dictatorship or communism," and in his commendation of the middle way, we come upon the process of ratiocination that was to characterize virtually all his later arguments on social or political matters. The existing social or political situation is the result of either extremity or apathy; the middle way, born of true faith, transcends both. Yet those possessing true faith are few in number. They constitute, in fact, a small aristocracy of proper understanding. And yet they make it impossible for the present authorities rightfully to retain control over certain aspects of human behavior. Politics, as Eliot had said, had become too serious a matter to be left to politicians.

He made it clear, moreover, that in order to survive, the man of letters would have to liberate himself from a provincial attachment to his private concerns: "the study of his own subject leads him irresistibly to the study of the others; and he must study the others if only to disentangle his own."[9] It must be noted, again, however, that the result of this disentanglement was, in Eliot's case, not necessarily a renewal of poetry as a medium strong enough to embody new political and social concerns. The major poetry he published after 1927, the year of these statements, cannot be seen to possess any new or more vital political life. *Animula, Ash-Wednesday, Marina, Sweeney Agonistes, The Rock, Four Quartets*—none of these can fairly be described as a political poem or as a poem clearly benefiting from a "disentanglement" of political concerns. To say this is to reveal the terms in which Eliot had grown to view the art of poetry: it simply could not, in his hands, incorporate one of his most basic preoccupations and anxieties, the political.

The years immediately after 1927 provide, I think, one of the most revealing periods in which to examine Eliot's political identity. During that time he not only discussed specific questions re-

---

[8] *Ibid.*, p. 319.
[9] "A Commentary," *Criterion*, 6 (Nov. 1927): 386.

lating to fascism and liberalism more explicitly than he ever would again, but committed himself to positions that marked the extremes of his political animosities. There is no evidence, however, to support a theory of correspondences between Eliot's growing reactionism and the rise of Hitler. He made no comments on Nazism; he did not look to Germany. With certain French and American philosophers and advocates of antidemocratic theories he had, as I have already pointed out, an explicit connection. And he was later to speak favorably of Mussolini. It is possible, of course, to find elements in Eliot's political writings that could be used to support fascism in Germany: assertions of the importance of authority could be pushed to the extreme of a defense of Nazi totalitarianism. But to posit any direct link between Eliot and National Socialism is simply to ignore the facts.[10]

Another explanation of Eliot's deeper interest in political issues during the late 1920's and early 1930's is provided by Dimitry S. Mirsky, the Russian critic of British literature and society who was to die in one of Stalin's infamous camps. In *The Intelligentsia of Great Britain*, Mirsky argues from a Marxist point of view that 1931 was a crucial turning point in English letters. England suffered a very serious depression that year, and

the events of 1930-1931 brought even the high-brows out of their proud timeless idealism. The sharp drop in the demand for intellectual labor struck one wing, and the terrible falling off of colonial tribute which enabled the other wing to be so civilised, had an immediate effect. However high they might have trained themselves to lift their eyebrows, this gentry now were compelled to recognise some connection between their position and balance sheets and the saturation point of industry—and the further dependence of those on the political activity of classes. The high-brows found themselves drawn into the general intellectual mobilisation for political work. And of course it goes without saying that the vast majority went to the right, into one or other form of fascism.[11]

---

[10] And it is also to ignore differences among the several forms of fascism. Ernst Nolte shows in detail some of the immense difficulties to be encountered in making any meaningful comparisons between Italian fascism, National Socialism, and the Action Française. See his *Three Faces of Fascism* (New York: Holt, Rinehart, 1966), pp. 275-76.

[11] *The Intelligentsia of Great Britain* (London: Gollancz, 1935), p. 131.

It is difficult, of course, to be sure that Mirsky had Eliot specifically in mind here; but it is also difficult to imagine that Eliot, as the editor of one of the most highbrow journals of the day, would have been omitted from such a survey. And other comments in the book seem to point directly at Eliot:

The British intelligentsia comes to fascism by various paths. The literary and artistic section go by way of "classicism" which amounts, in regard to general world outlook, to accepting some external authority in preference to personal persuasion; in political life, to accepting the authority of organisation as against liberty, and in artistic life, to the supremacy of form over content. "Classicism" carried out thoroughly leads to catholicism, and certainly catholicism shows the greatest likelihood of satisfying the fascised intelligentsia which thirsts for "system."[12]

Mirsky is correct in seeing that "classicism" can, in fact, have strong political implications, and in recognizing the strong desire of Eliot and those like him for form and system, but he does not succeed, for me at least, in establishing 1931 as the crucial turning point. Eliot's attitudes were present before 1930; they continued long after. He was already committed to Maurras, to Sorel, to Babbitt; he had long felt that democracy was alien to "the aristocracy of culture." The fact of the matter is that Eliot's politics were rarely susceptible to local or topical influences. They steadily made themselves felt. His was not a case of radical change or surprising developments; what went on instead was that new facets of an attitude already shaped revealed themselves over a period of years. History did not change abruptly, nor did Eliot. Moreover, his effort was not to react well to events, but to provide himself with explanations that would make events irrelevant. After he assumed British citizenship and was confirmed in the Church of England, his path would have to hold in balance the antidemocratic nature of his political philosophy, the loyalty he had declared to the King, and the faith he had found in Anglicanism. The facts of history, thus distanced from him, would have negligible effect. But he would become more British indeed than the British, more a part of English life and historical traditions, than

[12] *Ibid.*, pp. 41-42.

those around him. He would become an apotheosis of accumulated English belief. His individual talent would, so to speak, mirror forth that tradition.

The burden of responsibility entailed in these interlocking commitments can explain a rather casual comment made six years after Mussolini's March on Rome. In speaking of the *British Lion*, then the journal of Rotha Lintorn-Orman's British Fascists (a group soon to be succeeded by Oswald Mosley's British Union of Fascists), Eliot was at once a supporter and a denigrator:

> The accusations made by *The British Lion* against British Communists may all be true, and the aims set forth in the statement of policy are wholly admirable. The *Lion* wishes to support 'His Majesty the King, his heirs and successors, the present Constitution, the British Empire and the Christian Religion.' These are cardinal points. We would only suggest that the British Lion might very well uphold these things without dressing itself up in an Italian collar. It is not our business to criticize fascism, as an Italian regime for Italians, a product of the Italian mind. But is *The British Lion* prepared to accept *le fascisme intégral*? What of the fascist ideas of political representation, which may be excellent, but which hardly square with 'the present Constitution' which the *Lion* is sworn to defend?[13]

The appeal here is to English national feeling, to local patriotism, to King and Constitution. The consequent distrust of the only fascist alternative available to Britain in 1928 is therefore quite understandable. That distrust also explains why Eliot was never able, during his entire career, to form any relationship with English fascist groups.[14] And the evidence strongly suggests that it was on grounds other than absence of political affinity that Eliot made his objections to them. Perhaps those grounds were ones of refinement and taste. How indeed to reconcile, he perhaps wondered, the fragile intellectual tradition embodied by Babbitt, Sorel, Maurras, and the policy of *Criterion* with antidemocratic methods, as they were then all too sordidly displayed on London streets

---

[13] "A Commentary," *Criterion*, 7 (Feb. 1928): 98.

[14] No record of any claim on him by Oswald Mosley exists; nor does Colin Cross, the historian of *The Fascists in Britain* (New York: St. Martin's Press, 1963), think it worthwhile even to mention him.

by Mosley, Arnold Spencer Leese, William Joyce ("Lord Haw-Haw"), John Beckett, and their half-menacing, half-ridiculous ilk? One can imagine that Eliot's intellectual bearing might very well have made him say, "Fascism has become too serious a matter to be left to fascists." It is amidst such complications, then, complications of interlocking responsibilities and of a distaste that spurned involvement, that Eliot made his politics known. Those politics, to repeat, were ones of disposition, and not of active partisanship.

He was very soon (March 1928) to return to the intellectual tradition at whose head he saw Maurras. In one of his rare politically oriented articles in *Criterion*, "The *Action Française*, M. Maurras, and Mr. Ward," he tried to correct what he felt were errors concerning the sincerity of Maurras' faith in Leo Ward's *The Condemnation of the Action Française*. Ward had raised the question whether Maurras truly accepted Christian faith and went on thereafter to accept the Roman Catholic Church or, without faith, embraced Catholicism as an instrument for furthering a political philosophy. Maurras, says Eliot, is "an unbeliever who cannot believe, and who is too honest to pretend to himself or to others that he does believe,"[15] but he has had a beneficial religious effect. Eliot belittles Ward's suggestion that "the influence of Maurras, indeed the intention of Maurras, is to pervert his disciples and students away from Christianity. I have been a reader of the work of Maurras for eighteen years; upon me he has had exactly the opposite effect." A religious faith can draw sustenance from those who possess no faith. Sincerity in faith is therefore something of an irrelevancy; instrumentality is far more important. Eliot lends weighty support to this distinction when he explains why Maurras has no readership in England:

The majority of those who are in a position to advertise contemporary French literature are Liberals, horrified by such a word as Reaction, and by no means friendly to Catholicism; or Conservatives, indifferent to

---

[15] This quotation and the next two are from "The *Action Française*, M. Maurras, and Mr. Ward," *Criterion*, 7 (Mar. 1928): 197, 202, 196–97.

foreign thought and equally unfriendly to Catholicism; or Socialists, who can have no use for M. Maurras at all. The fact that he is also an important literary critic, and has written as fine prose as any French author living, makes no difference to his reputation. But if anything, in another generation or so, is to preserve us from a sentimental Anglo-Fascism, it will be some system of ideas which will have gained much from the study of Maurras.

The prospect of any kind of fascism, sentimental or unsentimental, is soon abjured in another of his infrequent contributions to *Criterion*. There he announces that although England is witnessing "the destruction of Democracy" through mass voting, he cannot embrace any local form of fascism. All such things are simply beneath his interest:

I am all the more suspicious of fascism as a panacea because I fail so far to find in it any important element, beyond this comfortable feeling that we shall be benevolently ordered about, which was already in existence. *Most of the concepts which might have attracted me in fascism I seem already to have found, in a more digestible form, in the work of Charles Maurras.* I say a more digestible form, because I think they have a closer applicability to England than those of fascism.[16] [Italics mine.]

Once again the cross-responsibilities of Eliot's position—antidemocratic and yet declared Englishman—make themselves felt. He goes on in the same article to explain what he means by "digestible":

The *Action Française* insists upon the importance of continuity by the Kingship and hereditary class, upon something which has some analogy to what the government of England was, formerly, at least supposed to be; it would protect the humble citizen against the ambitious politician. Now the idea of the Kingship does not seem to have played any great part in fascism: it looks rather as if it had been accepted as a convenience. In theory, the *Action Française* does not contemplate a powerful dictator and a nominal king—but the powerful king and the able minister. The other difference is that the aim of fascism appears to be centralization. The theory of the *Action Française* carries decentralization to the farthest possible point.

[16] Eliot's ideas on fascism cited here and in the following three paragraphs come from "The Literature of Fascism," *Criterion*, 8 (Dec. 1928): 288-90, 284.

What this sinuous reasoning seems to encourage, other than a careful study of the writings of Maurras, is the creation of a political state that could be characterized as "decentralized royalism, the humble citizen deriving his comforts from the privileged and hereditary class," the England, one might say, of George III. And it is not simply the peevish political realist who would be sure to draw attention to the crucial omission here: power. What would enforce the social reversions Eliot has in mind if the populace were unwilling?

Such anxieties can, perhaps, be soothed by looking at another aspect of this *Criterion* article. Eliot there explains that the reason why people have of late (1928) turned to easy political solutions and to isms like communism and fascism is that "the deterioration of democracy has placed upon men burdens greater than they could bear, and surreptitiously relieved them of those they could bear." The result, as he says, is spiritual anemia, the recurring human desire to escape the burden of life and thought.[17] Man cannot keep his attention steadily on practical problems, but is uselessly and continually wandering into worlds of theory with only his powers of improvisation to guide him. "Our newspapers," he says, "pretend that we are competent to make up our minds about foreign policy, though we may not know who is responsible for cleaning the streets of our own borough." In pointing thus to the question of competence, Eliot offers, I think, a key to his puzzling line of reasoning with respect to the Action Française. He himself, we know, must certainly have felt some of the burdens involved in the "deterioration of democracy." He spoke of those burdens, after all, for most of his life. In response to them, he exercised his competence in areas where one can sense at times that the powers granted by desperation are alone guiding him. How otherwise to understand his reactionary form of "decentralized royalism" but as a kind of fiction, the purpose of which is both to escape and

[17] One is reminded here of E. M. Forster's incisive comment that the appeal of a fascist leader like Oswald Mosley could be explained by his answering to "the boredom which devastates people who are not quite sure that they are gentlemen." See Wilfred Stone, *The Cave and the Mountain* (Stanford University Press, 1966), p. 363.

to belittle the heavy constraints of reality? How indeed to understand the means by which he reconciled his mind to politics but as the intrusion of the anachronistic?

That he was implicitly aware of the complex problems into which he had entered by envisioning such societies as he did is made clear by what he said, at virtually the same time, about writers like H. L. Mencken. He pointed out that it is easier to destroy than to construct and that it is easier for readers to understand the destructive than the constructive side of an author's thought. This is obvious, but it possesses a real immediacy if one thinks of Eliot's own murkiness in developing, at this time, a constructive and coherent alternative to what he had long felt were liberal errors, or, as he was later to call them, "heresies." Crippled in some way in piecing together the elements that would constitute such an alternative, he gestured toward a vague "orthodoxy."

The lack of constructive ideas in his writings is a problem that makes itself felt elsewhere. And at times it leads to a problem not merely of credibility, but of intelligibility. When he says, for instance, that he is "interested in political ideas, but not in politics," or declares that he intends to discover "whether Fascism is the emergence of a new political idea or the recrudescence of an old one," or says that "what matters is the spread of the fascist idea," one at first feels that an attempt is being made to grapple with ideas, be they good or bad, that promise deliverance from the tedium and the defects of liberal ideology. Presenting himself, that is, as a student of ideas, Eliot dismisses both communism and fascism because they "seem to me to have died as political ideas, in becoming political facts." Fascism, indeed, even before it is brought into effect by revolution or by other means, presents certain irregularities as a subject of pure intellection. Italian fascism, at least, has had a history irregular enough, he says, to make uncertain its relationship to ideas: "The singularity of the Italian revolution seems to be this, that it began with no 'ideas' at all, or rather as an offshoot of advanced socialism, and proved itself capable of transforming itself as occasion required, and of assimilating ideas as required."

The problem, then, in coming to terms with fascism, is one of deciding which part of it is the haphazard compound of elements arising from local circumstance and which the defining form. Or what, in Eliot's phrase, is the politics and what the political idea. He hints that the sensible answer is to distinguish the Italian revolution from fascism, allowing the former to be politics, the latter to be the political idea. Let this be so; one is still left with the implication (an implication Eliot chose not to pursue) that fascism has an existence in some ideal form anterior to its practical form.

Fascism, however, was not everywhere so understood, and it is instructive to contrast Eliot's attitude with that of Giovanni Gentile, Mussolini's Minister of Education and one of the chief philosophers and spokesmen of the Italian movement. "Fascism," he declared in 1928, "is not a philosophy. Much less is it a religion. It is not even a political theory which may be stated in a series of formulae. . . . The real 'views' of the *Duce* are those which he formulates and executes at one and the same time."[18] It is difficult to see here, or to see in Mussolini's own summary statement on the growth of his forces ("Doctrine . . . might be missing; but there was something more decisive to supplant it—Faith"[19]), any sense of an "idea" of fascism distinguishable from the practice, or any indication that the "idea" and the practice are not one and the same. To invert Eliot's remark about fascism, then, it might be said that fascism seemed not to have died, but to have come alive as a political idea in becoming a political fact.

Eliot seems, moreover, on the verge of recognizing the emphatically pragmatic nature of fascism when he declares that "it is conceivable that in particular circumstances fascism might make for peace, and communism for war."[20] "I end by reflecting that the developments of fascism in Italy may produce very interesting results in ten or twenty years."[21] So, of course, they did, but by continuing to change in ways so disturbing and violent that no one

[18] "The Philosophic Basis of Fascism," in Carl Cohen, ed., *Communism, Fascism, and Democracy* (New York: Random House, 1962), p. 365.

[19] As quoted in Cohen, p. 355.

[20] "Mr. Barnes and Mr. Rowse," *Criterion*, 8 (July 1929): 690.

[21] "The Literature of Fascism," p. 290.

who restricted his interest solely to its "ideas" could ever hope to find himself completely satisfied.

To infer, however, from Eliot's peculiar attitude toward the idea and the practice of fascism that he can be dismissed as a crypto-fascist is to ignore his lifelong scorn of any practice that found an easy way to function in a world so lost. Not only was he skeptical of, for instance, the Conservative Party (it had, he wrote in 1928, "a great opportunity, in the fact that within the memory of no living man under sixty, has it acknowledged any contact with intelligence"[22]); he simply presumed that nothing, not even something that suited him, and moreover worked in this time and place, could be good enough. Hence he could say, "The first requisite of any political movement which may hope to influence the future, should be *indifference to success* and loyalty to slowly formed conviction."[23] When Eliot says things like this, and like his remark about the First World War that "perhaps the most significant thing about the War is its *insignificance*,"[24] we are reminded not only of the distance he maintained from political events, but of the special handling even his most perfunctory political utterances demand.[25]

[22] "A Commentary," *Criterion*, 8 (July 1929): 579.

[23] *Ibid.*, 9 (Oct. 1929): 5. Italics Eliot's.

[24] *Ibid.*, 9 (Jan. 1930): 183.

[25] Denis Donoghue has pointed out ("Literary Fascism," *Commentary*, 44 [Aug. 1967]: 82) that in certain cases Eliot's words are "entirely in line with standard liberal opinion," and he has illustrated this by locating a remark, in the same issue of *Criterion* in which "The Literature of Fascism" appeared, hostile to the kind of Irish censorship against which Yeats was then fighting. Other illustrations of the same order can certainly be found; Eliot repeatedly expressed views on censorship that can be well received by liberals. But those views are undercut by other statements. Eliot, it seems, did not absolutely rule out all kinds of censorship. In "Thoughts After Lambeth," he says, "Some time ago, during the consulship of Lord Brentford, I suggested that if we were to have a Censorship at all, it ought to be at Lambeth Palace; but I suppose that the few persons who read my words thought that I was trying to be witty" (*Selected Essays*, p. 323n). What must be recognized is not simply the preponderant weight of *un*liberal opinions that place Eliot on the right, but the careful way in which even those statements "entirely in line with standard liberal opinion" must be read. Among other things, they are compromised, I believe, or lessened in impact, by his aversion to "the familiar."

He writes, for example, in the third of his major political contributions to *Criterion*, "Mr. Barnes and Mr. Rowse," that what
communism and fascism

> have in common is certainly *familiarity*. They have both been already
> partially absorbed by the popular mind, so that, in the intellectual sense,
> there is nothing "shocking" about them; and as they seem to be so easily
> absorbed by the popular mind, one suspects that they must have a good
> deal in common with what was in the popular mind already. They are
> both, in other words, perfectly *conventional* ideas.[26]

So, of course, are all standard liberal ideas and therefore even
Eliot's infrequent agreement with those ideas must be interpreted
as the agreement of one who is bored and is even yet seeking out,
with another part of his mind, the exotic. This sense of tedium, of
"spiritual anemia," also invades his relationship to fascism, and it
is therefore with a casual and untormented spirit that he can at
last announce, at the end of "Mr. Barnes and Mr. Rowse":

> I confess to a preference for fascism in practice, which I dare say most
> of my readers share; and I will not admit that this preference is itself
> wholly irrational. I believe that the fascist form of unreason is less re-
> mote from my own than is that of the communists, but that my form is
> a more reasonable form of unreason.[27]

Such an announcement, charged though it may be to our ears today, was not then a difficult one for the fatigued Eliot to make.
Nor is it so shocking to us if we note that every position mentioned
in the passage—including Eliot's own—is described as a form of
unreason.

Eliot's next opportunity for taking a political stance was an
essay on Charles Baudelaire. Like his essays on Arnold, Dante, the
Metaphysical poets, Lancelot Andrewes, F. H. Bradley, and Irving
Babbitt, this essay can be read as an exercise in self-scrutiny. Here,
if anywhere in Eliot's prose, is disguised autobiography.

The question of Christian belief is central to Eliot's consideration of Baudelaire. About Baudelaire's satanism and blasphemy, he

[26] *Criterion*, 8 (July 1929): 682-83.
[27] *Ibid.*, 690-91.

comments: "Genuine blasphemy, genuine in spirit and not purely verbal, is the product of partial belief, and is as impossible to the complete atheist as to the perfect Christian. It is a way of affirming belief."[28] The faith thus affirmed, moreover, need not be a perfect or wholly knowledgeable one; what is important is its function in some other, larger purpose. Eliot says as much when he remarks of Baudelaire that his task was not so much to practice Christianity, as, more importantly, "to assert its *necessity*." That necessity was born of a longing to feel, in an unmistakable way, his own existence and being. Faith, then, is not a connection with something external, but an internal stimulation of awareness.

Baudelaire's satanic involvements, we go on to learn from Eliot, were a means of promoting his own sense of exclusive transcendence; through faith he lifted himself above the beastly mass:

So far as we are human, what we do must be either evil or good; so far as we do evil or good, we are human; and it is better, in a paradoxical way, to do evil than to do nothing: at least, we exist. It is true to say that the glory of man is his capacity for salvation; it is also true to say that his glory is his capacity for damnation. The worst that can be said of most of our malefactors, from statesmen to thieves, is that they are not men enough to be damned. Baudelaire was man enough for damnation: whether he *is* damned is, of course, another question, and we are not prevented from praying for his repose. In all his humiliating traffic with other beings, he walked secure in this high vocation, that he was capable of a damnation denied to the politicians and newspaper editors of Paris.

This, then, is one side of faith. It separates one from the bourgeois many; it makes one man enough to scorn the "humiliating traffic." Eliot's stress on the psychological usefulness of religion must be seen as a response to his continuing disgust with the popular, the familiar, the myriad forces each with its own ugly design upon "the aristocracy of culture." There is much to be protected, and faith, for both Baudelaire and Eliot, is seen as a kind of high tariff.

The connection between the necessity of faith and the circum-

[28] The quotations in this and the following paragraphs are from "Baudelaire," *Selected Essays*, pp. 373, 380, 378, and 378-79, respectively. This first quotation is reminiscent of Sir Thomas Browne's religiosity; he had to retain his belief in devils and witches in order to keep a firm hold on his faith.

jacent social wasteland is made even more explicit by Eliot, when, after dismantling the stage-properties of Baudelaire's satanism ("Baudelaire is concerned, not with demons, black masses, and romantic blasphemy, but with the real problem of good and evil"), he makes it clear that a belief in sin provides one of the best escapes from liberalism. Thus religion and politics are fused:

In the middle nineteenth century . . . , an age of bustle, programmes, platforms, scientific progress, humanitarianism and revolutions which improved nothing, an age of progressive degradation, Baudelaire perceived that what really matters is Sin and Redemption. . . . the recognition of the reality of Sin is a New life; and the possibility of damnation is so immense a relief in a world of electoral reform, plebiscites, sex reform and dress reform, that damnation itself is an immediate form of salvation—of salvation from the ennui of modern life, because it at last gives some significance to living.

Only three years later Eliot put forward, in *After Strange Gods*, the idea that literature itself suffers "with the disappearance of the idea of Original Sin."

Eliot's religious declarations demand to be seen in the light of his political and social preoccupations. Private meditation is joined with social despair. They issue from the same source and must be weighed in the same balance. It is extremely difficult, after reading the essay on Baudelaire, not to feel an intimate connection between two statements made by Eliot in 1930 that might otherwise be felt to be disparate: "You must either take the whole of revealed religion or none of it"[29] and

The Roman empire left behind it at least a few ruined temples, aqueducts, and walls; one is sometimes inclined to wonder whether the British will leave, for the future archaeologist, anything better than the traces of innumerable golf courses, and a number of corroded fowling-pieces, scattered like primitive arrowheads, over the desolate wastes of Scottish moors.[30]

With faith, Eliot can perhaps be heard to say, the time shall be redeemed. As Baudelaire endowed himself with a full sense of sin

---

[29] [A review of] *God: Being an Introduction to the Science of Metabiology*, by J. Middleton Murry, *Criterion*, 9 (Jan. 1930): 336.

[30] "A Commentary," *Criterion*, 10 (Oct. 1930): 4.

and thereby elevated himself from contemporary dissolution, so Eliot in the late 1920's and early 1930's saw in the Church the only salvation for individuals caught in a society bent on mass self-destruction. Once again Eliot's affinity with Hulme is evident, and it is appropriate that the Baudelaire essay closes with an apostrophe to him. Baudelaire would have approved, Eliot says, Hulme's sense of Original Sin and Hulme's declaration that "institutions are necessary."

In calling Baudelaire a "fragmentary Dante," and in suggesting that his strength lay in his capacity to suffer immense pain, Eliot allows us to see the close kinship he must have felt for the earlier poet. He thought of him as the first "counter-romantic" in poetry, as a forerunner in the struggle he and his ally Pound were waging against romanticism, Protestantism, and liberalism in their many forms. Moreover, he saw how Baudelaire could somehow figure darkly as a comrade to his own figures of great passive suffering and tortured knowledge, Prufrock and Tiresias. Like them, he could reveal much of the world in all its sin, guilt, death, and evil through his ability to attract pain to himself.

Baudelaire's imagination was impaired, as was Eliot's, in attempting to recreate the Dantesque worlds of spiritual anguish and spirited ecstasy. Neither poet could provide in his verse a wholly stable structure of belief, a system of perfectly lucid discriminations in the realm of good and evil. Eliot had praised Dante above Shakespeare, saying the earlier poet understood "deeper degrees of degradation and higher degrees of exaltation." But it is just this amplitude and *mesure* that Baudelaire and Eliot are powerless to give. They attach themselves instead to the decadence, the hell, all around them. With disgust refined into something almost Platonic, they compulsively describe in detail a world they would do anything to forget. Their knowledge of their surroundings is oppressive. As Georg Lukács says in another context:

The striving of the great realists to remain true to the realities of life has for its inevitable result that when they portray life under capitalism and particularly life in the great cities, they must turn into poetry all the dark uncanniness, all the horrible inhumanity of it. But this poetry is real poetry: it comes poetically to life precisely because of its unrelieved horror. This discovery and revelation of poetic beauty in the dreadful ugliness of capitalist life is worlds apart from those photographic copies of the surface which use the hopelessness and desolation of the subject as a medium of presentation.[31]

Such a statement can also tell us much about Eliot and about Pound, particularly the Pound of Cantos 14 and 15; it can also reveal much about Baudelaire, indeed much about Conrad, Louis-Ferdinand Céline, Curzio Malaparte, and certain other contemporary writers, British, American, and European, whose compulsion is to describe a world they themselves cannot endure. In a sense, all such writers are fragmentary Dantes. All proceed to explore the greater horror underlying the horror of the surface, and none seems capable of figuring forth the world of illumination, rationality, and Dantesque splendor of which their own Infernos are the antitheses.

[31] *Studies in European Realism* (New York: Grosset and Dunlap, 1964), p. 158.

CHAPTER TEN

Renunciations and Prescriptions

Ash-Wednesday (1930) is a partial attempt to give substance to
Eliot's positive aspirations. But it arrives by the *via negativa* of
purgation ("Lord, I am not worthy / Lord, I am not worthy") and
enlightened despair ("Because I cannot hope to turn again / Consequently I rejoice, having to construct something / Upon which
to rejoice") at the position that withdrawal is the only proper response to the sordid crush of the world. One must detach oneself
wholly from such a world:

> As I am forgotten
> And would be forgotten, so I would forget
> Thus devoted, concentrated in purpose.

But this kind of devotion can bring only a mixed blessing; the
spirit is not truly liberated if it has no choice but detachment. *Ash-
Wednesday* is a disturbing poem because it seems an attempt to
convey the expectant spirit of a mind hoping for grace, but instead
it counsels that already troubled mind "to care and not to care /
Teach us to sit still." Eliot had explained Baudelaire's personal
malady as a form of *accidie*, "arising from the unsuccessful struggle towards the spiritual life." The words are also well-suited to
Eliot. His struggle toward the spiritual life in *Ash-Wednesday*
seems frustrated by the mesmerizing effect the world of oppression
has on him. He wishes to disentangle himself from that world, to
move onward to refined illuminations. But the world draws him
back—"Why should the agèd eagle stretch its wings?" Suspended
between heaven and hell, he turns his attentions to the possibilities

of shoring up certain social institutions that form part of the hell.

That "necessary" institution, the Anglican Church, is the subject of "Thoughts After Lambeth" (March 1931), a specialized investigation into the contemporary practices of the Church, and a criticism of some parts of the Report of the Lambeth Conference. (Eliot, as we might expect, proved somewhat more conservative than the Report, particularly on the issues of youth, science, and ecumenicism.) What is of interest is the way in which Eliot confirmed the attitudes toward religion revealed in the Baudelaire essay, and adopted attitudes toward the Church from which political inferences are easily drawn.

At one point he refers to his famous royalist, classic, and Anglo-Catholic declaration:

When . . . I brought out a small book of essays, several years ago, called *For Lancelot Andrewes*, the anonymous reviewer in the *Times Literary Supplement* made it the occasion for what I can only describe as a flattering obituary notice. In words of great seriousness and manifest sincerity, he pointed out that I had suddenly arrested my progress—whither he had supposed me to be moving I do not know—and that to his distress I was unmistakably making off in the wrong direction. Somehow I had failed, and had admitted my failure; if not a lost leader, at least a lost sheep; what is more, I was a kind of traitor; and those who were to find their way to the promised land beyond the waste, might drop a tear at my absence from the roll-call of the new saints. I suppose that the curiosity of this point of view will be apparent to only a few people. But its appearance in what is not only the best but the most respected and most respectable of our literary periodicals, came home to me as a hopeful sign of the times. For it meant that the orthodox faith of England is at last relieved from its burden of respectability. A new respectability has arisen to assume the burden; and those who would once have been considered intellectual vagrants are now pious pilgrims, cheerfully plodding the road from nowhere to nowhere, trolling their hymns, satisfied so long as they may be "on the march."

These changed conditions are so prevalent that any one who has been moving among intellectual circles and comes to the Church, may experience an odd and rather exhilarating feeling of isolation.[1]

1 "Thoughts After Lambeth," *Selected Essays* (New York: Harcourt, Brace, 1950), p. 325.

This exhilarating privateness, come to the Church as it stands almost vacant, is joined with a tired Olympian disdain: "the World is trying the experiment of attempting to form a civilized but non-Christian mentality. The experiment will fail."[2] For Eliot, then, the Church signified not union, but separation. The rhetorical climax of the cited paragraphs is the pleasure of escape. Paradoxically enough, even orthodoxy itself can be isolated. And it must be remembered that Eliot is here discussing not simply his confirmation in the Church of England, but the declarations of royalism and classicism made at the same time. These things together exhilarate Eliot. He goes on to say, in apocalyptic tones Babbitt would have liked, that we live "in a world which will obviously divide itself more and more sharply into Christians and non-Christians. The Universal Church is today, it seems to me, more definitely set against the World than at any time since pagan Rome."[3] Between the isolated Church, then, and the pagan world without, no contact exists or should exist. This absolutism, severe and ascetic, brings us to see Eliot's political attitude in yet another one of its infinite complexities. Civilization and all of its politics, be they of the right or the left, are doomed to extinction without Christianity and the Church. A man so believing could scarcely have placed any great trust in such wholly secular solutions as parties and ideologies. However strong his devotion to politics (and the greater part of his work in *Criterion* and three later books are testimony to that devotion), it must inevitably be diverted and bled.

It should also be kept in mind that there were other reasons for less than a full measure of political interest from Eliot. One of these reasons is exemplified by his response to the British fascist leader Oswald Mosley, a man who began his political career in England with the hope and encouragement of many of his countrymen, but disappointed them by his sordid and authoritarian ways. That response was, as I have said, minimal, and on one of the few oc-

[2] *Ibid.*, p. 342.
[3] *Ibid.*

casions in which Mosley figures in his writings, Eliot's stance is skeptical and coldly polite. Writing in April 1931, just before Mosley assumed central control of the various British fascist sects, Eliot said:

> The Mosley programme . . . though in some respects vague or feeble, contains at least some germs of intelligence; and a pronouncement by men who have had the courage to disassociate themselves from any party must be read with respect. It recognises that the nineteenth century is over, and that a thorough reorganisation of industry and of agriculture is essential. The fundamental objection to it, of course, is that it is not fundamental enough. The changes are propounded in the same old cautious and sensible, and at the same time catchy, phrasing, as any other political manifesto.[4]

What Eliot likes, then, in Mosley's movement (called, in 1932, the British Union of Fascists) is what he believed was its nonpartisanship and its "modern" awareness. What he dislikes is that it is not radical enough; it is, to use his favorite term of abuse, too "familiar." But Mosley and his men, let us remember, presented England in the mid-thirties with the most alarming fascist threat the country had yet experienced. They were, as Eliot suggests, the only group on the British right sufficiently alienated from traditional procedures and traditional obligations to be able to imagine England in a new political configuration. That they did not succeed, that their history was mostly comic opera rendered thoroughly unappetizing by random excursions into violence, is an index of a deeper stability in the nation that they were powerless to threaten.[5]

If we would imagine Eliot considering, even momentarily, an affiliation with Mosley, we must account for the fact that the very institutions blocking Mosley's path were those "necessary" in-

---

[4] "A Commentary," *Criterion*, 10 (Apr. 1931): 483.

[5] As Hans Rogger puts it, England was immune to Mosley "because established institutions (parliament, the party system, the class structure) had proved themselves resilient in absorbing the shocks of modernity and change, and had a longer time in which to do so than was granted any other country." "Afterthoughts," in Hans Rogger and Eugen Weber, eds., *The European Right: A Historical Profile* (Berkeley: University of California Press, 1966), p. 577.

stitutions that Eliot, out of deference to tradition, could never repudiate. And, perhaps most tellingly, the world Mosley shadowed forth was so repugnant that, with rare exceptions,[6] no English person of any intellectual stature could muster the bad taste to remain its friend for long.

Where indeed to go, Eliot might in those years of the 1930's have wondered, with his judgment of the world, with his politics, amidst such politicians? His situation reminds us not only of his statement about Baudelaire's "humiliating traffic with other beings," but also of that disturbing question that Eliot's very presence in Europe at that time raised in the American mind. Why, that is, was he an expatriate? Eliot's answer to the question is complex, and its irony reveals that he knew he would feel alien almost anywhere:

> The American intellectual of to-day has almost no chance of continuous development upon his own soil and in the environment which his ancestors, however humble, helped to form. He must be an expatriate: either to languish in a provincial university, or abroad, or, the most complete expatriation of all, in New York. And he is merely a more manifest example of what *tends* to happen in all countries.[7]

America was a barbarous land, but all lands were barbarous. Mosley's party was unthinkable, but all parties, involved as they are in the goverance of barbarous lands, were equally unthinkable. John Harrison has suggested that Eliot refused to associate himself with political parties "simply because he adhered to the principle of non-action."[8] It would be more precise to say that, antipathetic as he was to the demeanor of every current political party, he had little choice but to succumb to the principle of nonaction. Eliot's political interests lay neither in disposing human energy toward the solution of social problems (he believed that men sometimes prove very interesting as they challenge, or are crippled by, such problems) nor in liberating human energy from social

---

[6] Colin Cross lists only Arthur Kenneth Chesterton (second cousin to G. K.), W. E. D. Allen, Alexander Thomson, and Unity Mitford (*The Fascists in Britain* [London: St. Martin's Press, 1963]).

[7] "A Commentary," *Criterion*, 10 (Apr. 1931): 484-85.

[8] *The Reactionaries* (London: Gollancz, 1966), p. 148.

confines, but in showing how men failed to achieve a society in
which certain religious values could be appreciated.

It is in this context, perhaps, that Eliot's view of communism
can most profitably be discussed. He saw communism, not as
many people have seen it, as an ideology representing the objective reality of many people and their concrete needs, but as something pertaining solely to the subjective, personal quirks of under-
developed individuals: "Communism—I mean the ideas of communism, not the reality, which would be of no use in this way—
has come as a godsend (so to speak) to those young people who
would like to grow up and believe in something."[9]

This is to make communism relevant not to any corporate social
fact, but to personal psychology, and to deprive it of any power
it might have beyond the isolated individual. It is thereby rendered
no less adventitious than any other pagan belief of the day: "stupidity, for the majority of people, is no doubt the best solution
of the difficulty of thinking; it is far better to be stupid in a faith,
even in a stupid faith, than to be stupid and believe nothing. . . .
I would even say that, as it is the faith of the day, there are only
a small number of people living who have achieved the right *not*
to be communists." Eliot's Anglo-Catholicism, however, would
not let him conclude without emphasizing that communism was
a false faith. "My only objection to it is the same as my objection
to the cult of the Golden Calf."[10]

Eliot's belief that consciousness is more important than material
power leaves him dissatisfied with capitalism as well; in another
Commentary he relates them both to the Golden Calf cult. In this
same piece, Eliot describes desperate and unsatisfied people as
surrounded by a number of "faiths" arbitrarily established to fight
against ennui. Chief among these faiths are communism and capitalism. They both excite people, he says, just as much by giving
them "licence in ways which they had been brought up not to
expect, or else by telling them that the way in which they instinc-
tively behave is the right way, as by restraining them in ways in

[9] "A Commentary," *Criterion*, 12 (Apr. 1933): 472.
[10] *Ibid.*, pp. 472-73.

which they were not accustomed to be restrained. People like licence, and they like restraint. They like surprise. The one thing they do not like is boredom."[11]

No land can be Eliot's home, no party is worth his allegiance, all the modern ideologies are poor substitutes for faith—even political power itself is useless. Or so Eliot seems to be saying in his two-part poem *Coriolan* (1931). "Triumphal March," the first section, describes the tedious world of those who wait for the leadership that must inevitably come. The press of the crowd and the spectacle of military might benumb all emotions except the simple one of childish expectation. The awesome leader finally arrives (ll. 27-31):

> Look
> There he is now, look:
> There is no interrogation in his eyes
> Or in the hands, quiet over the horse's neck,
> And the eyes watchful, waiting, perceiving,
> indifferent.[12]

The initial feeling of satisfaction, however, vanishes in an instant. The poem ends with a retreat into serenity followed by anticlimactic banality (ll. 32-47):

> O hidden under the dove's wing, hidden in the
> turtle's breast,
> Under the palmtree at noon, under the running
> water
> At the still point of the turning world. O hidden.
> . . .
> (And Easter Day, we didn't get to the country,
> So we took young Cyril to church. And they rang
> a bell
> And he said right out loud, *crumpets.*)
> Don't throw away that sausage,
> It'll come in handy.

[11] "A Commentary," *Criterion*, 12 (July 1933): 644.

[12] F. R. Leavis calls this the "supreme public moment, climax of the day"; what is presented to our eyes is "the Hero, the Führer." "T. S. Eliot's Later Poetry," reprinted in Hugh Kenner, ed., *T. S. Eliot, A Collection of Critical Essays* (Englewood Cliffs, N.J.: Prentice-Hall, 1962), p. 115.

Immense power, even that of a dictator, is futile and absurd. Either
the transcendent or the embarrassingly human will nullify it. The
populace is to be ridiculed for its oafishness, and the leader is to
be ridiculed for his spectacular incompetence.

The second section, "Difficulties of a Statesman" (also 1931),
sees political power from the vantage point of those who wield it.
Amidst a profusion of committees and commissions, decisions and
appointments, the statesman still feels and speaks as a lonely man
(ll. 24-28):

> Meanwhile the guards shake dice on the marches
> And the frogs (O Mantuan) croak in the marshes.
> Fireflies flare against the faint sheet lightning
> What shall I cry?
> Mother mother

The plaintive whimperings of this hollow man culminate in despair. Having seen "the conventional importances" to be wholly
unimportant, and having recognized "political man" to be a hopelessly routinized creature, he turns away from the world (l. 55):

> RESIGN   RESIGN   RESIGN

Real power, where needed in the human situation, is not at all
forthcoming.

If society, then, as Eliot would have it, is to be built not upon
power and its corruptions, but upon a higher system of values, he,
like the exhausted statesman, must either depart completely from
contemporary political issues or enter upon a form of social planning that will embrace such values. That Eliot faced this decision,
and that he provisionally chose the latter alternative, is suggested
by his first book dealing directly and primarily with the question
of societal values and their effect on literary achievement. We may
note in moving on to that book that his exhaustion resembles that
of many politicians currently charged with the task of imagining
a future for England and America. So does his belief that if the
minds of men are changed, all else, including the nasty question of
power and material force, will be taken care of.

After Strange Gods (1933)[13] must be seen as a clear repudiation of Eliot's youthful dictum that literary analysis should not be "the expression of an attitude 'toward life' or of an attitude toward religion or of an attitude toward society." In 1924, he had warned of an obliteration of distinctions and said that it was most dangerous "to confuse literature with religion." A decade later, speaking at the University of Virginia in the worst year of the Great Depression, he almost effortlessly abandoned this dictum and even denied that he, as a poet, could give literary judgments: "I am uncertain of my ability to criticise my contemporaries as artists; I ascended the platform of these lectures only in the role of moralist" (ASG 10). Eliot announced that he did "not wish to preach only to the converted, but primarily to those who, never having applied moral principles to literature quite explicitly . . . are possibly convertible" (ASG 11). He then abruptly shifted his ground and presented his case not only in the role of moralist, but as a castigator of his age so aggrieved at its errors that he could see no help at all in dialogue (ASG 12): "in a society like ours, wormeaten with Liberalism, the only thing possible for a person with strong convictions is to state a point of view and leave it at that."

The tone of *After Strange Gods* is a shift, then, from the cautious to the positive, from the tentative to the declarative. The caustic quality of "wormeaten with Liberalism" embeds it in one's memory.

This shift can be sensed when Eliot talks about the authors of *I'll Take My Stand* and about the Neo-Agrarian movement in the American South, a movement including Allen Tate, Donald Davidson, John Crowe Ransom, and Robert Penn Warren (ASG 18):

It will be said that the whole current of economic determinism is against them, and economic determinism is today a god before whom we fall down and worship with all kinds of music. I believe that these matters may ultimately be determined by what people want; that when anything

---

[13] This book was issued in one edition only, with printings in both London and New York (*After Strange Gods, A Primer of Modern Heresy* [New York: Harcourt, Brace, 1934]); hereafter cited as ASG.

is generally accepted as desirable, economic laws can be upset in order
to achieve it; that it does not so much matter at present whether any
measures put forward are practical, as whether the aim is a good aim,
and the alternatives intolerable.

Here the tone is urgent, the choices few, the enemy (economic laws
and liberal thought, one presumes) clearly in sight. No notion of
economic determinism will be allowed to justify the intolerable.
That kind of determinism must be overcome and a society founded
on "tradition" must be established. Eliot explains tradition by
saying that it involves all those habitual actions that represent the
blood kinship of "the same people living in the same place." Tradition he then associates with the central doctrine of orthodoxy,
but not until a few now notorious remarks are made concerning
"blood kinship" (ASG 20):

Stability is obviously necessary. You are hardly likely to develop tradition except where the bulk of the population is relatively so well off
where it is that it has no incentive or pressure to move about. The population should be homogeneous; where two or more cultures exist in the
same place they are likely either to be fiercely self-conscious or both to
become adulterate. What is still more important is unity of religious
background; and reasons of race and religion combine to make any large
number of free-thinking Jews undesirable. There must be a proper balance between urban and rural, industrial and agricultural development.
And a spirit of excessive tolerance is to be deprecated.

Let us remember the date of this extraordinary statement: 1933.
The great years of American immigration were over. The exclu-
sionary Immigration Act of 1924, drafted by Senators Albert Johnson and David A. Reed, had had its effect. But from 1820 to 1930,
no less than thirty-eight million people had immigrated. Two and
one-half million Jews had entered the country between 1880 and
1913 alone. In 1933, one hundred and twenty million people,
fourteen million of them foreign-born, were living in the United
States. It is in this context that Eliot's praise of a homogeneous
citizenry must be seen.

This praise provides a good introduction to the society Eliot
hoped orthodoxy would bring about. Bound by tradition, organic
and self-referential, it would be in large part directly opposed to

the humanitarian-liberal tradition of tolerance, free thought, and belief in diversity. The impact of *After Strange Gods* is generated, in fact, not by its very few constructive suggestions, but by its terse censure of certain adversaries (foreign races, self-consciousness, Jews, and excessive tolerance). Without these adversaries, and without its flavor of imprecation, Eliot's argument would have been inert and listless, a vague plea for social homogeneity. *After Strange Gods* is a political work because of the prejudices it expresses, not for the political vision it establishes.

Its central term, "orthodoxy," is rather elusive, although Christian orthodoxy is clearly meant. Eliot distinguishes orthodoxy from "tradition" by saying that whereas tradition is "a way of feeling and acting which characterizes a group throughout generations" and must largely be unconscious, orthodoxy, or at least the maintenance of orthodoxy is a matter that calls for "the exercise of all our conscious intelligence" (ASG 31). This distinction is subtly refined when Eliot says that whereas "tradition, being a matter of good habits, is necessarily real only in a social group, orthodoxy exists whether realised in anyone's thought or not." In fact, "a whole generation might conceivably pass without any orthodox thought; or, as by Athanasius, orthodoxy may be upheld by one man against the world" (ASG 31-32). Eliot's position is, of course, a traditionally Christian one: the faith lives on, but not as the amalgam and accretion of man's efforts through history to define it. To save his soul, man can exercise his conscious mental powers to arrive at orthodoxy, but such a process neither strengthens nor weakens orthodoxy; it survives, unaffected.

The relevance of this sort of thinking to Eliot's politics becomes clear when we recognize that it is a theological reinforcement of his attempt, even though interested in politics, to find a place secure beyond faction and partisanship. All varieties of politics in the world are familiar variations of an old theme, *mutatis mutandis*, and however deeply they may affect human beings, they are simply too transient for much serious consideration. Orthodoxy, however, is in eternal repose above political solutions.

The complications of this argument become apparent, however, when Eliot tries to translate orthodoxy into a literary criterion in a brief discussion of three short stories, "Bliss" by Katherine Mansfield, "The Shadow in the Rose Garden" by D. H. Lawrence, and "The Dead" by James Joyce; the hell pictured in his friend Pound's *Draft of XXX Cantos*; the religious growth of William Butler Yeats; and the poetry of Gerard Manley Hopkins. Miss Mansfield's story simply neglects "the moral issue of good and evil"; Lawrence's story is flawed by "the absence of any moral or social sense"; Pound's hell possesses neither dignity nor tragedy and, ignoring "essential Evil," implies a heaven "equally trivial and accidental." Yeats shows what happens when "a highly sophisticated lower mythology" is put in the place of "a world of real Good and Evil, of holiness or sin"; Hopkins, surprisingly enough, is no better—he is too "verbal," and offers only "technical tricks" (ASG 38, 39, 47, 50, 52-53). Joyce alone created works "penetrated with Christian feeling"; he is, Eliot says, "the most ethically orthodox of the more eminent writers of my time" (ASG 41).

The common flaw of all these works, Joyce's excepted, is their manifestation of the radical weakening of Christian values that can be charted in history and felt everywhere in modern life. "The chief clue to the understanding of most contemporary Anglo-Saxon literature," Eliot declares, "is to be found in the decay of Protestantism" (ASG 41). Thus literary criticism comes, in his hands, to resemble the search for heretics. But there is more to it than this. The rejection of Christianity has meant that the notion of original sin has fallen into general neglect, robbing literature of profundity. And that has, in turn, led to even more extreme dangers (ASG 45-46):

with the disappearance of the idea of Original Sin, with the disappearance of the idea of intense moral struggle, the human beings presented to us both in poetry and in prose fiction today, and more patently among the serious writers than in the underworld of letters, tend to become less and less real. . . . If you do away with this struggle, and maintain that by tolerance, benevolence, inoffensiveness and a redistribution or increase of purchasing power, combined with a devotion, on the part of an élite, to Art, the world will be as good as anyone could require, then you must expect human beings to become more and more vaporous.

With original sin gone, liberalism begins its treacherous encroachment. When liberalism holds sway, writing will collapse.

This neat formulation is not unique to Eliot; Frank Kermode argues that Pound, Yeats, and Hulme also understood history as a sequence in which a secular or religious equivalent of the Fall dictates rightness or wrongness for the time thereafter.[14] What is striking about Eliot's explanation is the speed and dexterity with which he moves from an elucidation of orthodoxy to a denunciation of liberalism. For this last is precisely the direction of his argument—toward a position from which to attack liberalism once again. Then all of the positive terms, "tradition," "orthodoxy," "wisdom," "race," are fused into a single instrument with which to purge Hopkins, an incidental figure, and reopen greater battle (ASG 53):

from the struggle of our time to concentrate, not to dissipate; to renew our association with traditional wisdom; to re-establish a vital connexion between the individual and the race; the struggle, in a word, against Liberalism: from all this Hopkins is a little apart, and in this Hopkins has very little aid to offer us.

It is not enough, in the antiliberal struggle, merely to defend tradition. Those who adopt that strategy are "mere conservatives," defending the bad with the good, both "the permanent and the temporary, the essential and the accidental" (ASG 67-68). They manifest, in other words, simply one more unorthodox approach to the problem. The orthodox is, to be perfectly explicit, what is true. Everything else is erroneous, even doctrines that as Edmund Burke would say, let the weight of what has been speak for what should be.

This kind of argument would seem to suggest that Eliot's stance would logically become evangelical or proselytizing. Since he believes so strongly, and since the truth is so accessible to him, should he not try to make that truth available to one and all? At one moment he seems to consider the idea, but he quickly veers away (ASG 33-34):

[14] *Romantic Image* (New York: Vintage Books, 1964), p. 145.

That an acceptance of the validity of the two terms ["tradition" and "orthodoxy"] as I use them should lead one to dogmatic theology, I naturally believe; but I am not here concerned with pursuing investigation in that path. My enquiries take the opposite direction: let us consider the denial or neglect of tradition in my mundane sense, and see what *that* leads to.

And then follows the more or less private study of heresy, the investigation of deviants who, pursuing "strange gods," have abandoned tradition (tradition and orthodoxy seem very similar here, if not identical). Hence the concentration on the plague of liberalism.

But very little time indeed is spent in elucidating the orthodoxy by which all else is damned. Kathleen Nott has pointed out that Eliot rarely allows any inspection of his own positive beliefs: "Is it not remarkable that this considerable amateur of the Church Fathers has nothing to say about theology, except allusively in his verse, until he blossoms into full orthodoxy? . . . Can we not call this skirting of all philosophical discussion a method?"[15] Of course it is his method. Eliot is everywhere the adversary, or, to use Wyndham Lewis's term, "the enemy." He takes strategic positions, but feels no compulsion to explain them. Neither "tradition," "orthodoxy," nor "classicism" is fully delineated, but this wasted land (the West) is full of vivid examples—often personifications—of heresy, of romantic individualism, of liberalism. Sigmund Freud is nothing but a "parvenu scientist." Marx is no more than a "Jewish economist" who has "inverted" Hegel for his own purposes.[16] The effect of this method, more cavalier as it approaches thinking of great magnitude and influence, is to cast upon everything a political shade. As "classicism," we remember, was bent to politics and was ultimately to be understood as a synonym for "anti-democratic," so "orthodoxy" is gradually bent to politics and is to be understood as "anti-liberal." The end-re-

[15] Kathleen Nott, *The Emperor's Clothes* (London: William Heinemann, 1953), pp. 110-11.

[16] Eliot's remark about Freud comes from "Freud's Illusions," *Criterion*, 8 (Dec. 1928): 353; his remark about Marx from "A Commentary," *Criterion*, 14 (Apr. 1935): 433.

sult is that Eliot's one clear and precise act, amid innumerable vague ones, is the arraignment of his age on political grounds. The substantive implications of this fact, however, are almost nowhere to be found in his writings. Only rarely did he acknowledge that the kind of complete transformation he desired would entail other, more mundane changes. Once, in speaking of the memory of A. R. Orage, he was so candid. Orage, he said, "saw that any real change for the better meant a spiritual revolution; and he said that no spiritual revolution was of any use unless you had a practical economic scheme."[17] And elsewhere, speaking of certain theories of Social Credit, he said that "I hope that Major Douglas is right from top to bottom and copper-plated."[18] This is, however, as far as practicality would lead him. His reluctance to enter upon such discussions is perhaps to be explained by his belief that the spiritual and the worldly are always uneasy company. Thus what he put forward about Douglas and a "practical economic scheme" with one hand, he took back with the other. Obviously a practical economic scheme would be necessary lest the spiritual vision be a vagary; just as obviously, anything that would embody the spirit would corrupt it. Several months later, in the spring of 1935, he said: "The Christian view is, I think, essentially dualistic. The City of God is at best only realizable on earth under an imperfect likeness: ἐν οὐρανῷ ἴσως παράδειγμα ἀνάκειται."[19]

This dualism prevents us from considering Eliot a reactionary thinker in any of the customary modern senses. He was reactionary, but quick to acknowledge the irrelevancy of reaction; anti-Semitic, but quick to note the superficiality of such religious designations as Jew or gentile. But we can say that Eliot rather soon

[17] "A Commentary," *Criterion*, 14 (Jan. 1935): 262.
[18] "A Commentary," *Criterion*, 13 (Oct. 1933): 120.
[19] "A Commentary," *Criterion*, 14 (Apr. 1935): 435. The Greek means, "Perhaps it is laid up as a pattern in heaven. . . ." The source is Plato's *Republic*, the conclusion to Book 9, "Imperfect Societies." Plato's sentence goes on, "where those who wish can see it and found it in their own hearts." The next sentence—which sounds almost as if Eliot had written it himself—says, "But it doesn't matter whether it exists or ever will exist; it's the only state in whose politics [the intelligent man] can take part" (H. D. P. Lee translation).

repented of his tentative engagement with social planning. His condemnation of modern ideologies grows more pointed (*Criterion*, Jan., July 1936):

between the Christian and the communist there is a great gulf fixed . . . in this country we are in danger from amiable bridge builders.

The movement toward the Right so-called . . . is far more profound than any mere machinations of consciously designing interests could make it. It is a symptom of the desolation of secularism, of that loss of vitality, through the lack of replenishment from spiritual sources, which we have witnessed elsewhere, and which becomes ready for the application of the artificial stimulants of nationalism and class.

The "artificial stimulants," in all their variety, deceive men and bribe them away from the truth, the orthodox, the Church. They are then led to the error of our age, an error clothed in two forms —communism or the isms of the political right. Eliot's chief poem of the early and middle 1930's solemnly reflects his disappointment. In *The Rock* (1934, third section), the Chorus knells:

> O weariness of men who turn from GOD
> To the grandeur of your mind and the glory of
>   your action,
> To arts and inventions and daring enterprises,
> To schemes of human greatness thoroughly discredited,
> Binding the earth and the water to your service,
> Exploiting the seas and developing the mountains,
> Dividing the stars into common and preferred,
> Engaged in devising the perfect refrigerator,
> Engaged in working out a rational morality,
> Engaged in printing as many books as possible,
> Plotting of happiness and flinging empty bottles,
> Turning from your vacancy to fevered enthusiasm
> For nation or race or what you call humanity;
> Though you forget the way to the Temple,
> There is one who remembers the way to your door:
> Life you may evade, but Death you shall not.
> You shall not deny the Stranger.

The Stranger calls men back to what is eternal, and reminds them that "However you disguise it, this thing does not change: / The perpetual struggle of Good and Evil." We can assume that he also

brings Eliot himself away from worldly involvements and into a
solitude of faith reminiscent of the solitary joy that was his upon
being received into Anglicanism:

> There is no help in parties, none in interests,
> There is no help in those whose souls are choked and
>   swaddled
> In the old winding-sheets of place and power
> Or the new winding-sheets of mass-made thought.
> O world! forget your glories and your quarrels,
> Forget your groups and your misplaced ambitions,
> We speak to you as individual men,
> As individuals alone with GOD.

CHAPTER ELEVEN

The Theater

If the lines that end Chapter 10 sound Eliot's true voice, and if solitude, negation, and the reactionary defense of time long since past (and even, perhaps, time largely fictitious) sum up his real position, how are we to understand his career in the theater? Much has been written about this aspect of his achievement, and one hypothesis holds that his plays represent a desire to provide for his public a communal enterprise, an incorporation of playwright with audience in which mutual sentiments may be expressed and enjoyed. This hypothesis, I think, overlooks the extent to which Eliot limited his dramatic offerings to a coterie "public." His plays, the superficial appearance of *Murder in the Cathedral* notwithstanding, do not revive the spirit and the appeal of an *Everyman*. Still less do they cultivate, in the manner of a Shakespeare or even a Yeats, the latent aspirations, nationalistic and otherwise, of the people who might be watching them. They are a severely restricted drama. They advance notions to which few individuals in this century easily and naturally respond; they pronounce doctrines *ex cathedra* in ways most unlike Shakespeare, who expressed, without pontification, aspirations widely shared.

Much has been made of Eliot's proposal in the *Dial* of November 1920 (and in *The Sacred Wood* of the same time) that "our problem should be to take a form of entertainment, and subject it to the process which would leave it a form of art." This suggests that he wanted to do precisely what he thought Shakespeare had done: create a form of drama for a public that wanted to be crudely entertained, "but would stand a good deal of poetry."[1] In other words, one coats the pill, and looks first to the pre-existing tastes of the audience upon whom one has designs. The elitist direction of this line of reasoning is soon apparent. What Eliot does, and Shakespeare had no need of doing, is to proceed from a clearly entrenched minority position to oppose the interests of a mass society he found lacking in refinement (he calls that society formless). Thus the artist represents in this case an adversary culture and, knowing far better than the public what its true tastes are, manipulates that public to his own specific ends. He is, to return once more to Wyndham Lewis's term, "the enemy."

Thus Eliot's admiration for the theater as a means to illuminate class divisions, to demarcate the differences that exist, on more or less economic grounds, between people. In his *Criterion* obituary for the famous music-hall artist Marie Lloyd, for instance, Eliot talked of using the cultural tastes of the lower class to keep that class aware of itself, and of its incompatibility with the "protoplasmic" bourgeoisie:

> The middle classes, in England as elsewhere, *under democracy*, are morally dependent upon the aristocracy, and the aristocracy are subordinate to the middle class, which is gradually absorbing and destroying them. The lower class still exists; but perhaps it will not exist for long. In the music-hall comedians they find the expression and dignity of their own lives; and this is not found in the most elaborate and expensive revue.[2]

Class divisions must remain; they alone could impede the all-devouring progress of the bourgeoisie. And certain forms of art could reinforce those divisions. Not, of course, the cinema, a tool of the democracy that threatens all (Eliot thinks of film, as a matter of fact, as a cancer so threatening to established order that he feels civilization is sure to die of boredom in the movie house), but perhaps his plays, such as *Murder in the Cathedral*, written for the Canterbury Festival of June 1935.

---

[1] Eliot, "The Possibility of a Poetic Drama," *Dial*, 49 (Nov. 1920): 447.
[2] "Marie Lloyd," *Selected Essays*, p. 407. Italics mine.

Pertinent to this view of the play is the role of the Chorus, the Women of Canterbury. They represent the mass, the people who know and yet do not know, who live and yet only partly live. We have seen them before, filing over London Bridge, being killed in wars, aimlessly populating cities, or carelessly abusing the past. For Eliot, they are somehow a lower order of being, capable of faith but more likely to commit some insupportable vulgarity. They suffer much, yet true perception is usually inaccessible to them:

> For us, the poor, there is no action,
> But only to wait and to witness.

Looking to Becket to give their lives significance, they suffer when he does, finding their own release in his. When he finds his God, they find theirs. Thus a kind of hierarchy of faith, as of social class, is established. Just as there are levels of importance in the "unreal" world of mundane society, so are there levels of faith, of action, and of suffering. The Women do suffer, and they do take up the lessons of pure resignation, but they do so as agents secondary to Becket, and dependent upon him; he in turn is secondary only to the world above.

This kind of stratification, in which the capacity for religious understanding and salvation is subtly linked with social standing, reaches its fullest expression in Eliot's *Idea of a Christian Society* and *Notes towards the Definition of Culture*. There, faith is seen in the social context. But in this early play, faith is seen primarily in no context at all. Utterly pure, it abjures a world compounded of equal parts illusion and pain. One suffers to the degree that one takes "suffering" seriously, but one can eventually learn to rise above even suffering. One learns, at least, the nature of the perfect anodyne.

In *The Family Reunion*, which saw its premiere in March 1939, six months before England went to war, we are again invited to inspect characters who can best be defined by their capacity to embrace faith. They are the profoundly self-willed Amy, Dowager Lady Monchensey; her self-knowing sister Agatha and her tor-

mented son Harry; the invincibly stupid brothers Gerald and
Charles Piper; and Amy's two other sisters Violet and Ivy. To
Harry, Amy represents control, discipline, and mechanical rigidity.
Agatha represents the promise of inward understanding gained
through suffering. All those present, save the various servants, are
of the same social class and thus their differing capacities for faith
cannot be attributed to their social origins. But a stratification is
nonetheless in force; characters in the play are differentiated according to the various levels of reality and spiritual understanding to which they can ascend.[3] This stratification is emphasized
by frequent references to the utterly static nature of all things under the sun: "Harry: O God, man, the things that are going to
happen / Have already happened."

We never learn either the reasons for such stratification or the
nature of Harry's redemption, which involves his departure:

> Amy: But why are you going?
> Harry: I can only speak
> And you cannot hear me. I can only speak
> So you may not think I conceal an explanation,
> And to tell you I would have liked to explain.

We gather that his future life will be one of spiritual devotion,
not unmixed with the discipline of the ascetic and the other de-
privations usually associated with Christianity in its most self-
lacerating forms. But anything we know is gained in darkness,
amid doubt. We are not unlike the dullard Charles, who confesses
so touchingly that:

> It's very odd,
> But I am beginning to feel, just beginning to feel
> That there is something I *could* understand, if I were
>   told it.

Perhaps one might say in defense of the play that it magnifi-
cently aspires to do that which cannot be done in our time: to portray faith newly acquired. One is then able to argue that Eliot's

---

[3] Grover Smith speaks of the "different orders of reality according to the
potentialities of the characters" in his *T. S. Eliot's Poetry and Plays* (Chicago:
Phoenix Books, 1956), p. 197.

difficulties are those of anyone who has chosen to speak devoutly of faith in a godless age. Harry's solitude, his fidelity to a creed untold, can then be seen as inevitable. His faith would naturally find no language.

Moreover, the fact that *Family Reunion* eschews the chorus that gave *Murder in the Cathedral* so much of its power and resonance is one indication that Eliot felt more strongly in 1939 than in 1935 that he had been deprived of the sustaining power of a society agreeing with him on matters of faith. The chorus had once represented that agreement, but no such spiritual consensus or ambience can properly be said to have existed in the England of 1939. The pressures of commercialism, of industrialization, of colonialism and imperialism gradually collapsing, had seen to that. The beginnings of war merely completed the collapse. The kind of drama Eliot might have wished to write, a drama in which the individual can find faith in a religious community everywhere surrounding and encouraging him, was impossible. The wellsprings of anxiety were fully open by 1939. For him to reach, with Harry, toward faith was to attempt to transcend historical forces over which he had no real control. As England plunged into the long and convulsive nightmare of war fought in desperation, Eliot was plunged into a despair which his own phrase at the time, "depression of spirits," only hints at.

His response to that emotional state was not, I suggest, unlike that of his character Harry. It was to move "somewhere on the other side of despair," to attempt once again a transcendence of historical pressures by the superimposition of a faith only cryptically described. Eliot would wish for that state to which Harry had once aspired: to be "liberated from the human wheel." Alessandro Pellegrini has pointed out that Eliot "deduces his faith almost by a process of logical ratiocination from the historical situation."[4] This comment may help confirm our sense that everywhere in Eliot the importance of religious faith resides not in matters of doctrinal substance, but in its utility for fending off historical con-

4 Alessandro Pellegrini, "A London Conversation with T. S. Eliot," *Sewanee Review*, 57 (Spring 1949): 288.

ditions. It is, primarily, an instrument. (We remember that Charles Maurras, who did not even believe in God, supported Catholicism on the ground that it would provide order.) In some instances, such as *Family Reunion*, faith fails as an instrument because it is employed but nowhere explained. Moreover, the hero's spiritual pilgrimage in that play is too solitary, too bereft of communal support, to serve as credible evidence of Christian power. In other instances, such as *Murder in the Cathedral*, the whole society is configured as a Christian one, albeit with flaws abounding, and the instrument can prove convincing. But the one play is not the other. Nor was 1935, a time of possibility and post-Depression recovery, the same as 1939, a time of war and upheaval. "The great poet," Eliot can remind us, "writes his time." As historical pressures alter, so must the responses of a poet armed with the sword of faith.

CHAPTER TWELVE

Middle Way and Apocalypse

Examining the later drama, as it seemed logical to do in conjunction with the earlier, has taken us out of chronology. Let us go back a few years to the time of the Spanish Civil War. The transcendent attitude that had been forming in Eliot's mind for many years best explains his response to this event, which many people have regarded as the central political and moral challenge of his time: "While I am naturally sympathetic [presumably with the Republic], I still feel convinced that it is best that at least a few men of letters should remain isolated, and take no part in these collective activities."[1] This response, enervating in its mixture of formal correctness and moral antisepsis, is given greater substance when Eliot speaks of what taking sides implies, and suggests again how far removed he is from men engaged, dangerously and sometimes heroically, in direct political activity:

any eventual partisanship should be held with reservations, humility and misgiving. That balance of mind which a few highly-civilized individuals, such as Arjuna, the hero of the *Bhagavad Gita*, can maintain in action, is difficult for most of us even as observers, and . . . is not encouraged by the greater part of the Press.[2]

[1] *Authors Take Sides on the Spanish War* (London: Left Review, 1937), n.p. Eliot's policy of nonintervention followed on the heels of that of his government. By autumn of 1936, Great Britain had decided to prohibit the export of war goods to Spain. The one-sided effects of this "neutrality" were soon obvious. The power and the prestige of the right-wing nationalists were exalted. The British left soon recognized the self-delusory qualities of this hands-off attitude. At last, no one was pleased with it.

[2] *Criterion,* 16 (Jan. 1937): 290.

Having relegated partisanship to the realm of the uncivilized, Eliot goes further and denounces one of the most frequently used means for achieving partisan goals: violence. Thus, of course, he denounces both sides in the Spanish conflict ("whichever side wins will not be the better for having had to fight for its victory"). In support of his views on violence he cites his early friend in England, Bertrand Russell, saying that in opposing violence Russell shows himself clearly able to separate partisan or political goals from the means necessary to achieve them—to distinguish political theory and political actuality. Political actuality, as Arjuna would be sure to know, belongs to a lower domain. For "the people who think, and that is a small minority,"[3] there must obviously be something higher.

Practically in the same breath, however, Eliot criticizes Russell —and by implication, Arjuna—for refusing to go into the detailed world of means and actuality. What Russell has ignored in his writings, it seems, is the fact that real social transformation will demand profound practical changes, and although he speaks of economic readjustment, he does no more. "If he could write a book," says Eliot, "which would show us exactly what economic readjustment would do the trick, he would be performing a great service."[4]

The inconsistency inherent in this turnaround is easily explained even if not comfortably resolved for Eliot: he was too clear-sighted not to see the real consequences of his views, the real nature of all politics. Consequently, no sooner did he engage either political theory (like Russell) or political actuality (like Spain), than he repudiated it.

The repudiation ultimately makes itself felt in a pessimism deep enough to sunder, apparently, *any* relationship to politics. This pessimism is manifested in the last pages of *Criterion*, written after the collapse of the Spanish Republic, and after the most strenuous decade of political involvement for Englishmen in this century. The penultimate Commentary, a counsel of despair, includes a sug-

[3] *Ibid.*, p. 292.
[4] *Ibid.*, p. 291.

gestion so radical in its political implications and so Catonic[5] in its philosophy that it is, in effect, an antipolitical suggestion:

To understand thoroughly what is wrong with agriculture is to understand what is wrong with nearly everything else: with the domination of Finance, with our ideals and system of Education, indeed with our whole philosophy of life. . . . What is fundamentally wrong is the *urbanization of mind* of which I have previously spoken, and which is increasingly prevalent as those who rule, those who speak, those who write, are developed in increasing numbers from an urban background. To have the right frame of mind . . . it is necessary that the greater part of the population, of all classes (so long as we have classes) should be settled in the country and dependent upon it. One sees no hope either in the Labour Party or in the equally unimaginative dominant section of the Conservative Party. There seems no hope in contemporary politics at all.[6]

Out of such hopelessness about politics in October 1938 is born the suggestion that only a return to the soil can bring salvation. Weary and scornful, Eliot proposes a retreat from the world that had only days before witnessed Neville Chamberlain abdicate to Hitler in Munich, had seen the League of Nations head toward collapse, had lived through Britain's embarrassing policy of nonintervention in the Spanish Civil War, and seemed about to be convulsed by yet another great war.

But Eliot's withdrawal and negativism actually indicate, I believe, that he had seized upon a new way of working out his complex negotiations with the world. His despair was not so profound as to silence him forever. In just two months, in fact, he was to lecture at the invitation of Corpus Christi College, Cambridge, and (in October 1939) to publish those lectures as *The Idea of a Christian Society*. He there returns, as one feels he was bound to do, to politics, but with a new emphasis. He will now try, as he

[5] I am thinking here of Cato the Censor, 234-149 B.C., the Roman moralist and statesman. Adamant against both extravagance and new customs, he sought to restrict Senate seats to the worthy and advised his countrymen to destroy Carthage because of the quality of her life. Retiring to the country, he affected rustic manners while complacently accepting class divisions and treating his servants harshly.

[6] Eliot, "A Commentary," *Criterion*, 18 (Oct. 1938): 59-60.

did only hazily before, to envision society as he would wish it to be.

The tone of *The Idea of a Christian Society*, written in time of war, is tentative and diffident. Gone are the harsh magisterial attitudes of *After Strange Gods*; gone also is the sense of hopeless exhaustion pervading the last issues of *Criterion*. Eliot is once again the attentive and self-effacing amateur. The introduction offers little reason to believe that any great problems will be solved within; but the problems that are posed will nonetheless demand the attention of everyone. Eliot's aim, as the book begins, is the modest one of definition, not persuasion; this is no plea for a religious revival. The study shall be objective, even technical: "I am not at this moment concerned with the means for bringing a Christian Society into existence; I am not even primarily concerned with making it desirable; but I am very much concerned with making clear its difference from the kind of society in which we are now living."[7]

But as the book proceeds, Eliot appears to have modified his aims, and to be making an unmistakably revolutionary plea (ICS 8):

my primary interest is a change in our social attitude, such a change only as could bring about anything worthy to be called a Christian Society. That such a change would compel changes in our organisation of industry and commerce and financial credit, that it would facilitate, where it now impedes, the life of devotion for those who are capable of it, I feel certain.

Seldom, surely, has economic revolution been so quietly understated. Seldom, surely, has it been considered simply as the happy and coincidental result of some more urgently needed change. Eliot never surrendered the belief that altered consciousness could alter all of society. However, his argument is even more imperious than this. For after denouncing liberalism in terms familiar to readers of *After Strange Gods* (for "destroying traditional social habits of the people," etc.), it moves into a position from which

---

[7] Eliot, *Christianity and Culture: The Idea of a Christian Society* and *Notes towards the Definition of Culture* (New York: Harcourt, Brace [A Harvest Book], n.d.), p. 6. *The Idea of a Christian Society* is hereafter cited as ICS.

the advantages of Christianity are considered wholly beyond argument (ICS 16):

If we have got so far as accepting the belief that the only alternative to a progressive and insidious adaptation to totalitarian worldliness for which the pace is already set, is to aim at a Christian society, we need to consider both what kind of a society we have at this time, and what a Christian society would be like.

Eliot does not have to seek far for a description of existing society. It is the same society that he condemned in *After Strange Gods* in 1933. It is a society best defined by its susceptibility to the deleterious forces of liberalism ("wormeaten with Liberalism"). Liberalism is bad because it becomes what it is by opposing something else; "it is something which tends to release energy rather than accumulate it, to relax, rather than to fortify. It is a movement not so much defined by its end, as by its starting point; away from, rather than towards, something definite" (ICS 12). A civilization strong enough to be permanent, then, must recognize its positive elements, the very elements against which liberalism acts. Eliot chooses not to accept the fashionably gloomy teaching of those who say that all positive elements have ceased to exist in so liberal a society, and that we must all presently endure chaos. He suggests, rather, that although culture is mainly negative, positive elements do survive proving that liberalism can never control a society. Equating "positive" and "Christian," he maintains that "a society has not ceased to be Christian until it has become positively something else" (ICS 10).

Modern society, as Eliot pictures it in this book, is composed essentially of these two elements—the Christian tradition and its adversary, the liberal tradition. Liberalism is too negative and Christianity too weak to assume control (Rome to the contrary notwithstanding). The worst that liberalism can do to society is to set loose the chaos that is its own logical extension. Until then, however, liberalism and Christianity exist in a symbiotic relationship, the reactive parasite gaining its definition from the weak host on which it feeds, the positive host knowing it is positive by virtue of the fact that so many negative elements surround it. "A Christian society only becomes acceptable after you have fairly examined the alternatives" (ICS 18).

In seeking to set forth what he calls, with a characteristic blend of painful modesty and Promethean resolve, "not a programme for a party, but a way of life for a people" (ICS 14), he must tell us what a positive Christian society, free of symbiotes, would be like.

He starts off by imagining a structure consisting of the Christian State, the Christian Community, and the Community of Christians. Of primary importance in this imaginary society is faith. As a general rule, people would be trained to think in Christian categories, but each of the three elements would come to faith in its own special way (ICS 23):

> Among the men of state, you would have as a minimum, conscious conformity of behaviour. In the Christian Community that they ruled, the Christian faith would be ingrained, but it requires, as a minimum, only a largely unconscious behaviour; and it is only from the much smaller number of conscious human beings, the Community of Christians, that one would expect a conscious Christian life at its highest social level.

The salient term here, as in *After Strange Gods*, is "conscious." The term crops up often, in a variety of important ways, in Eliot's discussions. Leaving aside the actual leaders, those engaged in the exercise of power central to any society, there remain two "faithful" groups. The actual leaders are not, we see, unfriendly to faith; they simply are irrelevant to it. They lead, but need not believe. Those who can be regarded, however, as the "unconscious" beings, those whom Eliot patronizingly describes as "occupied mostly by their direct relation to the soil, or the sea, or the machine" (ICS 23), are to find their faith in rituals and traditions. They have, after all, little capacity for thinking about the objects of faith. Even for those who do have such capacity, formed habits are needed; the reason is that the Christian direction of thought and feeling can only occur "at particular moments" during the day and week. (We should know by now that Eliot never urged confidence in any human ability.) The conscious and believing Christians, moreover, can act to offset the possibility of cynical manipulations on the part of the political leaders. They would provide, like the "clerisy" of Coleridge (which Eliot mentions), an ethical leadership; they would exert guidance in education and in what he fervently hopes would be a revival of monastic orders.

This three-part division, then, is the structure of Eliot's Christian society. He is quick to see that it might be thought too frail and chimeric—and he anticipates such criticism of it by saying, as usual, that he is not presenting an idealized picture of a rural retreat. He seems to recognize that society cannot be reduced to such basic forms and he is aware of the myriad forces that today oppose a truly Christian orientation of society. "A great deal of the machinery of modern life," as he says, "is merely a sanction for un-Christian aims . . . not only hostile to the conscious pursuit of the Christian life in the world by the few, but to the maintenance of any Christian society *of* the world" (ICS 27). But then he proposes, while admitting that his idea might sound bigoted, that nothing less than a Christian organization of society will do. In other words, where he finds un-Christian behavior, he proposes uniform Christian belief. This, in all of its astonishing simplicity, is the instrument of his proposed society.

Kathleen Nott has voiced the question that is in many minds when she asks whether there is any ". . . *power* which will operate the machine for which Mr. Eliot has given us a blueprint."[8] What, in the crudest sense, will make Christianity *work* in a world of coercions the bases of which are not spiritual, but material? Nott continues her questioning by asking of the structure of Eliot's society:

Now what exactly can it be that *obliges* a statesman who, in spite of a Christian education, is sceptical or indifferent to Christian belief, to work within a Christian frame or "to design his policy for the government of a Christian society?" And what would oblige a Community which was unable to think about the objects of belief, to accept his government, unless it conferred obvious and immediate material benefits which the Community would have to be advanced enough, in an intellectual sense, to realise or "think about"?[9]

[8] Nott, p. 129.
[9] *Ibid.*, p. 131.

Eliot's answer would obviously be that each group would act in a Christian manner, with or without being involved in "belief," because it would simply feel it the best thing to do. The Community of Christians would act to promote that general feeling. Composed of "both clergy and laity of superior intellectual and/or spiritual gifts" (ICS 30), and including "some of those who are ordinarily spoken of, not always with flattering intention, as 'intellectuals,' " this Community would be able to form the conscious mind and the conscience of the nation. The question of power thus becomes no more than a question of influence. Conscience answers to coercion, answers even to brute force.

Eliot admits, however, that the system he has set forth would be extremely fragile, that there would still be a State, and that there would be "no safeguard against its proceeding, from un-Christian acts, to action on implicitly un-Christian principles, and thence to action on avowedly un-Christian principles" (ICS 35). What Eliot seems in fact to be confessing, as he draws our attention to the gap separating Christian society from the political State, is that power can never be exorcised, but will always have its own unstoppable way. What he is also admitting is that even after a Christian society is envisioned and established, it could prove once again the easy prey of history and of power and follow the same melancholy direction as such societies have in the past. "We have no safeguard for the purity of our Christianity," he regretfully announces, "for, as the State may pass from expediency to lack of principle, and as the Christian Community may sink into torpor, so the Community of Christians may be debilitated by group or individual eccentricity and error" (ICS 35).

Forced to make some damaging admissions about power, Eliot redoubles his efforts to minimize history. But history is simply the arena time provides for power. Noting that "Christendom has remained fixed at the stage of development suitable to a simple agricultural and piscatorial society," and that Christian social forms are thus ill-suited to the complex modern world, Eliot sees two possible solutions. The first is, in his phrase, a "neo-Ruskinian" position, and would call for a return to a much more basic and primitive mode of life. The second would "accept the modern world as it is and simply try to adapt Christian social ideals to it" (ICS 25). Since he cannot, or at least feels he should not, accept a Catonic glorification of rustic simplicity, and since he knows that for Christianity to embrace the modern world is for Christianity to be sullied, he has reached a logical impasse. He tries to escape by simply declaring that the society he has in mind "can only be realised when the great majority of the sheep belong to one fold" (ICS 37). Logical contradictions are met by pontification.

"The Christian," he says, and here he would seem to include the Christian like himself who finds that he is enmeshed in historical circumstances from which there is respite neither in a simple past nor in a compromised future, "can be satisfied with nothing less than a Christian organisation of society. . . . a society in which the natural end of man—virtue and well-being in community—is acknowledged for all, and the supernatural end—beatitude—for those who have the eyes to see it" (ICS 27). But this, we must understand, is neither logic nor argument. It is special pleading. It is to gaze, as a Christian must, at a world not of his own making, and to ask plaintively for something entirely different.

It is, in fact, to plead for his own variety of elitism. Eliot's quaint modesty of style can sometimes obscure from us that disturbing fact. His repeated admonitions to think only of the "idea" of a Christian society and to ignore anything so drably practical as considerations of power and structural details can make us forget that we are dealing with modern industrial society and not a Platonic abstraction. We are made to feel vulgar if we descend to a query about means. We also feel the peculiar disadvantage of being allowed only to view a "positive" society, one stripped of the tensions and contradictions our experience tells us are characteristic of all forms of social life. Such a pure creation allows for nothing but simple assent or rejection, never a comparison of real alternatives.

At only one crucial point in this troubling book does Eliot descend from Utopia. In a lengthy footnote he exhibits a concrete understanding of England's contemporary condition that belies his portrayal of himself as a political amateur. He knows quite clearly where he stands, with whose interests he is allied, and who opposes him (ICS 61):

Britain will presumably continue to be governed by the same mercantile and financial class which, with a continual change of personnel, has been increasingly important since the fifteenth century. I mean by a "lower middle class society" one in which the standard man legislated for and catered for, the man whose passions must be manipulated, whose prejudices must be humored, whose tastes must be gratified, will be the lower middle class man. He is the most numerous, the one most necessary to flatter. I am not necessarily implying that this is either a good or a bad thing: that depends upon what lower middle class Man does to himself, and what is done to him.

The necessary implication is, of course, that "lower middle class man" must be restrained. That is what must be "done to him." Eliot's argument cannot avoid carrying such a sinister burden. With interests such as his to defend, surrounded by adversaries, he necessarily has malign plans for the class threatening to devour him. The opposition he feels is neatly described when he divides culture between "the producers and the consumers of culture—the existence of men who can create new thought and new art (with middlemen who can teach the consumers to like it) and the existence of a cultivated society to enjoy and patronise it" (ICS 60). The consumers who will be taught to "like it," are, we may presume, that same political entity: the lower-middle class, the petty bourgeoisie. Against that class, it is fair to say, his plea is made here, just as it had been made earlier in his career.

Sir Richard Rees thinks well of such pleading. He says that Eliot's proposal "can be described as a dogmatic but nevertheless mild and tolerant authoritarianism, imposing no more than a Christian frame of reference upon the State."[10] Here Sir Richard, like so many others who have found little to criticize in Eliot, seems

---

[10] Sir Richard Rees, "T. S. Eliot on Culture and Progress," in Walter Laqueur and George L. Mosse, eds., *Literature and Politics in the Twentieth Century* (New York: Harper and Row, 1967), p. 101.

to incorporate in his thinking some of the same odd relationship to power that Eliot himself favored. What is mildly described as "no more than a Christian frame of reference," an imposition of Christian authority on a state hardly Christian in all its parts, would offer a challenge to the existing order so profound that to think of its success is surely to envision antagonisms, convulsions, perhaps even violence. Yet Sir Richard speaks in a way innocent of radical change or force, an innocence that Eliot, so versed in systems of despair, does not share. It is to his credit that Eliot summons the strength to remind us "that whatever reform or revolution we carry out, the result will always be a sordid travesty of what human society should be" (ICS 47). We may legitimately infer that he includes in the reckoning his own kind of religious transformation.

In contrast to this characteristic wariness, there is heard a note at the close of *The Idea of a Christian Society* that, although inaudible to Sir Richard in his gentle satisfactions, reverberates through the whole. That note is, once again, the apocalyptic one (ICS 49):

I would not have it thought that I condemn a society because of its material ruin, for that would be to make its material success a sufficient test of its excellence; I mean only that a wrong attitude towards nature implies, somewhere, a wrong attitude towards God, and that the consequence is an inevitable doom.

The condemnation and the apprehension of coming doom combine to give the last paragraph of the book its peculiar eloquence. Eliot there intimates that his reason for writing *The Idea of a Christian Society* was that "the events of September, 1938," as he decorously refers to them, had brought into open play all of his suspicions, all of his fears, and that he had at last to announce his doubt of the validity of his civilization. War had made him ask (ICS 51):

Was our society, which had always been so assured of its superiority and rectitude, so confident of its unexamined premises, assembled round anything more permanent than a congeries of banks, insurance companies and industries, and had it any beliefs more essential than a belief in compound interest and the maintenance of dividends?

Raymond Williams is correct when he says that in *The Idea of a Christian Society* "Eliot's business is to confess an attitude, and it is an essential part of this attitude that the formulations of programmes cannot have priority."[11] They can never have priority because of his logical procedures. Eliot pledges himself not to be, like the liberals, "negative"; he states that he wants a wholly new "way of life for a people." But, depriving himself of power because it corrupts, he seeks to actuate his ideal society by querulous pleading, and not by force, the necessary tool of every planner as dissatisfied as himself. The past cannot offer him his answer, and sickened by the present, he vaguely and apprehensively surveys a future he denies himself the means to bring into being:

> Wandering between two worlds, one dead,
> The other powerless to be born.

The Idea of a Christian Society is, as one critic has said, "indigestible,"[12] because it is written by a man who, having judged the world and all its possibilities, employs a logic enforcing his separation from that world. Once again Eliot reveals the nature of his alienation. Once again his exclusive reliance on consciousness and the alteration of consciousness guides him to despair. The mind alone, faith alone, proves insufficient to his cause.

Perhaps faith appears insufficient because it is insufficiently explained. For Eliot to rely so heavily upon it, and yet to be so chary of disclosing to us its inward true nature, is to arouse doubt in the minds of all save the most devoted. This problem, of course, is what Kathleen Nott touches upon when she calls "skirting of all philosophic discussion" Eliot's principal method. To gesture toward, but not to reveal; to pursue, but not to unravel, this is Eliot's procedure. Its greatest successes lie in deflecting the insistent probings of those who remain unsatisfied by the proclamation of "faith" as the means to cure, or move beyond, all worldly ills. To give the exact lineaments of faith, after all, would be to usher in a host of unwanted opinions about "faith true" and "faith impure," about "correct" and "counterfeit" doctrine. Better mys-

[11] *Culture and Society, 1780-1950* (New York: Doubleday, 1960), p. 246.
[12] Rees, p. 102.

tery and gestures of submission than such conflict, such violations of the inner sanctum. This is not to say that Eliot's faith was a sham. But it is to say that his faith had uses in worlds other than the private and personal one, and that one such use proved strategic in argument. Eliot need never have feared the sometimes devastating lucidity of rational analysis—not so long as he held preserves off limits to analysis. Nor need he have worried that his license to prescribe, from his ultramundane position, recommendations to his worldly neighbors would expire. The introduction of faith would always suspend for him the rules of the game.

CHAPTER THIRTEEN

'Four Quartets'

As we now know, historical pressures can be felt in Eliot's great poem of late maturity, *Four Quartets*. "Burnt Norton" was born of the disparate remains of *Murder in the Cathedral*, and published in *Collected Poems 1909-1935* (1936), but the four-part poem we now know was born of the Second World War. Confusion and demoralization in public life had given the inwardness of private existence a new meaning:

> Even 'Burnt Norton' might have remained by itself if it hadn't been for the war, because I had become very much absorbed in the problems of writing for the stage and might have gone straight on from *The Family Reunion* to another play. The war destroyed that interest for a time: you remember how the conditions of our lives changed, how much we were thrown in on ourselves in the early days? 'East Coker' was the result—and it was only in writing 'East Coker' that I began to see the Quartets as a set of four.[1]

The critical reception of *Four Quartets* has itself been a war, or at least a skirmish, between those who see the poem as a breathtakingly successful exposition of modern Christian mysticism and self-transcendence, and those who see it as the wholly bankrupt expression of a poet whose pessimism and spiritual dessication had at last exerted their terrible triumph upon him. The division has been there from the beginning. In 1944, Curtis Bradford, for instance, wrote of "East Coker" that, "as the poem is about to end with images of desolation, the poet recollects that his end, his

[1] T. S. Eliot, "The Genesis of *Four Quartets*," *New York Times Book Review*, Nov. 29, 1953; as quoted in Bernard Bergonzi, ed., *T. S. Eliot*, Four Quartets: *A Casebook* (London: Macmillan, 1969), p. 23.

death, is his true spiritual beginning. There has been a triumphant reversal of the statement with which the poem began: "In my beginning is my end."[2] In direct opposition to this laudatory sentiment is that of George Orwell, writing at roughly the same time. Citing Eliot's "gloomy Pétainism," and viewing the Anglican Church as little more than a bleak harbor for Eliot's "escape from individualism,"[3] Orwell sees the poet as following a path sure to lead to defeatism or worse.

The struggle, in its larger sense, is actually between two very general groups of people: those who believe that the accumulated cultural reflexes of Europe, England, and America, including their religious traditions, can still provide strength and support and shape poetry of the highest order, and those who believe these reflexes have deteriorated to the level of superstitions, and thus can inspire only meretricious poetry. For the former group, Eliot reaches something fine, something whole and pure, a true moment of awful understanding. For the latter, Eliot has brought together largely uninspired lines and phrases, lacking both *frisson* and drama, leading steadfastly into a domain of inert melancholy.

Both the apologists and the radical skeptics have overlooked something. Any sense of triumph in the poem, any sustained moment of mystical penetration, is greatly endangered by the almost compulsive admission of inadequacy made by the poet. Whatever he finds to say is not enough. Wherever he turns to find strength in words, his hands grasp only the unsteady instrument of false speech:

> Words strain,
> Crack and sometimes break, under the burden,
> Under the tension, slip, slide, perish,
> Decay with imprecision, will not stay in place,
> Will not stay still. Shrieking voices
> Scolding, mocking, or merely chattering,
> Always assail them.
>   ("Burnt Norton," V, 149-55)

[2] Curtis Bradford, "Footnotes to 'East Coker,'" *Sewanee Review* (1944); as quoted in Bergonzi, p. 63.

[3] George Orwell, review in *Poetry London* (1942); as quoted in Bergonzi, p. 85.

That was a way of putting it—not very satisfactory:
A periphrastic study in a worn-out poetical fashion,
Leaving one still with the intolerable wrestle
With words and meanings. The poetry does not matter.
It was not (to start again) what one had expected.
("East Coker," II, 68-72)

So here I am, in the middle way, having had twenty years—
Twenty years largely wasted, the years of *l'entre deux guerres*
Trying to learn to use new words, and every attempt
Is a wholly new start, and a different kind of failure
Because one has only learnt to get the better of words
For the thing one no longer has to say, or the way in which
One is no longer disposed to say it. And so each venture
Is a new beginning, a raid on the inarticulate
With shabby equipment always deteriorating
In the general mess of imprecision of feeling,
Undisciplined squads of emotion.
("East Coker," V, 172-82)

This agony, this "intolerable wrestle," is as much the subject of *Four Quartets* as the divine illumination that his words alone can merely approximate. It may be argued, moreover, that the greatest rewards in the poem lie not in the fully achieved sense of spiritual accomplishment described in the concluding lines ("And all shall be well . . . When . . . the fire and the rose are one"), but in the perception of the way in which life must uneasily, even tortuously, be maintained by one who has been driven to the margin of existence. The modern Christian Eliot so faithfully represents is he who, in poetry, equipped only with words ("words alone are certain good"), can hardly do more than attempt the impossible ("For us, there is only the trying") and to know that failure lies clearly in the offing. The cruel paradox of *Four Quartets* stems from the poet's careful and stubborn reliance upon words as the single instrument for evoking and substantiating faith, coupled with an equally strong conviction on his part that in this world, an un-Christian world doomed to internal decay, no labor and no zeal can matter very much. The contemporary Christian fatalist, such as Eliot, is to be seen poised in stasis, surrounded by his motionless yet struggling comrades ("Who are only undefeated / Because we have gone on trying"). Everything they see about them, every turn society has taken, every modern heresy, serves manifold purposes: to show how deeply the seeds of ruination have been planted, to reveal the powerlessness of the Truth, and to remind the comrades once again that they were not created to live in this world, but only to serve as unwilling spectators of its somber folly. Thus are the *Quartets* inert, static; thus can Eliot employ so resourcefully the line from Mary, Queen of Scots, "In my beginning is my end." The poem does not move from its fixed point of powerless aspiration. We are not far from the blocked struggle of *Ash-Wednesday*.

What leftist adversaries of the poem have, for their part, neglected is the essential justice of the statement by one of their number, Orwell himself, that it is absurd to attack Eliot for being a "reactionary" and to imagine that he "might have used his gifts in the cause of democracy and Socialism."[4] To imagine that Eliot might thus have written, and to castigate him for not so doing, is an exercise in one of the more egregious forms of politically radical fatuity. It assumes that he, unlike the rest of us, is an unencumbered force acting with "free will," and can bring himself smoothly into conjunction with the more "progressive" aspects of some grand historical movement.

But Eliot, let us remember, is as much confined by history as anyone else. He lacks, as we all lack, the mythical lever of Archimedes by which one moves the world and thereby one's position with respect to it. He writes in defense, sometimes muted, sometimes full-voiced, of the socioeconomic structure he knows best. That structure has, in centuries past, possessed considerable, even overwhelming strength. It is hardly extinct today. Its defenders and allies are to be found in walks of life where poetry, even that reputed as highly as Eliot's, does not reach. That which Eliot defends might indeed be a regressive aspect of what is now meant by the class society of the West, but the regressive and progressive aspects of this society have more in common with each other than they do with the forces that threaten or would like to threaten it.

---

4 *Ibid.*, p. 87.

Eliot's poetry, then, is the utterance of one who believes that a chorus of supporting voices does somewhere surround him, the relative thinness and uncertainty of the religious voices in the chorus notwithstanding. It is his understanding that he speaks not his own mind alone.

Nevertheless, his consciousness is at times plagued by doubts, anxieties, and feelings of impotence. As has been mentioned above, *Four Quartets* is partly about the impossibility of doing or even saying certain things. It is about the inarticulateness of words, the ineffectiveness of activity, the conflation of time into a single instant, and the claim of the transcendent, the suprahuman on us. Things are put forward, only to be withdrawn.

> There is, it seems to us,
> At best, only a limited value
> In the knowledge derived from experience.
> ("East Coker," II, 81-83)

> I said to my soul, be still, and wait without hope
> For hope would be hope for the wrong thing; wait without love
> For love would be love of the wrong thing; there is yet faith
> But the faith and the love and the hope are all in the waiting.
> Wait without thought, for you are not ready for thought:
> So the darkness shall be the light. . . .
> ("East Coker," III, 123-28)

> And the way up is the way down, the way forward is the way back.
> You cannot face it steadily, but this thing is sure,
> That time is no healer: the patient is no longer here.
> ("The Dry Salvages," III, 129-31)

> In order to arrive at what you are not
> You must go through the way in which you are not.
> And what you do not know is the only thing you know
> And what you own is what you do not own
> And where you are is where you are not.
> ("East Coker," III, 142-46)

The dialectics (if one may use a term so apparently inappropriate to Eliot) of the poem are closed. Possibilities are evoked, only to be negated; each thing meets its opposite only to grind to a halt in the confrontation. Any higher synthesis that might otherwise emerge is checked. One finds that the answer such a synthesis might provide is to be gained not dynamically, but statically: one "understands" the situation one faces by recognizing that it is *that* situation and no other, that change is illusory, that differences are always latently similarities, and that one would do well to regard, with care, the immutable. How else explain England?

> You are not here to verify,
> Instruct yourself, or inform curiosity
> Or carry report. . . .
> . . .
> Here, the intersection of the timeless moment
> Is England and nowhere. Never and always.
> ("Little Gidding," I, 43-45; 52-53)

Or the melding of age-old political tensions:

> We cannot restore old policies
> Or follow an antique drum.
> These men, and those who opposed them
> And those whom they opposed
> Accept the constitution of silence
> And are folded in a single party.
> ("Little Gidding," III, 186-91)

Or the futility of seeking transformation:

> We shall not cease from exploration
> And the end of all our exploring
> Will be to arrive where we started
> And know the place for the first time.
> ("Little Gidding," V, 239-42)

One is left at last with what is. It is, has been, and shall be. One does not so much "recognize" it, as swallow it while being swallowed. In so devouring, and in being devoured, one is at harmony with the Word. The Word, of course, is God.

This is a doctrine that cannot be adduced to the support of any ideology. Everything political is absorbed, only to become no more than ephemerally political. The vanity of every aspiration, from whatever political or economic motive, is revealed. The poem sweeps away both right and left, leaving satisfaction nowhere:

O dark dark dark. They all go into the dark,
The vacant interstellar spaces, the vacant into the vacant,
The captains, merchant bankers, eminent men of letters,
The generous patrons of art, the statesmen and the rulers,
Distinguished civil servants, chairmen of many committees,
Industrial lords and petty contractors, all go into the dark,
And dark the Sun and Moon, and the Almanach de Gotha
And the Stock Exchange Gazette, the Directory of Directors,
And cold the sense and lost the motive of action.
And we all go with them, into the silent funeral,
Nobody's funeral, for there is no one to bury.
                                        ("East Coker," III, 101-11)

One can take a certain amount of pleasure in seeing so many of one's enemies perish so neatly—until one's own name appears on the list. Moreover, he who enumerates the death of others is himself to die and will take absolutely every spectator of death along with him. Darkness indeed. No ideological position can be formed amid such darkness.

Eliot removing politics and ideology in all of their customary senses from serious contention or discussion and reducing them so devastatingly to the world of sublunary vanity—this is the poet at his most religious. The world is folly. The world is devoid of sense. Differences are eroded. Polarities dissolve. The life of woe meets the life of weal, but to no purpose. The supernal life, indescribable, is the one thing of importance. To see ourselves "surrounded / By a grace of sense, a white light still and moving, / *Erhebung* without motion, concentration / Without elimination, both a new world / And the old made explicit" ("Burnt Norton," II, 71-75), is to be removed once again to the terrain Eliot always occupied when he sought to rise to a diffidence wholly outdistancing contradictions. Since, as one might put it, contradictions are so ineradicably a part of life, but since the importance of life, of "living and partly living" has, Eliot would say, traditionally been so fatuously overestimated, it is fitting that Eliot move to a position beyond life. This, a part of his Christianity, was also a part of that oscillation between politics and life and positions very much elsewhere that we have remarked so often before.

CHAPTER FOURTEEN

'Notes towards the Definition of Culture'

Eliot was jarred out of his Christian fatalism in the mid-1940's by the impact and aftermath of the Second World War. He shared the general recognition in 1945 that England, and all of Europe, had suffered shocks so profound as to call into question the entire organization of society. With Europe moving toward change and recovery, with England again pulling itself together, and with the United States emerging as the most powerful force of industrial capital in the world, the time was right for new theories of economic and social development, and several such theories appeared. Prominent among the new theorists, as Eliot knew, was Karl Mannheim.[1] Eliot's own *Notes towards the Definition of Culture*, complete at last in 1948, may be read in part as a late rejoinder to Mannheim and to the idea of reconstituting society through conscious planning. Eliot's declaration of acknowledgment is clear: "my debt to [Mannheim] is much greater than appears from the one context in which I discuss his theory."[2] Indeed it is. Throughout the *Notes* Mannheim is a kind of unnamed adversary, representing the modern tendencies that most repelled Eliot and most threatened the social interests he would defend.

Eliot's *Notes*, appearing fully nine years after *The Idea of a Christian Society*, is the last, and the fullest, discussion of prob-

---

[1] Mannheim's *Man and Society in an Age of Reconstruction* was first available in English in 1940.

[2] *Christianity and Culture: The Idea of a Christian Society* and *Notes towards the Definition of Culture* (New York: Harcourt, Brace, n.d.), p. 83; hereafter cited as NTDC.

lems that had occupied his mind for approximately twenty-five years. What distinguishes it from the earlier work is not only its greater sophistication, but also its explicit resistance to *all* ideas of social and political planning. *The Idea of a Christian Society* had been ambivalent on the subject of planning, at first speaking hopefully of it, but in the end casting enormous doubt on it. The later work is devoted to demonstrating that a proper society cannot be planned at all.

Eliot was fascinated with Mannheim partly because he grasped in absolute terms Eliot's central dilemma: "the apparent necessity," in Eliot's own words, "of choice between freedom and organisation."[3] Since, as Eliot had written earlier, "society cannot return to any earlier degree of simplicity," the apparent choice is no real choice at all, for society can only proceed "to a more intelligent and thorough organisation."[4] Mannheim had, of course, long before come to this same conclusion, and it can be seen as a tribute to the power of Mannheim's thought that Eliot not only praises his book at length, but also gives up any pleasure he might have in positing a return to agrarian simplicity as a solution to mankind's problems. Such reversionary impulses had, we know, played a key role in *After Strange Gods* and *The Idea of a Christian Society*. But here, no longer permissible, such impulses are rebuked as part of:

the "dark age attitude"—waiting, perhaps for many generations, for the storm of the machine age to blow over; retiring, with a few of the best books, to a small, self-contained community, to till the soil and milk the cow. That, like extreme pacifism, is an attitude with which there is no argument. But if we still look for any other attitude to adopt we must adjust our minds to consider Mannheim's proposals with equanimity.[5]

With equanimity, but not with agreement. Mannheim's *Man and Society in an Age of Reconstruction* was an important book by a prophetic scholar. Its ideas, and the ideas it inspired for the

[3] Eliot, "Man and Society" [a review of *Man and Society in an Age of Reconstruction* by Karl Mannheim], *The Spectator*, 164 (June 7, 1940): 782.
[4] *Ibid.*
[5] *Ibid.*

next several years, struck at the heart of Eliot's social and political principles. The basic disagreement can be discussed in terms of what "consciousness" meant to the two men. Mannheim projected a society in which there would emerge a specially trained group of people to handle the enormously complicated problems engendered by high-powered industrialism. He argued that only through a vastly increased measure of conscious planning, of the conscious deployment of extant and potential social forces, could the problems he saw be solved. Not only would planning be inevitable, but, "the new form of policy can only succeed at a much higher level of consciousness, a consciousness with a taste for experiment."[6] Arguing from a somewhat idealistic, or nonmaterialist, position, Mannheim wanted primarily to change the way men think. Then, perhaps, the way they act and the conditions enveloping that activity would change. But the order he had in mind is crucial. We need the courage, said Mannheim, "for the kind of thought necessary in our age."[7] Correct action would presumably follow, in time, from such courage and such thought. Thus his almost complete reliance on those who have attained a high degree of consciousness and have, as he would put it, transcended class constraint. Such a *freischwebende Intelligenz* emerged as the hope for the future: "The freedom of the intellectuals from 'high society' and their development into a section more or less detached from other sections, and recruited from all social classes, brought about a wonderful flowering of a free intellectual and cultural life."[8]

Even though this classless group might be internally threatened by its own excess of numbers in the future, it alone could resolve the destructive antagonisms sure to arise between class-bound interests. The elites, once formed, would become as the extraterrestrial lever Archimedes needed to move the world. "One can already see that unless the principle of equalizing opportunities is linked

[6] Karl Mannheim, *Man and Society in an Age of Reconstruction* (New York: Harcourt, Brace, 1940), p. 7.

[7] *Ibid.*, p. 143.

[8] *Ibid.*, p. 101.

up with objective criteria of achievement and just principles of social selection, mass society is bound to degenerate into Fascism."[9]

It is directly to the proposals of "objective" criteria and "just" principles that Eliot's own argument responds. Eliot is sensitive, indeed hypersensitive, to the danger of disturbing existing class structures and relationships. Seeing those relationships as part of an organically shaped society, and believing that certain religious sentiments, such as traditional Anglo-Catholicism, serve to unify that society, he is forced to take exception to even so vaguely liberal a critic of society as Mannheim: "However moderately and unobtrusively the doctrine of élites is put," Eliot says, "it implies a radical transformation of society" (NTDC 109). And since he has already presumed that any change whatsoever will result in a loss, a radical transformation is bound to trigger the apocalypse. When he says, therefore, that Mannheim's view "posits an *atomic* view of society," he is talking about the very cancer that he and other well-placed "mandarins" of this society must fear more than all other maladies. Such a society functions, as he sees it, on the basis of an attenuated consciousness and a class rigidity that encourages no great vertical mobility or constructive power on the part of a *freischwebende Intelligenz* or anyone else. To allow such mobility there would be in the end to allow mobility elsewhere; and to increase consciousness in one place would be to increase, or even to inflame, it in another. Hence Eliot must say that "it would appear to be for the best that the great majority of human beings should go on living in the place in which they were born" (NTDC 125). The possibly incendiary friction otherwise resulting would, he thinks, pose too great a threat to traditional structures.

The idea that society is an organic structure is certainly not original with Eliot, or new to him in *Notes towards the Definition of Culture*. An idea with its deepest modern roots in Burke and Coleridge, it is emphasized by Eliot in such a way, however, that to define a word like "culture" turns out to be a most difficult

[9] *Ibid.*, p. 92.

undertaking. "Society" becomes in his hands very much like "culture," and "culture" is seen to be of three essential parts: that of the individual, that of the group, and that of the whole society. These three parts are actually one whole body, but that whole body is more than just a collection of its parts. Such a paradox is perfectly in accord with organicist thinking, and Eliot goes on to say that there is danger in identifying culture with a mere collection of distinct cultural constituents or activities. The whole is certainly greater than the sum of the parts. Instead, then, of providing a collective description, he provides two partial definitions of culture, one essentially anthropological and the other essentially qualitative. One states that culture is "the *whole way of life* of a people," the other states that culture is "that which makes life worth living" (NTDC 103, 100). Between these two definitions Eliot's mind travels. The result is that "culture," whatever it is, attaches to itself a certain mysteriously elusive quality. It at once defies description, is to be seen objectively as an anthropological condition, and is something to be praised.

This mysteriousness permits him to introduce a key dictum: culture, he says, "is the one thing that we cannot deliberately aim at" (NTDC 91). If culture, that is, were susceptible of precise definition, it might also prove to be susceptible of management. But such is not the case. Much of his argument is given over to enumerating the elements of cultural strength—"the persistence of social classes," religion, the family, regional identification, and even "the club"—but he makes no claim that one could produce a "society" (in the good sense) by mixing all these things together. He simply says that "you are unlikely to have a high civilisation when these conditions are absent" (NTDC 88). This is another subtle way of saying that "culture" cannot be trapped by any definition.

Even with these necessary, if not sufficient, elements in place, however, all is not well. For culture is prey to mutability. When Eliot declares that "our own period is one of decline . . . the standards of culture are lower than they were fifty years ago . . . the evidences of this decline are visible in every department of human activity" (NTDC 91), he points to a situation over which, dismayingly enough, mortal beings seem to have absolutely no control. Culture is naturally subject to decay — hence its greatest enemy is time. (Pound, as we recall, was also of this opinion.) "The one thing that time is ever sure to bring about is the loss [of earlier values]," he says; "gain or compensation is almost always conceivable but never certain" (NTDC 98). Against such a decline, little can be done. Some of Eliot's scorn is directed against those who innocently think that something can be done, that some force of the human will and imagination can stave off the inevitable. But culture will soon disintegrate. Moreover, the sort of unity he has in mind is not expressible as a common enthusiasm or purpose, anyway: "enthusiasms and purposes are always transient" (NTDC 125).

When he speaks, then, of the unity of Christendom, or when he calls it an essential part of the highest culture the world has ever known, the reader cannot help feeling that Eliot is speaking of something that, impervious though it be to analysis, is hopelessly vulnerable to all the forces of nature, both human and otherwise. Almost anything, in fact, that human intelligence can bring to it will deform or corrupt it; better the human mind bring to it nothing other than pure faith.

Out of this severe doctrine comes a further sharpening of Eliot's own thinking about consciousness. *Notes* suggests that one of the central obstacles to the progress of culture, even if the family, social classes, religion, and anchored population remain just as they are, is excessive consciousness. Consciousness, as he understands it, inevitably works to divide society and culture. It makes culture too aware of itself and of its own elusive workings, the springs of which are the slow turning of history and the inarticulate communications between past and present. The "introspectiveness" of consciousness is dangerous. When Mannheim suggests, then, that culture and society can be saved by elites and that only technocratic manipulations by gifted minds at every important station of life can keep chaos away, Eliot's unfriendly response draws upon one of his two definitions of culture—culture "as a whole way of life"—and he says that the idea of elites posits "an atomic view of society."

Raymond Williams has seen how hostile Eliot must necessarily be to such atomicist thinking, and has himself endorsed Eliot's recognition that the doctrine of elites, implying as it does "a radical transformation of society," presents that society with innumerable dangers. Not only would such a society quickly become functionally authoritarian, but it would also possess "a kind of Utopian sanction, which makes criticism difficult or impossible."[10]

These seem legitimate criticisms insofar as they derive from a theory positing a "whole way of life." But Eliot's antagonism to elites goes much further than this. When he speaks with anxious foreboding of a "radical transformation of society," he carries in his mind the expectation that Mannheim's elites would bring about a further development of the culture in organic complexity: "culture at a more conscious level, but still the same culture" (NTDC 110). This would seem perfectly acceptable—until one recognizes that it would also mean, as Eliot makes explicit, a lack of those contacts and mutual influences "at a less conscious level, which are perhaps even more important than ideas" (NTDC 110). Mannheim would understand culture as something open to rational investigation, but Eliot would contend that rational investigation is precisely the wrong tool. Cerebration is not enough; perhaps plumbing the chthonic depths of a culture through religion can be. Living culture is the only way to understand it. Thus we are drawn back, slowly but surely, to Eliot's devotion to consciousness negated, to the unconscious absorption of society by self, self by society. All does gradually become One, just as in *Four Quartets*.

This implicit devotion to the unconscious life is indeed surprising for a man apparently so hostile to some of D. H. Lawrence's celebrations of the unconscious life. Eliot's sour comments on education, the customary panacea of the liberal-minded, point out the absurdity of any artificial means to induce or transmit culture. Too much talk about education, in fact, can create problems where none before existed: "Those who are conscious of their lack of

[10] *Culture and Society, 1780-1950* (New York: Doubleday, 1960), p. 257.

education are discontented, if they cherish ambitions to excel in occupations for which they are not qualified" (NTDC 176). With discontent comes dislocation and, once again, the disintegration of culture.

With so many contagions ready to infect culture, Eliot seems apprehensive of any cure that would inadvertently heighten consciousness. In his solicitude for culture, and for cultural unity (things that sometimes seem to him too frail to survive), his only recourse is to prescribe something the mere prescription of which can only raise our consciousness: "The unity with which I am concerned must be largely unconscious" (NTDC 125). But one cannot be told to be unconscious without thereby becoming more conscious.

Eliot does allow, however, for the existence of one active form of consciousness within the society. That special exemption is the aristocracy. Classes can be characterized by their respective holds on consciousness; certain classes preside over society with a consciousness virtually unrestricted, and others operate with a consciousness greatly diminished. "It is important to remember," he says, "that we should not consider the upper levels as possessing *more* culture than the lower, but as representing a more conscious culture" (NTDC 121). Thus are higher and lower degrees of consciousness controlled, the end being the total stabilization of society. Class structure is not preserved out of anything so sentimental as nostalgia, but because such structure alone can guarantee that those on top will know each other intimately and will therefore be able to resist any tendency to isolation and lack of continuity, such as the "atomic" elites would suffer. Consciousness, in other words, will reside in that one special place where it can exert a maximum of control, with the least interference from any parties hostile to it or from any groups whose sudden advent to their own kind of heightened consciousness would invite general disunity. Consciousness, as much for Eliot as for Marx, is one index to society and its makeup. For Marx, however, it is the inevitable result of society's economic relationships. For Eliot, it is a property, a possession, of one particular group within society, and it is transmitted to other groups only at great risk of being impoverished, and endangering the fragile wellbeing of the entire social enterprise.

As a corollary of this, it may be said that culture is the exclusive preserve of the class that controls it and that, under peril of vulgarization, must prevent it from spreading. Although other cultural life may exist, there is little doubt that, since the bourgeoisie and the aristocracy are nearest the regions of real *political* power the culture they share will have a primacy denied to the culture of other classes. Moreover, one essential condition of preserving the quality of the culture of the minority is "that it should continue to be a minority culture" (NTDC 184). When Eliot speaks, then, of his governing elite, and says that "a greater responsibility would be inherited by those who inherited special advantages, and in whom self-interest, and interest for the sake of their families ('a stake in the country') should cohere with public spirit" (NTDC 159), we know that we are once again witnessing the way in which political power and cultural control are wedded in Eliot's eyes. This system might be described as *noblesse oblige, a fortiori.* Those who, as he decorously puts it, have "a stake in the country," are precisely those privileged with "the higher consciousness" in cultural matters.[11]

It should be obvious, then, as this special "exemption" of the aristocracy indicates, that two contrary forces are alive at once in Eliot's thinking. One stresses the wholeness, the homogeneity, of culture. The other emphasizes the separateness of cultural elements. Culture may be "a whole way of life," but its constituent

[11] One is reminded here of Christopher Caudwell's trenchant paraphrase of this idea: "The rulers are free in the measure of their consciousness. Therefore the exercise of art becomes more and more their exclusive prerogative, reflecting their aspirations and desires." *Illusion and Reality* (New York: International Publishers, 1937), p. 42. But perhaps a more realistic, down-to-earth appraisal of Eliot's thinking here is provided by E. M. Forster: "One has a feeling at moments that the Muses are connected not so much with Apollo as with the oldest country families. One feels, moreover, that there is never all this talk about tradition until it has ceased to exist, and that Mr. Eliot, like Henry James, is romanticizing the land of his adoption." *Abinger Harvest* (London: Edward Arnold, 1936), p. 111.

parts would do well to stand at a good distance from each other. Political management is not to be considered the common concern of all those involved in the society, but is the special prerogative of one group. That Eliot thus recommends a rather atomic and undemocratic social structure is, for all its irony in the context of his disagreement with Mannheim, perfectly in keeping with his second definition of culture: "that which makes life worth living." Only special prerogatives and special controls, we see, can make life worth living.

But even such class-oriented and authoritarian principles are themselves undercut by one of Eliot's most devastating admissions. Culture, as it turns out, exerts as much force upon its elite as that elite exerts upon it. The explanation of this surprising reciprocity lies, as one would by now expect, in "consciousness." As Eliot says, "the culture of which we are wholly conscious is never the whole of culture: the effective culture is that which is directing the activities of those who are manipulating that which they *call* culture" (NTDC 184).

Thus we return, by a sinuous process of reasoning on Eliot's part, to the central fact about his diagnosis of our situation: that diagnosis necessarily reveals and reinforces an almost total social paralysis. Even the governing elite and those possessed of the maximum consciousness can have but little effect in shaping bodies so refractory as culture and society. Whatever the blights on the existing landscape—hierarchies of power and powerlessness, perpetually warring classes, urban racial tension, an unsettled younger generation, and torpid religious sects—it is a landscape for which Eliot would argue. In defending it in his own oblique and fitful way, he saw it then (as he would, I think, see it today) as the legacy of all greatness in Western culture, "the highest culture that the world has ever known" (NTDC 106).

Unfortunately, and ironically, the only way he could actually defend such a landscape was to write in its defense, and this he did, as I have argued, with as much energy as his faith would permit. But truly to defend any political system or class structure is to envision the use of power in its behalf. And Eliot eschewed power.

The force thus remaining to him, the force of the written word, is linked with consciousness, however, and we remember that consciousness is linked with the dissolution of culture and the disintegration of classes. *Notes* is a disturbing book because it embodies this fundamental contradiction. For Eliot to wish to restrain consciousness is to draw attention, or to sound alarm, where dumb assent is alone to be desired.

Hence one must agree with Raymond Williams, who, in speaking of Eliot's "fundamental" conservatism, says "it is clear, when the abstractions are translated, that what he recommends is substantially what now exists, socially."[12] But his recommendation is not, as Williams might seem to imply, a mere point of personal preference with Eliot. It is rather the logical consequence of positions set forward with respect to both the definition of society and the response society must make to consciousness. In establishing those positions, he was articulating as clearly as he could a social, not a personal, preference. He sought to defend the common interests of those like himself, not his private interests alone.

Eliot himself recognized that such a defense was inevitably flawed by deep contradictions, such as the one noted above. Throughout *Notes*, he attempts to resolve this contradiction, as before, by claiming that he is "pre-political" and that he occupies a station beyond questions of power. He merely "studies" political phenomena, but nowhere incites to action. He supports this modesty by, among other things, two epigraphs. The first is from Lord Acton: "I think our studies ought to be all but purposeless. They want to be pursued with chastity like mathematics." The second is from Samuel Johnson (on George Lyttleton): "Politics did not, however, so much engage him as to withhold his thoughts from things of more importance."

In 1955, some years after *Notes*, he returned to the same hope that he could write, could talk about politics, could defend in his own way the status quo, and could do so without fear of supporting either consciousness or the deployment of power. He then said that he was "preoccupied in penetrating to the core of the matter, in trying to arrive at the truth and to set it forth, with-

12 Williams, p. 258.

out too much hope, without ambition to alter the immediate course of affairs, and without being downcast or defeated when nothing appears to ensue."[13] The halfheartedness of all this is striking. If *The Idea of a Christian Society* views power (the only means to social change) as corrupt and therefore useless, *Notes* attempts to say that consciousness itself is corrupt and will inevitably lead to chaos. But nothing at all is said about the enormous constraints that must be brought into play if both power and consciousness are to be nullified and if society is to survive as Eliot would wish. Consciousness and power, indivisibly wedded, will always have their own gradual and absolutely compelling way. Trying to constrain both consciousness and power is like trying to fight against the waves of the sea. But Eliot lacks the vigor of Cuchulain, or even the curmudgeonly zeal of more steadfast political reactionaries. Thus, although his thought is momentarily invigorated by Mannheim's threatening arguments, his demeanor, one of quietude and resignation, joins with his class bias to guarantee his affinity with "dark-age attitudes." By his own kind of transcendent lassitude, he is absorbed into a class of people that wills no change, sees all progress as hostile, and would return to a state of affairs (usually imaginary), in which the restless motion of men and of their minds toward greater awareness and liberation would be stilled. Thus the reactionary impulse, whether or not he so desires, everywhere guides his arguments to their forbidding final implications.

Simone de Beauvoir has described the modern reactionary thinker in a way that sheds some light on Eliot and on his defense of a certain social order: "Gloomy or arrogant, he is the man who says no; his real assurances are all negative. He says no to the 'modern world,' no to the future, in other words, to the living action of the world: but he knows that the world will prevail over him."[14]

The knowledge that the world will indeed prevail over him is

---

[13] Eliot, *The Literature of Politics, A Lecture Delivered at a C.P.C. Literary Luncheon* (London: Conservative Political Centre, 1955), pp. 21-22.

[14] Simone de Beauvoir, "La pensée de droit, aujourd'hui," in *Privilèges* (Paris: Éditions Gallimard, 1955), p. 199. The translation is my own.

the most profound knowledge Eliot possesses. It serves, as it must all Christians, to drain the blood and vigor from all their worldly pronouncements, their designs and ambitions, their schemes and hostilities. The landscape at which they are thus left, singly, to stare is pure, bleak, and empty.

Notes towards the Definition of Culture represents, I think, the climax of Eliot's career as a writer concerned with political problems. During the last fifteen years of his life Eliot was satisfied to shore up in minor ways the positions established in *Criterion* and in his three principal political and cultural studies.

A patient exploration of the political attitudes revealed in these positions will show that two strong and absolutely contradictory forces were at work in Eliot's mind. The first urged him to attend to the reasons why the social order he wished to defend seemed about to collapse; the second urged him to turn away from all such mundane considerations. The first explains why politics fascinated him, almost obsessed him, engaging his mind in matters his poetry often seems powerless to touch. The second explains why his responses to politics could never be completely political in any ordinary sense.

The interaction in Eliot's mind between these two forces dictates the strange, repetitive oscillation of his political engagements: beginning in fascination, they changed first to disgust, then to repudiation, then to transcendence. The transcendence would eventually give way to fascination again, and so on.

An exploration of Eliot's political attitudes will also reveal three central concerns: the first of these is an aversion to the *familiarity* of all political thought, whether of the right or the left. The second is an aversion to political *power* and the corruptions it involves. The third is an aversion to political *consciousness*. Eliot evaluated these concerns variously at various times during his life. From an early emphasis on the first, he grew into a greater awareness of the importance of both the second and the third, and was to end by conferring immense importance on the third.

Eliot's plea against consciousness, ending as it did his involvement in the affairs of society and in politics, remains his most interesting and significant gesture. It recognizes, directly and radically, one great force of politics, and does so in a manner much more cogent than his earlier plea against power. Eliot's development, from the early comments in *Criterion* to his late statements in *Notes towards the Definition of Culture*, reveals a progress toward discovering the ultimate springs of political activity—first power, then consciousness. He saw quite clearly that without consciousness, the kinds of political development he opposed would be less likely to occur.

This realization on his part can help explain his attitudes toward fascism and toward social reversion. Power for the sake of power, devoid of anything approaching full consciousness, is at the root of fascism. But Eliot abjured both power and consciousness and, in so doing, negated not only fascism, but all contemporary ideology. Moreover, he ruled out the idea that any earlier, more idyllic, political arrangement could satisfy him. Any such arrangement would possess the seeds of consciousness and would therefore soon grow into a stage of greater awareness. He had to settle, then, for a thorough scorn of the direction in which the world was headed, and a faint hope for stasis—for an ideal society that would never change and, severely limited in consciousness, would never permit its members even to imagine change. Not only did Eliot want to remove consciousness, which colors and informs all political action, from the political arena, but he also wanted to introduce faith, just as Maurras had introduced it, to make sure that all ideologies, save the favored one, could be classed as "heresies."

Faith, for Eliot, was less a positive doctrine than a means by which he could retire from all conflict. Searching throughout his career not for a middle way, but for an escape from all confines, he found in faith something appropriate to his wish to be both inaccessible and silent. Faith could simply be announced, not explained, and could at the same time reduce politics to the utterly trivial or the outright heretical.

As a consequence, a cloak of such anonymity (or "invisibility," as Hugh Kenner has called it) is thrown around Eliot that we can be sure of only one thing: from within the cloak this fallen age, his age and ours, has been absolutely condemned.

Conclusion

We may now return to the discomfiture experienced in reading Pound at his most wrathful or Eliot at his most intolerant. Let us examine this discomfiture—especially as it is felt by liberals—more closely.

The visions of order embraced by Pound and Eliot confirm the notion that a search for unity, for a means whereby the many can become the One, characterizes the work of many of the most influential writers of our time. That is what a certain kind of modern "image" is all about: a way of stopping the senseless flux, of finding wholeness in the tumult. Factitious or not, such an image serves to stabilize a world that would otherwise seem wholly threatening in its volatility, in its lurchings toward total breakdown. Frank Kermode observes that Pound and Eliot (along with Yeats, T. E. Hulme, and others) imposed such images upon history in order to create a stability of "unity, indissociability." For one of them, Anglo-Catholicism was inseparable from royalism and classicism. For the other, Social Credit was inseparable from faith in the bounty of nature, from Ovidian multiplicity, Il Duce, and the struggle against the Jews. The strengths of imaginative verbal autonomy would stave off the chaos impending because of middle-class democracy, because of all the leveling elements of the age.[1]

Yet these stays against confusion yielded a design for the age to which the age failed to conform. Adhering to the design in the

[1] I am indebted to Professor Yosal Rogat of Stanford University for discussing this idea with me.

face of this failure may now seem to us either presumptuous or oddly heroic. In either case, it must be seen as a great modern instance of the display of authority, inherent in which is always the danger of reliance on the authoritarian. Thus the total configuration is first imagined, and then, if means become available, imposed. The readiness to impose was veiled and sporadic in Eliot and naked and steady in Pound. It can startle and dismay readers who at first do not recognize some of the darker implications of an imaginative superintendence of the world.

Alike in spurning the all-pervading mediocrity they felt democracy had fostered, the two poets agreed on other matters as well: the advantages of a prescriptive, rather than a descriptive, reading of cultural history; the superiority of the artist-pioneer in the consciousness of a generation; the advantages of having that consciousness be local, particular, and rooted in a specific geography. If the vulgar masses ever ascended to power, and total enfranchisement were extended to the middle-class democratic man, things would surely worsen.

Other similarities between the two poets are evident. Neither was really able to withstand societal tensions. Eliot sought God and meditated on a social order free of divisive strains. Pound ransacked history for the one great error to blame for the myriad dysfunctions of society. Having found it, he focused single-mindedly upon it, and lashed his age for not correcting it. And he was as eager for a world free of the oppositions between abstract ideas as he was for a world free of the alien, the Jew, the "other." No more than Eliot did he have the capacity to engage intellectual complexity and deep contradictions. Eliot entered his plea for an order of life simplified to almost feudalistic dimensions; Pound adhered to a metaphysics composed only of those elementary mechanical means whose functioning would assure social perfection. Their supreme confidence reflects their common ability to ignore what was around them. Neither Pound, alone with a lucid vision of civilization purged of usury, nor Eliot, alone with God, felt any impetus to move with other men. Convinced that they had seen through much and had alone defied the general crassness, they held forth. Toward literature and toward society they held the same attitude, an aristocratic attitude that would write off a considerable number of people with no more hesitation than it would a pile of bad books.

Because they had proceeded so far with ways of thinking that repudiated conflict, Pound and Eliot could do little more than practice the exclusiveness, and the cruel reductive mastery, that alone could produce the kind of wholeness they wanted. Fusing aesthetic and political sensibilities, they found themselves wanting a world from which a great many things had been swept away. It is in this light that some of their chilling hostilities and prejudices should be seen. The world, once cleansed, was to reveal to Eliot an unbroken vista of Christian piety and agrarian simplicity; to Pound a Provençal landscape in which a generous nature would give forth riches, and poets their music, unhindered. In dedicating their minds to such prospects, and in finding everything else a vulgar counterfeit, however, they turned away from what another poet, perhaps wiser in his idiosyncrasies than they in theirs, had called "the uncontrollable mystery on the bestial floor."[2] Many of the ungovernable complexities that the world had to offer they found pathological but otherwise uninteresting. As they demonstrated, the price of a "unified" sensibility can be a remote sensibility.

Thus separated from society, and yet eager to make the strongest impositions on it, they now serve us in a special way. In judging them, we are forced to see how difficult it is for the engaged imagination to make an entry into the world, to dominate circumstance. By the spasmodic involvement and detachment characterizing their own attempts at entry, which took a political form, Pound and Eliot give evidence of the gap separating any subjective consciousness with designs on the world from that world itself. The gap, never to be closed, can be felt by poet and nonpoet alike.

The difficulties of political entry have been recognized for centuries. Plato's *Republic* describes a common human plight in a conversation between Socrates and his pupil. The intelligent man,

[2] W. B. Yeats, "The Magi."

says Socrates, who speaks first here, will not grasp for the material things of this world:

"If he thinks they will destroy the order within him, he will avoid them."
   "If that is his object, he won't enter politics," he [the pupil] said.
   "Oh yes, he will," I replied, "very much so, in the society where he really belongs; but not, I think, in the society where he's born, unless something very extraordinary happens."
   "I see what you mean," he said. "You mean that he will do so in the society which we have been describing and which we have theoretically founded; but I doubt if it will ever exist on earth."
   "Perhaps," I said, "it is laid up as a pattern in heaven, where those who wish can see it and found it in their own hearts. But it doesn't matter whether it exists or ever will exist; it's the only state in whose politics he can take part."[3]

That state, then, in which the intelligent man can enjoy political participation is far removed from the real world of political antagonisms and their resolution. Plato's ancient judgment of the situation has modern implications. We may see in it a way of understanding both Pound's and Eliot's politics, and our agonizing difficulties in judging those politics. For these difficulties are rooted in the same dilemma as the politics themselves: the disjunction between the subjective sensibility seeking to observe and dominate, and the objective weight of real historical situations.

Plato knows and calmly accepts the fact that the disjunction is not to be closed; the intelligent man lives only in his mind. When we turn from the ancient judgment to the modern instance, we are faced with a situation that has ceaselessly commanded attention from observers of every sort: the inability of the private sensibility to escape its own subjectivity. Estranged from the world without, the interior sensibility establishes a cosmos of its own. Exterior circumstances appear crazed, fragmented, and in motion without meaning. Thus we have, for our own examples, Eliot in *Four Quartets* attempting with the frail instrument of language ("Words strain, / Crack and sometimes break, under the burden") to reconcile his inward comprehension with outward reality, and yet rec-

---

[3] *The Republic*, trans. with an Introduction by H. D. P. Lee (Baltimore, Md.: Penguin Books, 1955), p. 369.

ognizing the implicit difficulties of such a task ("every attempt / Is a wholly new start, and a different kind of failure"); or Pound, in the Pisan cantos, writing in solipsistic defense of his isolated memories ("certain images be formed in the mind / to remain there / *formato locho*") now buried under the collapse of history. In both cases, the impossibility of fusion between inward consciousness and outward event is distressing in the extreme.

It is dramatically distressing in Pound's case. He was, among American poets, the greatest of the modern instigators, the most dynamic and the most resourceful. His energies, acknowledged by all who had encountered him, were the single strongest catalyst in the development of a new literary sensibility. New programs, campaigns, isms, provocations, and encouragements: he was involved in them all. And he espoused fascism when he saw it—or at least its leader in Italy—as something new. His influence had transformed the new poetry; he presumed it could transform the new politics as well. But Mussolini was not so tractable as, for instance, the *Waste Land* manuscript. Italian fascism collapsed, and Pound's inward sensibility could deal only haphazardly with the chaos Pound perceived all around him.

The fusion between the inner and outer worlds was no more complete for Eliot. But he eased the agony of his problem by the security of his assimilated relationship to England. He sought to create, in his mind, an established English order that would be a shield against the exterior confusion he could not tolerate. That order would embrace his faith in the English church and the English throne; it would rest on his idealized structuring of a state whose inhabitants would maintain a "direct relation to the soil, or the sea, or the machine." In meditating upon the perfection of his imagined paradigm, he was safely held back from the reality that threatened always to coarsen it. Pursuing a penitential and ecclesiastical consciousness, he challenged the development of other forms of consciousness. Fearing the chaos that would erupt were most people to achieve a fully conscious understanding of their lives and social positions, he who had liberated the poetic imagination chose to liberate nothing else. In the end, Eliot attained a position from which matters of this world, preserved at a distance, were made to seem everlastingly inconsequential.

The paths taken by Pound and Eliot have been pursued by poetic travelers before. These paths had been precisely described in the 1930's by Edmund Wilson in his well-known comparison of Axel and Rimbaud:

> If one chooses the first of these, the way of Axel, one shuts oneself up in one's own private world, cultivating one's private fantasies, encouraging one's private manias, ultimately preferring one's absurdest chimeras to the most astonishing contemporary realities, ultimately mistaking one's chimeras for realities. If one chooses the second, the way of Rimbaud, one tries to leave the twentieth century behind—to find the good life in some country where modern manufacturing methods and modern democratic institutions do not present any problems to the artist because they haven't arrived.[4]

Pound and Eliot, of course, wished to go beyond disillusionment and hopelessness. They wanted to travel to the public world and there find their speaking voices. But their journeys ultimately proved circular and always brought them back to their inner world again. There, the two found themselves alone with private manias, or with lonely struggles to leave the twentieth century behind.

Wilson, who by turns deplored and praised the achievement of the Symbolists and their followers, and who hoped that future writers would learn much from them without succumbing totally to their influence, envisioned a literature that would reconcile the individual to his society. His vision, however, was not to be realized. As a patrician 1930's liberal fascinated by revolutionary possibilities, he hoped for a union of the technical literary possibilities of high culture and the forward progress of society. But the union was not forthcoming. By the end of the decade, politics had become monstrous; global war raged; totalitarianism grew with the terrible strength of a cancer. Wilson's liberal hopes were without foundation in a world dominated by Hitler and Stalin.

---

[4] Edmund Wilson, *Axel's Castle: A Study of the Imaginative Literature of 1870-1930* (New York: Scribner's, 1931), p. 287.

His plight can prove instructive to us. We must acknowledge the difficulties experienced by contemporary liberal and scholarly opinion in the presence of Pound's and Eliot's achievements. Robbed of certitude by seeing political absolutism on both right and left during this century, that opinion is paralyzed and incapable of choice. It is enclosed in its own kind of solipsism. Entry into the world of profound political consequence is as difficult for today's liberal as it was for Pound or Eliot. In this important sense, it is no matter that Pound and Eliot had fears of certain classes and ethnic groups, shrank from intellectual complexity, dreaded the fullest development of human consciousness. No matter that they added a cruel edge to the doctrine of *épater le bourgeois*, or that their apparent mastery over art and life was based on intolerance. What matters is that they reached a plateau of structured belief that liberals may desire, but cannot attain. The step from being authorities in poetry and criticism to thinking well of authoritarianism in general is the most important step Pound and Eliot took. That they failed of other steps, and nowhere found the important reconciliations they desired, is clear. That first step, however, is one closed to liberal intellectuals, who, scrupulously concerned with political power and its abuses, live at odds with its use for their own direct benefit. Driven even further from a reconciliation of life and politics than Pound and Eliot, liberals will continue to be haunted by the two poets' example. And uneasy judges will always judge partially.

Appendixes

Pound and Eliot: The Alliance

Although Pound and Eliot have been shown here as having a remarkable kinship in simultaneously influencing and fending off their age, they were not wholly of one mind. Their long friendship was riven relatively early by the same forces, among them the political, by which they are today to be defined. As Eliot, looking back, once put it: "There did come a point, of course, at which difference of outlook and belief became too wide; or it may have been distance and different environment; or it may have been both."[1] Pound, summarizing their initial agreement, noted the same disagreement: "at a particular date in a particular room, two authors, neither engaged in picking the other's pocket, decided that the dilutation of *vers libre*, Amygism, Lee Masterism, general floppiness had gone too far and that some counter-current must be set going. . . . Results: Poems in Mr Eliot's *second* volume, not contained in his first ('Prufrock,' *Egoist*, 1917), also 'H. S. Mauberley.' Divergence later."[2]

This divergence can best be described as Pound or Eliot might himself have chosen to describe it: by direct citation of the particular, by an echoing of history, by a flow of related quotations. Let us allow the two voices once again to speak for themselves with a minimum of textual assistance.

I. RETROSPECTION

Pound, 1925: I pointed out . . . in the beginning that there was no use of two of us butting a stone wall; that he wd. never be as hefty a battering

---

[1] "Ezra Pound," *Poetry*, 68 (Sept. 1946): 335.

[2] "Harold Monro," in *Polite Essays* (London: Faber and Faber, 1937), p. 14. First published in *Criterion*, 11 (July 1932).

ram as I was, nor as explosive as [Wyndham] Lewis, and that he'd better try a more oceanic and fluid way of sapping the foundations.[3]

Eliot, 1949: I think of a friend who, in the early days, was as much concerned with the encouragement and improvement of the work of unknown writers in whom he discerned talent, as with his own creative work; who formulated, for a generation of poets, the principles of good writing most needful for their time; who tried to bring these writers together for their reciprocal benefit; who, in the face of many obstacles, saw that their writings were published; saw that they were reviewed somewhere by critics who could appreciate them. . . . To him, several other authors, since famous, have owed a great deal.[4]

Pound, 1957: It is perhaps time to interrupt the flow of legend before exaggeration swells much farther. Mr. Eliot had already written *Prufrock* and other works of considerable interest before arriving at the shadowed portals of 5, Holland Place Chambers. He either disapproved of some of my practices or was puzzled as to why I committed them. We found certain points of agreement.[5]

Eliot, 1959: He was a marvelous critic because he didn't try to turn you into an imitation of himself. He tried to see what you were trying to do.[6]

Pound, 1962: Eliot and I started diverging from the beginning. . . . We started disagreeing about a number of things from the time we met. We also agreed on a few things and I suppose both of us must have been right about something or other.[7]

II. AFFINITY

Eliot, 1917: Eeldrop [Eliot] was a sceptic, with a taste for mysticism, and Appleplex [Pound] a materialist with a leaning toward scepticism. . . . Eeldrop was learned in theology, and . . . Appleplex studied the physical and biological sciences.

There was a common motive which led Eeldrop and Appleplex thus to separate themselves from time to time, from the fields of their daily

[3] As quoted in Donald Gallup, "T. S. Eliot & Ezra Pound: Collaborators in Letters," *Atlantic Monthly*, 225 (Jan. 1970): 60. I am much indebted to Gallup's extensive gathering of quotations in this article.

[4] "Leadership and Letters," *Milton Bulletin*, 12 (Feb. 1949), as quoted in Gallup, p. 49.

[5] "Mr. Eliot and Mr. Pound," Letter to *Times Literary Supplement*, London, 2, 891 (July 26, 1957): 457.

[6] "T. S. Eliot: An Interview," [Donald Hall], *Paris Review*, 1959, as reprinted in *Writers at Work, Second Series* (New York: Viking, 1963), p. 96.

[7] "Ezra Pound: An Interview," [Donald Hall], *Paris Review*, 1962, as reprinted *ibid.*, p. 48.

employments and their ordinary social activities. Both were endeavoring to escape not the commonplace, respectable or even the domestic, but the two well pigeonholed, too taken-for-granted, too highly systematized areas.[8]

Eliot, 1946: It was in 1922 that I placed before him in Paris the manuscript of a sprawling, chaotic poem called *The Waste Land* which left his hands, reduced to about half its size, in the form in which it appears in print. I should like to think that the manuscript, with the suppressed passages, had disappeared irrecoverably: yet on the other hand, I should wish the blue penciling on it to be preserved as irrefutable evidence of Pound's critical genius.[9]

Pound to Eliot, 1921. Subject: Completion of *The Waste Land:* Complimenti, you bitch. I am wracked by the seven jealousies, and cogitating an excuse for always exuding my deformative secretions in my own stuff, and never getting an outline.[10]

Eliot, 1922: I sincerely consider Ezra Pound the most important living poet in the English language.[11]

Eliot to Pound, 1923. Dedication of *The Waste Land:* For Ezra Pound *il miglior fabbro.*

Eliot, 1923: I have to keep an attitude of discipleship to him (as indeed I ought). . . .[12]

III. DIVERGENCE

Eliot, 1928: I confess that I am seldom interested in what [Pound] is saying, but only in the way he says it.[13]

Pound, 1930: Mr. Eliot who is at times an excellent poet and who has arrived at the supreme Eminence among English critics largely through disguising himself as a corpse once asked in the course of an amiable article what 'I believed.'

Having a strong disbelief in abstract and general statement as a means of conveying one's thought to others I have for a number of years an-

---

[8] "Eeldrop and Appleplex, I," *Little Review*, 4 (May 1917), as reprinted in Margaret Anderson, ed., *The Little Review Anthology* (New York: Hermitage House, 1953), p. 103.

[9] "Ezra Pound," *Poetry*, 68 (Sept. 1946): 330.

[10] D. D. Paige, ed., *The Letters of Ezra Pound, 1907-1941* (New York: Harcourt, Brace, 1950), p. 169.

[11] As quoted in Noel Stock, *The Life of Ezra Pound* (New York: Pantheon Books, 1970), p. 249.

[12] As quoted in Gallup, p. 61.

[13] "Isolated Superiority," *Dial*, 84 (Jan. 1928): 6.

swered such questions by telling the enquirer to read Confucius and Ovid.[14]

Eliot, 1934, *After Strange Gods:* If you do away with [moral and spiritual] struggle, and maintain that by tolerance, benevolence, inoffensiveness, and a redistribution or increase of purchasing power, combined with a devotion, on the part of an élite, to Art, the world will be as good as anyone could require, then you must expect human beings to become more and more vaporous. This is exactly what we find of the society which Mr. Pound puts in Hell, in his *Draft of XXX Cantos.* . . . If you do not distinguish between individual responsibility and circumstances in Hell, between essential Evil and social accidents, then the Heaven (if any) implied will be equally trivial and accidental.[15]

Pound, 1934: Mr. Eliot's book [*After Strange Gods*] is pernicious in that it distracts the reader from a vital problem (economic justice); it implies that we need more religion, but does not specify the nature of that religion; all the implications are such as to lead the reader's mind to a fog. . . . He is in fact treating the sickness of the age. His diagnosis is wrong. His remedy is an irrelevance.[16]

Eliot, 1934: Mr. Pound does not make clear to me what *is* the peculiar malady of my logic. I should like to know. Naturally, *if* my diagnosis is wrong, my remedy is likely to be an irrelevance.

I had no intention of distracting my readers from the vital problem of economics; and Mr. Pound's objection seems to depend upon the assumption that this is the *only* vital problem.[17]

Pound, 1934: If Mr. Eliot weren't head and shoulders above the rank of the organised pifflers, and if he didn't amply deserve his position as recognized head of English literary criticism I would not be wasting time, typing-ribbon and postage, to discuss his limitations at all.[18]

Eliot, 1938: [Pound] has given thirty-odd years of close study to his art, and . . . at the very least, occupies a high place in the poetical history of a generation.[19]

Pound, 1939: In so far as Mr. Eliot's letch after God, or his groping

[14] "Credo," *Front* (Albuquerque, N.M.), 1 (Dec. 1930): 11, as quoted in Stock, p. 295.

[15] *After Strange Gods: A Primer of Modern Heresy* (New York: Harcourt, Brace, 1934), pp. 46-47.

[16] "Mr. Eliot's Quandaries," *New English Weekly*, 4 (March 29, 1934): 559.

[17] "Mr. T. S. Eliot's Quandaries," *New English Weekly*, 4 (Apr. 12, 1934): 622.

[18] "Mr. Eliot's Solid Merit," *New English Weekly*, 5 (July 12, 1934): 297.

[19] "On a Recent Piece of Criticism," *Purpose*, 10 (Apr./June 1938): 90-94, as quoted in Gallup, p. 62.

towards right theology, is a desire for a central concept it is constructive and vital, it is a move toward the totalitarian . . . a revolt against European schizophrenia.[20]

Pound, 1942: Eliot, in this book [*After Strange Gods*], has not come through uncontaminated by the Jewish poison.

Until a man purges himself of this poison he will never achieve understanding. It is a poison that lost no time seeping into European thought. Already by the time of Scotus Erigena it had begun to make a bog of things. Grosseteste thinks straight when his thought derives from European sources. And the best poets before Dante were Ghibelline.

To want to settle ethical relationships, i.e., to settle the ethical problem without confusing it with the metaphysical, is quite a different matter. In the essays Eliot falls into many non sequiturs. Until he succeeds in detaching the Jewish from the European elements of his particular variety of Christianity he will never find the right formula. Not a jot or tittle of the hebraic alphabet can pass into the text without danger of contaminating it.

Cabbala, black magic, and the whole caboodle. Church against Empire, Protestantism against the unity of the Mother Church, always destroying the true religion, destroying the mnemonic and commemorative symbols.

It is amusing, after so many years, to find that my disagreement with Eliot is a religious disagreement, each of us accusing the other of Protestantism.[21]

IV. RECONCILIATION

Eliot, 1946: If I am doubtful about some of the *Cantos*, it is not that I find any poetic decline in them. . . . In the *Cantos* there is an increasing defect of communication . . . apparent . . . for instance, whenever he mentions Martin Van Buren. . . . But the craftsman up to this moment— and I have in mind certain recent and unpublished cantos—has never failed. There is nobody living who can write like this: how many can be named, who can write half so well?[22]

Eliot, 1954: Mr. Pound is more responsible for the XXth Century revolution in poetry than is any other individual.[23]

---

[20] "The 'Criterion' Passes," *British Union Quarterly*, 3 (Apr./June 1939): 68.
[21] *A Visiting Card* (London: Peter Russell, 1952), p. 22. This is the first English-language edition of Pound's *Carta da Visita* (Rome: Edizioni di Lettere d'Oggi, 1942).
[22] "Ezra Pound," *Poetry*, 68 (Sept. 1946): 335-36.
[23] Introduction to *Literary Essays of Ezra Pound* (Norfolk, Conn.: New Directions, 1954), p. xi.

Pound, 1965: [Eliot's] was the true Dantescan voice—not honoured enough, and deserving more than I ever gave him.

... Let him rest in peace. I can only repeat, but with the urgency of 50 years ago: READ HIM.[24]

A religious disagreement? So Pound thought it to be, "each of us accusing the other of Protestantism." But that Protestantism should be understood as a heresy that also held them together and defined them, a mutual deviation from visions of order that both men embraced. And those visions of order embraced, in turn, politics.

[24] "For T. S. E.," in Allen Tate, ed., *T. S. Eliot, The Man and His Work* (New York: Dell, 1966), p. 89.

Ezra Pound Speaking:
A Broadcast from Rome

The following text is an attempt to reproduce, in its entirety, Pound's shortwave broadcast from Rome for March 15, 1942. In subject, theme, and degree of argumentative coherence, this broadcast is representative of the 125 such broadcasts made by Pound between December 7, 1941, and July 25, 1943, and monitored by the Foreign Broadcast Intelligence Service (FBIS) of the United States government. It was largely on the basis of these broadcasts, some of which are specifically named in the bill, that Pound was indicted for treason on July 26, 1943.

Pound's mind is focused here, with incantatory fervor and its customary concern for specific detail, on the question of the health of one national culture, the English. The mechanical rigidity of mind that I have noted as characteristic of Pound is apparent. Also apparent, of course, is his anti-Semitism, more extreme in these speeches than anywhere else. Pound here mixes, as he did throughout his life, the simplistic with the recondite, the vulgar ethnic diatribe with the abstruse historical interpretation.

This Appendix is based on two sources: a recording and a typed transcript of the broadcast, both made by the FBIS. (Copies of the tapes of many broadcasts are available at the United States National Archives to anyone professing scholarly or educational interest in them; and the transcripts, on microfilm at the Library of Congress, are available to anyone.) I have also compared this text with the script prepared by Pound for the broadcasts and now part of his papers at the Beinecke Library, Yale University. Collating the transcript and the recording produces a better text than using either of them alone, but still an imperfect record of what Pound said that day. The transcript is laced with errors; those monitoring Pound regularly misheard him. The recording is also imperfect; the shortwave transmission was not free of static, and the recording techniques were flawed. Nor does Pound's script answer all the textual problems, for Pound sometimes wrote one thing and said another. However, it has served to clear up some passages that were neither audible on the tape nor present in the FBIS transcript. Annotations of some possibly unfamiliar terms and names are provided.

[Announcers:]
One of our special lecturers will now read a talk entitled "England."

The Italian Radio, acting in accordance with the Fascist policy of intellectual freedom and free expression of opinion by those who are qualified to hold it, following the tradition of Italian hospitality, has offered Dr. Ezra Pound the use of the microphone twice a week. It is understood that he will not be asked to say anything whatsoever that goes against his conscience, or anything incompatible with his duties as a citizen of the United States of America.

[Pound:]*
Parlando da Roma. Ezra Pound speaking from Rome. *Parlando da Roma.*

The enemy is *das Leihkapital.* Your enemy is *das Leihkapital.* The international wandering loan capital. Your enemy is not Germany; your enemy is money on loan, and it would be better for you to be infected with typhus and dysentery and Bright's Disease than to be infected with this blindness, which prevents you from understanding how you are undermined, how you are ruined. The big Jew is so bound up with his loan capital that no one is able to unscramble the omelet. It would be better for you to retire to Derbyshire and defy New Jerusalem; better for you to retire to Gloucester and find one spot that is England, than to go on fighting for Jewry and ignoring the process.

It is an outrage that any clean lad from the country—I suppose that there still are a few English lads from the country—it is an outrage that any clean lad from the country or any nice young man from the suburbs should be expected to die for Victor Sassoon.[1] It is an outrage that even a drunken footman's by-blow should be asked to die for Sassoon.

* Pound's speech Copyright © 1973 by the Estate of Ezra Pound.

[1] Sir Victor Ellice Sassoon (1881-1961), a fifth-generation descendant of the original founder of a family of Jewish merchants, philanthropists, and men of letters. The Sassoons have been called the Rothschilds of the East because of their origin in Baghdad. Like his forebears, Victor Sassoon con-

As to your Empire, it was not always won by clean fighting; but however you got it, you did for a time more or less justify keeping it on the ground that you exported good government, or better government than the natives would have had without England. But you let in the Jew and the Jew rotted your Empire, and you yourselves outjewed the Jew. Your allies in your victimized holdings are the *bunya*,[2] that is, the moneylender. You stand for usury, and above metal usury you have built up bank usury, 60 percent as against 30 and 40 percent, and by that you will not be saved.

Corrupting the whole earth, you have lost yourselves to yourselves, and the big Jew—not the little Jew—that big Jew has rotted every nation he has wormed into. A millstone. Well, an exceptionally good swimmer might conceivably be cast into the sea with a millstone tied round his neck; he might perhaps untie it. If he were a Scotsman he would remember his jackknife before being thrown overboard. You seem to remember nothing.

It were better to be infected with typhus.

And as to this federal union or Jewnion, there is no question of race in Streit's proposition. It is, as proposed, a union of slaves under Jewry, offered by liars and abettors of thieves. You have stolen land from your late allies, and land slips from your control. The only conquests Britain and Roosevelt have made are conquests from their alleged allies. Franklin Delano can swipe all South America, Canada, and Australia, and ruin the United States of America while he is doing it, and what's that to you? It is not England's salvation.

Will you ever look at the story of empires? You are not even in the mercantile system. You are in a fake mercantile system that is not even mercantile, though it was for a time called mercantile or the mercantilist system. And it was defined as considering that the happiness of a nation consists in the amount of money it owns, and its process was to consist in stealing, welching, pouching the greatest possible amount of money from other nations. That defines the usury system—the only system Anglo-Saxons have known or used in our time, and it will not save you, nor will Judaized Russia, nor will the Kahal,[3] that is, the Jews' Central Committee of Leaders.

What is their system? It is, unvaryingly, cheap goods, sweated out of

---

tributed to the development of industry in India. He was a leader of British Indian Jewry and after 1933 worked strenuously to help refugees from Nazism.

[2] Hindi *bunya*, or *banya*: moneylender.

[3] Hebrew: a Jewish congregation; in Eastern Europe, until the nineteenth century, the organized Jewish community possessing autonomous rights and responsible for taxation.

cheap labor, dung dust hurled on the world and the world conceived as sweatshop. And to hell with the eight-hour day! Down with abundance! It means dumping of sweated goods, sweated goods dumped against any and every nation that pays a just price for labor. That is your ally, your Soviet Jew ally.

And in your path there is a trail of blood and infamy: you bought Hessians to kill your own blood in America; you bought them from a stinking Jew overlord who was in the hands of the Rothschilds.[4] That is history. You stirred up the American savages against your own kin in America. And now Eden and Cripps have called in the Muscovite to burn and destroy all Eastern Europe and kill Finland, for the sake of a stinking Jew's nickel mines.[5] Your infamy is bound up with Judea. You cannot touch a sore or a shame in your Empire, but you find a Mond, a Sassoon, or a Goldsmid.[6]

You have no race left in your government. God knows if it can be found still scattered in England. It *must* be found scattered in England. The white remnants of England, the white remnants of the races of England, must be found and must find a means to cohere. Otherwise you might as well lie down in your graveyards.

You have for years had cheap goods dumped in from Russia. Your alliance with Moscow will bring no relief to that wound. Your Jews have ruined your home manufactures. Loans from the city of London, loans to the Orient, interest paid in cheap cotton goods, loans to the

[4] The House of Rothschild, the most distinguished and powerful dynasty of Jewish financiers and bankers, began with Meyer Amschel Rothschild (1743-1812) in Frankfort.

[5] Sir Anthony Eden (1897-   ), a former Prime Minister of England (1955-57), served as Foreign Minister from 1935 to 1938. Sir Stafford Cripps (1889-1952) became Ambassador to the USSR in 1940 and leader in Commons in 1942. Mining rights to nickel ores in Finland's Petsamo region were leased to the Mond Nickel Company (date not given; *Encyclopedia Britannica*, 1953 ed.).

[6] Alfred Moritz Mond (1868-1930) greatly expanded his father's firm, Brunner, Mond and Co., which became Imperial Chemical Companies. Subsequent to the time of this broadcast, he became first Baron Melchett. He served in Parliament as both a Liberal and a Conservative. Although he was not reared as a Jew, he was frequently the butt of anti-Semitism. He became an ardent Zionist. The reference to Goldsmid is perhaps to an Anglo-Jewish family descended from Aaron Goldsmid (d. 1782). The Goldsmids became prominent financiers during the French Revolutionary wars, and also gained close familiarity with George III and Lord Nelson. Sir Isaac Lyon Goldsmid (1778-1859), who made a large fortune through financing railway construction, became the first professing Jew to receive an English hereditary title.

South American countries, interest paid in beef from the Argentine, meaning the ruin of English grazing.

Now the laws of durable government have been known since the days of King Wan.[7] When empires go to rot, they go to rot for known reasons. *The Times, Telegraph, Manchester Guardian* are there to conceal these reasons. Your press is an infamy, and has been throughout our time. The laws of a durable government have been known from the days of King Wan; and when the Roman Empire, the old Roman Empire, perished, it perished from the same follies that your kikes, your Rothschilds, Beits, Sieffs, Schiffs, and Goldschmidts have squirted into your veins.[8]

While England was still in the old Roman Empire, it started to go down with cheap grain dumped in from Egypt, meaning the ruin of Italian farming. Usury and more usury. That is the answer; that is what rocked the Empire. For two centuries, ever since the brute Cromwell brought them back into England,[9] the kikes have sucked out your vitals. A mild penetration. For a hundred years they have bootlicked your nobility, and now where is your nobility?

You had at least a semblance of control over England; you had, let us say, some influence with the lords of Judea, as long as they wanted your titles. As long as Levy-Levenstein-Lawton wanted to be addressed as Lord Burnham[10] you could turn the worst edge of their avarice. Or,

[7] Wên Wang (1231-1135 B.C.), the title of canonization of Ch'ang, Duke of Chou, known as the Chief of the West. In prison he wrote the *Book of Changes* (*I Ching*).

[8] Beits may refer to Sir Alfred Beit (1853-1906), the South African financier and co-founder, with Cecil Rhodes, of Rhodesia. He was given some help during his career by the Rothschilds. Baron Israel Moses Sieff (1899-   ), British industrialist, Zionist, and philanthropist, was a close friend of Chaim Weizmann, the first president of Israel, and was involved in labors issuing in the Balfour Declaration. He was also chairman (1931-39) of Political and Economic Planning (P.E.P.). The Schiff reference is probably to the prominent American financier and philanthropist Jacob Henry Schiff (1847-1920). A member of the banking firm of Kuhn, Loeb & Co., he became its head in 1885. Many of the most powerful American industrialists of the nineteenth century were financed through his efforts.

[9] Oliver Cromwell, Lord Protector of England (1653-58), was largely responsible for the readmission of Jews to England after their exclusion under Edward I in 1290.

[10] Although he scrambles names here, Pound is probably thinking of Sir Harry Lawson Webster Levy-Lawson, Viscount Burnham (1862-1933), who succeeded his father as owner of *The Daily Telegraph* in 1903, selling it in 1928. He was not a professing Jew.

rather, you could turn it off the upper or huppar clawses and turn it onto the poor, as you did without mercy. But when the same scrougers[11] have moved over to New York City, how will you manage them?

The same bloody-minded extortioners, or their descendants, the same financial houses, the same Rothschilds, who plotted with Sherman and Vandergould[12] to kill the American nation; who betrayed the American nation in the 1860's—head office in London, agents in U.S.A. Well, now the address is altered: main office in Wall Street and Cohen in London.

You send Willie over to spy on us Americans; you send 5,000 usurers' pimps over to Washington and give them special passports—diplomatic passports—to inveigle the United States into your glory games, your plans to get cannon fodder from Idaho and from Iowa to weld your slave collar on Europe.

And this time *you* get dumped into the ash can. You have forgotten your Kipling. Piggy Baldwin had forgotten his cousin if his obscene and treacherous mind ever grasped the meaning of Rudyard's stories.[13] Let me recall one passage. "The Americans," wrote Rudyard, "obligingly slaughtered each other in order that the Czecho-Slovaks might inherit Boston Common." Great pity! Tomorrow is your turn. Damn it all, you slaughtered the flower of England in the Boer War. Then in 1914 in the first three months the best of you went out and got slaughtered—in a Jew's war. The encirclement idea, idea of encirclement, idea that barbarians will provide cannon fodder, with which you can kill Europe.

God knows who saw it then, but it has been seen in the interim. It has been seen only too clearly, and your foul papers, the filth of your newsprint has been subsidized to keep your mind off it. A dirty bit of meat by the name of Gollancz has used the book trade to conceal it.[14]

[11] Pound may mean "scroungers" here, but no *n* sound is audible on the recording.

[12] John Sherman (1823-1900) served as chairman of the United States Senate Finance Committee and as Secretary of the Treasury (1877-81) under President Rutherford B. Hayes after playing a leading role in government finance during Reconstruction. Vandergould might be Pound's conflation of Vanderbilt (Cornelius, 1794-1877) and Gould (Jay, 1836-92), American railroad magnates and speculators. Gould was involved in the gold scheme that caused the Black Friday panic of 1869. But see Pound's *A Visiting Card* (London: Peter Russell, 1952), pp. 10, 12.

[13] Stanley Baldwin, First Earl Baldwin of Bewdley (1867-1947), was Prime Minister of England in the 1920's and 1930's (1923-24; 1924-29; 1935-37). He and Rudyard Kipling were first cousins.

[14] Sir Victor Gollancz (1893-1967) was an English publisher and author;

You have almost no means of communication. When a Brooks Adams writes five volumes that would help you see it, six copies reach England.[15]

You have lost the help of the mind. God knows how the scattered handful of Englishmen still in England can still speak one with another. I see no remedy in your Parliament. I don't mean as Parliament; I mean in the personnel. It is your problem. You do not now even elect your own Parliament. Whether with an election you could get anything, save old dead meat, I do not know. But during the last war a few men had a glimmer of instinct of whatever formula. They called it pacifism. Was it? Oh my, all of 'em I ever met were pugnacious!

Was it an instinct to save the butt end of the race by not fighting? Is there "a race" left in England? Has it any will left to survive? You can carry slaughter to Ireland, but will that save you? I doubt it. Nothing can save you, save a purge. Nothing can save you, save an affirmation that you are English.

Hore-Belisha is not.[16] Isaacs is not.[17] No Sassoon is an Englishman racially. No Rothschild is English, no Streiker is English, no Roosevelt is English, no Baruch, Morgenthau, Cohen, Lehman, Warburg, Kuhn, Kahn, Schiff, Sieff, or Solomon was ever yet born Anglo-Saxon.[18] And it

---

in 1936, with John Strachey and Harold Laski, he established the Left Book Club.

[15] Brooks Adams (1848-1927) was an American historian and the author of *The Law of Civilization and Decay* (1895) and *The Degradation of the Democratic Dogma* (1919).

[16] The British politician Lord Leslie Hore-Belisha (1898-1957) served as financial secretary to the Treasury (1923-34) and Secretary of State for War (1937-40). He resigned from the latter office after being subjected to vigorous attacks, some of them involving anti-Semitism.

[17] The Isaacs family, an American Jewish family prominent in New York City, was founded by Samuel Myer Isaacs, who emigrated to the United States in 1839 from London. It has included philanthropists, rabbis, teachers, and musicians.

[18] Although the recording clearly says "Streiker," the script says "Strakosch"; both references unknown. The Roosevelts, though not Jewish, have nevertheless been the targets of many anti-Semitic attacks. The Baruch, Morgenthau, Lehman, and Warburg families are all prominent American Jewish families. The Baruchs and Morgenthaus have supplied two internationally known figures: Bernard Baruch (1870-1965), stock analyst and advisor to presidents from Woodrow Wilson to Harry Truman, and Henry Morgenthau, Jr. (1897-1967), Secretary of the Treasury (1934-45) and early champion of preparation for American entry into World War II. The Warburgs, a family long active in banking, philanthropy, and the arts, are connected by

is for this filth that you fight. It is for this filth that you have murdered your Empire. It is this filth that elects, selects, elects your politicians. You have lost your tradition. You have not even learned what George Gordon Lord Byron told you. You are, as even that foul rag the *Times* tells you, a little late in making a start. In the year 1942 Anno Domini, there is only one start that you can make, and that is a start towards being England. A refusal to be a province of Israel, a refusal to be an outpost of Yanko-Judea. *Quando tutti saremo forti.*[19] Pound speaking from Rome. *Parlando da Roma.*

[Announcer:] You have just heard a talk by Ezra Pound entitled "England." The news in English follows immediately.

---

marriage to the Loeb and Schiff families. By Cohen, Pound probably means the Cohen family that has been prominent in Anglo-Jewish life for almost two centuries. Financiers and bankers, they are connected by marriage to the Rothschild and Montefiore families. The Kuhn reference is probably to Kuhn, Loeb & Co., founded by Abraham Kuhn (1819-92) and Solomon Loeb. And the Kahn mentioned is probably Otto Hermann Kahn (1867-1934), American banker, arts patron, and philanthropist. Married to the daughter of a partner in Kuhn, Loeb & Co., he joined that firm in 1897.

[19] Italian: Until we shall all be strong.

Index

Index